THE
GOVERNMENT
OF SCOTLAND

THE GOVERNMENT OF SCOTLAND

Dr Michael Keating · Dr Arthur Midwinter

MAINSTREAM
PUBLISHING

Published by
MAINSTREAM PUBLISHING,
25a South West Thistle Street Lane,
Edinburgh EH2 1EW.

ISBN 0 906391 39 3

Printed and bound from copy supplied by
Spectrum Printing Company, Edinburgh

The Publishers gratefully acknowledge financial assistance from the
Scottish Arts Council in the production of this volume.

CONTENTS

LIST OF FIGURES

LIST OF TABLES

PREFACE

THIS book is about policy making in Scottish government. It is not a comprehensive account of how Scotland is governed. That would require a detailed analysis of the British and, indeed, international forces determining the pattern of public policy in Scotland. Rather, it is about government's distinctly Scottish aspects. The framework which we adopt is that of a policy network in which Scottish, United Kingdom and European elements interact. If we concentrate our attention on the Scottish elements, it is because in the past these have been given too little attention in the standard accounts of British government. We see these Scottish elements operating at two levels, the Scottish level in which there is a degree of autonomy for Scottish political interests to agree on policy independently; and the UK level where Scottish distinctiveness, where it exists, is focussed upon gaining special consideration within a wider policy framework.

Our researches have shown that, in certain fields, there is a surprisingly large scope for independent Scottish initiative and action. This is traced in our chapters on the Scottish Office, Scottish Agencies and Channels of Influence. The overall conclusion, however, is that the United Kingdom is in practice as well as theory a largely unitary state and that Scottish administrative devolution has had little impact upon this. This is confirmed by our case studies of policy making in the three key areas of housing, economic and industrial affairs and public expenditure. Our chapters on local government, which are the first full text-book treatment of the Scottish local government system, show that, even within Scotland, the trend towards centralisation is apparent.

We did not commence this book in order to convey a message. Its purpose was, and is, to explore the network of policy making in Scotland and to present a full account of Scottish central and local government. However, a message has emerged and we present it in our conclusion. This is that the relentless trend of centralisation is damaging both the efficiency of our governmental arrangements and the quality of our democracy. It can only be halted by a determined exercise of political will.

Many people from all aspects of political and administrative life, past and present, have assisted us in our research, some of whom would not thank us for naming them. We acknowledge their help but accept that the responsibility for interpretation from such a multiplicity of sources is ours alone. We would like, in particular, to thank Yvonne MacLeod for coping with successive drafts of the manuscript and scattered references. We also thank the Carnegie Trust for the Universities of Scotland and the University of Strathclyde for grants for the research upon which the book is based.

University of Strathclyde.   MICHAEL KEATING
December 1982.   ARTHUR MIDWINTER

Part One:

INTRODUCTION

LOCAL GOVERNMENT (SCOTLAND) ACT 1973
REGIONS & DISTRICTS

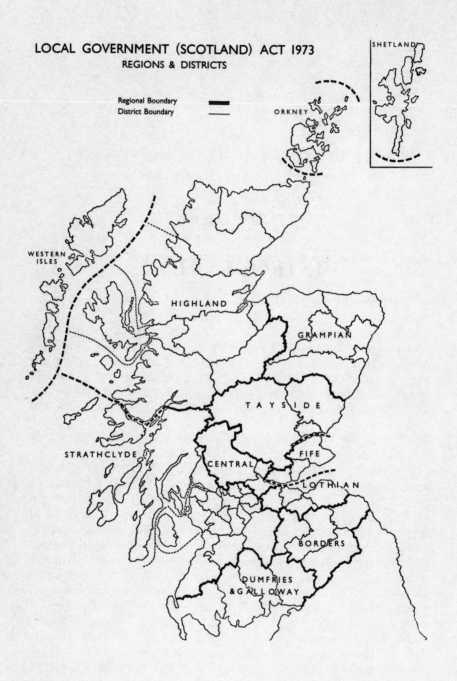

Regional Boundary
District Boundary

SHETLAND

ORKNEY

WESTERN ISLES

HIGHLAND

GRAMPIAN

TAYSIDE

STRATHCLYDE

CENTRAL

FIFE

LOTHIAN

BORDERS

DUMFRIES & GALLOWAY

CHAPTER ONE

THE ENVIRONMENT OF SCOTTISH POLICY MAKING

AT one time, a book on policy making in Scottish government might have appeared something of an oddity. Britain was regarded as a unitary and homogeneous state and a model of political stability. As recently as 1970, Finer could write that while Britain had, like many new states, its nationalities, languages, religious and constitutional problems, these belonged to past history (Finer 1970).

Since then, it has been generally recognised that regional and cultural diversity and territorial politics are not simply relics of history or characteristics of new states but a prominent feature of industrial and post-industrial societies. The nationalist upsurge of the 1970s in Scotland might have left little in the way of constitutional change but it dramatically highlighted the continuing heterogeneity of UK politics and profoundly altered perceptions of the nature of the state. In fact, managing diversity has long been one of the tasks of British government but the fact that the UK is a unitary state with a single Parliament and Cabinet has often blinded observers to the diversity of political activity within it.

The emphasis of this book is on the way public policy is made and applied in the distinctive conditions of Scotland. Of course, our approach is necessarily selective. A great deal of public policy for Scotland is identical with that for the rest of the UK — for example the conduct of foreign policy or setting the rate of income tax. On the other hand, there are areas of policy in which Scotland stands out as being, to a greater or lesser extent, different and these are our main concern. We describe the principal institutions of Scottish central and local government and the actors within them, but the contribution of a policy approach is to enable us to get beyond static institutional description to observe the dynamics of government at work. We rely heavily on the concept of 'policy networks', seeing Scottish government not as a 'political system' since ultimate authority lies outwith Scotland, nor as simply part of the 'British political system' since it is undeniably different, but rather in terms of a series of complex networks, linking Scottish actors to one another and to non-

Scottish networks. Some decisions are taken entirely within the Scottish networks. Others are taken at the 'UK level' with Scotland providing a distinctive input. In yet other matters there are no specifically Scottish issues at stake though Scottish politicians and administrators may be involved as part of the UK policy community. Power and influence within these networks are dependent not only upon formal responsibilities but also upon the relationships established and the political conditions prevailing. It is only through an examination of the policy making process that these power relationships can be understood and appraised.

In this chapter, we look at some of the factors which make up the policy environment in Scotland and thus make for a distinct mode of policy making.

* * * * *

The origins of Scotland's political personality are to be found in its history, in particular the experience of independent nationhood up until 1707. It is this which gave Scotland a political identity and constantly poses the question of whether the Union could or should be broken and independent statehood resumed. The teaching of Scottish history, especially in primary schools, brings home to each generation the tradition of Scottish independence and the struggles to assert it. Scottish history, like all history, is used by contemporaries to bolster their own arguments and, as the tradition of statehood has been available to be taken up by a variety of social and political movements in pursuit of their own aims, a number of historical myths have been spawned. Pre-union Scotland has been idealised and historical figures made to serve a variety of purposes, representing at once national self-assertion and social change. Thus the concept of an independent Scotland, redefined in each generation, has remained as an alternative model of political development.

The persistence of a Scottish national identity after 1707 is also to be explained by the nature of the Union itself. An incorporating but not an assimilating union, it abolished the Scottish Parliament (and also, it is often forgotten, the English one) but left intact the institutions of 'civil society' regarded by many contemporaries as more important than an ambiguous statehood. The most important of these were the legal system, the established Church of Scotland and the royal burghs. In turn they served as carriers of Scottish identity and as a focus for a distinctive Scottish politics after the Union.

The legal system is of immense importance in the assertion of Scotland's identity. It requires the passage of separate legislation for Scotland on many matters even where the policy content is identical to English legislation. It allows for the law on a variety of matters to differ from that of England; and it is linked to a separate judicial system allowing for the development of a distinctive case-law. There are no hard and fast rules as to which matters should be dealt with by Scottish law and which by UK legislation but, generally speaking, matters subject to administrative decentralisation to the Scottish Office are legislated for separately, as are many matters of private law and morality. The law on industrial, economic and commercial matters is usually the same throughout the UK as are laws on 'new' matters of state responsibility such as race relations or consumer protection. Some Scots lawyers have bemoaned a tendency to convergence of the Scottish and English legal systems and the consequent threat to some traditional principles of Scots law. On the other hand, the trend, as we shall see later, is for separate Scottish legislation to be used increasingly for the translation of policy into legal form, rather than trying to adapt English law to Scottish conditions.

The Union left Scottish administrative arrangements largely intact but the present institutions are later developments. There was a Secretary for Scotland until 1746 when his post was abolished and the country came under the 'management' system in which patronage was distributed to leading Scots notables in return for support for the government of the day. Outside the Highlands, other Scottish native institutions were largely untouched and such administration as government undertook was in the hands of the burghs and *ad hoc* boards. The fall of the management system in 1828 did mark the start of a period of assimilation but this was checked in 1870 when a rising Scottish consciousness, at a time of expanding state activity, succeeded in obtaining a separate Scottish Education Act. This set the trend for subsequent extensions of state activity. In 1885, a Secretary for Scotland was appointed, beginning the process of administrative decentralisation which we trace in the next chapter.

The growth of the twentieth-century state has subsequently taken a rather different form in Scotland. Local government was reformed in 1929 and 1975 and, while the royal burghs have disappeared, they have been replaced by a home-grown Scottish system. The expansion of 'quasi-government' and 'fringe bodies' in Scotland, too, has taken on distinct characteristics as governments sought effective means of policy delivery in the peculiar Scottish environment. These are examined in Chapter Three.

It would be wrong to exaggerate the institutional distinctiveness of Scotland. Over all remains the unitary Parliament normally under the effective control of a united Cabinet. Even within Parliament there are opportunities to play out distinctively Scottish issues and a range of committees dealing with Scottish legislation and administrative scrutiny; but at the end of the day it is the will of Parliament as a whole which prevails.

Scottish governmental institutions have developed to allow certain issues to be resolved differently for Scotland and at the same time allow

Scottish considerations to influence certain types of UK-level decisions. What are the distinctive Scottish questions involved here and how do they arise? The answer is to be found in the geographical, economic, social and political structure of Scotland.

Scotland accounts for about a third of the landmass of Britain but only a tenth of the population and this is concentrated in the central belt and the North East, leaving the Highlands and Islands very sparsely populated. The uneven population distribution gives rise to its own problems, such as the provision of transport and other public services to remote areas and meeting the costs of such provision. The remoteness of the Highlands and Islands, together with their other peculiar problems has given rise to a range of special initiatives for the area (see Chapter Three). In contrast, Glasgow has until recently suffered from problems of overcrowding.

As we shall see in Chapter Nine, it is difficult nowadays to talk of a 'Scottish economy' but Scotland does present particular economic and industrial problems different, if only in degree, from those of other parts of the UK. There is a high concentration of declining heavy industrial sectors and a poor record of indigenous growth compensated to some extent by a high rate of inward investment. On the other hand, the North Sea oil boom has transformed some parts of the country, bringing the problem of coping with expansion and development.

Agriculture and fishing in Scotland possess their own characteristics. In the case of agriculture, climate, soil and topography dictate a different range of products from those predominating elsewhere in the UK. The fishing industry, in contrast to that of England, has always concentrated on inshore waters. It was thus less affected by the closure of the North Atlantic fishing grounds but more likely to come into conflict with fishermen from other parts of the UK in the coastal waters of Britain.

Social conditions vary greatly within Scotland but it is possible to make some general remarks. Industrial decline has produced consistently higher unemployment rates than the UK average though, for those in work, male industrial earnings are relatively high. Health in Scotland has tended to be worse than in other parts of the UK, with particularly high rates of coronary and lung disease. It is not clear precisely why this should be so but poor environment and high rates of smoking appear to play their part.

Housing in Scotland has long been a major problem. There is a tradition of poor amenities, high densities and low rents. Since the war, a great deal of redevelopment has been undertaken by public authorities so that Scotland now has a much higher proportion of publicly owned housing than the rest of the UK and a low rate of owner occupation. We examine in Chapter Eight the effects of this upon the development of housing policy in Scotland.

Like many other western countries, Scotland has experienced a crisis in its cities in the 1970s and 1980s. Census indicators have shown very high rates of multiple deprivation and population loss; but the crisis has taken its own form in Scotland. There have not been the racial tensions of English cities or the outbreaks of violence so that the problem has not come onto the political agenda in a racial or law-and-order form. Nor is the problem primarily an 'inner city' one. Deprivation tends to be more prevalent in the council housing schemes built on the periphery of the cities and to be related to a complex of causes.

The religious structure of Scotland marks it out from the rest of the UK. Most of the population belong, at least nominally, to the established Church of Scotland whose influence on Scottish values and practices has been immense. Though the beliefs of the early reformers and of the Covenanters may have on occasion been distorted to fit the needs of later propagandists, the Protestant tradition in Scotland has left an emphasis on egalitarianism and democracy and a veneration for education. In the West of the country particularly, the large Roman Catholic minority originating in Ireland has left its mark on politics and policy. Sectarianism was long a major issue in Scottish politics and controversies continue over the status of Catholic schools within the state system. On 'social' questions of private morality, such as divorce or homosexuality, Catholic and Presbyterian leaders have often been united in taking an anti-permissive line. Overall, religious issues, once of major importance in defining a separate Scottish politics, are of declining importance, though the troubles in Northern Ireland have found echoes in western Scotland to an extent unknown elsewhere on the mainland.

Culturally, Scotland has always been a heterogeneous country, with divisions between the Gaelic Highlands and Islands and the English-speaking Lowlands as well between Catholics and Protestants in the latter. One of the striking features of the twentieth century, however, has been the strengthening of a Scottish identity as a result of the waning of these divisions and the emergence of new symbols and issues. Brand (1978) mentions the revival of Scottish history, the folk song movement, the Church, the Scottish army regiments and football as helping to create the new Scottish identity. As a result, most Scots can now wear a dual identity, as both Scots and British and view issues from a Scottish perspective as well as a class, partisan or 'British' one.

At the same time, the development of Scottish administrative institutions by internalising much Scottish debate and presenting even 'UK' questions from a Scottish perspective, has reinforced the Scottish political identity. In this, the media, too, have played an important role. The Scottish press is quite distinct from that of England in both the popular and quality sectors and provides a considerable amount of local and Scottish news. Independent television in Scotland is run by Scottish

Television, Grampian and Borders (based in Carlisle) and generally seeks a Scottish angle for features and current affairs programmes, though the main news is taken from ITN, with Scottish headlines at the end. Similarly, the BBC, through its television output in Scotland and the Radio Scotland channel, devotes a significant amount of broadcasting time to Scottish issues.

Electoral behaviour in Scotland has frequently diverged from that of England, though not always in the same direction. Following the 1832 Reform Act, the Liberal Party enjoyed an almost undisputed hegemony in Scotland up to the First World War. Thereafter, it was squeezed out by the two major parties and Scottish election results between the wars show little divergence from the English pattern. In 1945, Labour did slightly worse, and the Conservatives slightly better, in Scotland than in England and for the next three elections there was little divergence between Scotland and England. However, as on class grounds alone one could have expected Labour to be stronger in Scotland (Miller 1981), there does seem to have been a countervailing Conservative influence in Scotland. The most likely explanation is the persistence of religious patterns of voting, especially among the older generation (Butler and Stokes 1969). In 1959, Scotland swung to Labour while England moved to the Conservatives. While this meant that Scottish voting was coming into line with the expected class patterns, the continued trend to Labour over the next twenty years even against the English swings must be explained by peculiarly Scottish factors. The 1979 General Election gave Labour a 10% lead over the Conservatives in Scotland, while they trailed by 7% in England.

One of the most striking differences between Scottish and English elections, of course, is the presence of the Scottish National Party. In the 1960s, the SNP made a short-lived advance, winning the Hamilton by-election and a clutch of council seats but it was in the mid-1970s that they began to change the electoral map of Scotland, making direct comparisons with England virtually impossible. After winning the Govan by-election in 1973, the SNP gained 22% of the votes and seven seats in February 1974. In October of that year, they pushed this up to 30% and eleven seats, forcing the Conservatives into third place. By 1979, their vote slipped back to 17% and they lost all but two of their seats but retained pockets of substantial strength.

Liberal successes in Scotland have been patchy. During their 1960s revival, they gained a number of rural seats, helped by the concentration of their vote which in 1966 gave them five seats for 172,447 votes while in England more than two million votes brought them only six seats. In the 1970s, they were largely eclipsed by the SNP and managed only sporadic local successes before the formation of the alliance with the Social Democrats.

So Scottish political behaviour has shown distinctive patterns particularly under Conservative governments which have had to rule without a majority of Scottish seats in 1959-64, 1970-74 and from 1979, in the latter two cases in a clearly minority position. As we shall see, this has its effects on the policy process in Scotland and on the degree of autonomy which might be conceded to Scottish decision makers.

So the environment of policy making in Scotland differs in significant respects from that of the rest of the UK. Much of this distinctiveness is self-reinforcing. So the establishment of Scottish institutions leads to issues being appraised from a Scottish perspective, thus emphasising Scottish distinctiveness. With the expansion of state activity, two levels of policy making have developed, the Scottish level and the UK level, each with its own concerns but with complex links between the two, through the political parties, interest groups and the machinery of the state itself. It is this network and the dynamics of policy making within it which is the subject of the rest of this book.

Part Two:

CENTRAL GOVERNMENT

CHAPTER TWO

THE SCOTTISH OFFICE

T HE Scottish Office, it has often been said, is exceptional among British government departments in being organised on the 'area' principle, bringing together under a single Secretary of State a number of tasks which, in England, would be the responsibility of several 'functional' departments. This arrangement has been given a variety of labels — 'administrative devolution', 'decentralisation', 'proconsular government'. None of these terms really fits and, indeed, the terms themselves lack clarity but the most useful label is probably 'decentralisation' denoting a particular way for central government to organise its own structure and activities rather than the handing over of responsibilities and powers to bodies outside central government. For the Scottish Office is an integral part of central government, albeit with some distinctive characteristics of its own. As a territorial department of the UK government, it performs a variety of distinctive roles which can be summarised under three headings:

(a)   To administer those functions which, because of the Scottish legal system or traditional features, need separate management. In the absence of a Scottish Office this would have to be provided, in any case, by special divisions of UK departments.

(b)   To allow for some measure of distinctiveness in policy making for Scotland, a capacity to respond to special Scottish demands and conditions.

(c)   To 'lobby' within government for extra resources for Scotland.

In this chapter, we consider the structure and functions of the Scottish Office, the policy process and the.'Scottish lobby' in terms of these three roles.

Structure and functions

The necessity for Scottish administrative machinery dates from the Act of Union, which laid down that certain Scottish institutions, like the burghs, the Kirk and the Scottish legal system, were to be preserved within the Union. A Secretary for Scotland existed in the years following the Union and, with the Lord Advocate, was responsible for such administration as was necessary. After the abolition of this post in 1746, power was shared between the Lord Advocate and whoever was currently recognised as the Scottish 'manager'. The 'manager' was usually given a free hand in the management of, and particularly the distribution of patronage in, Scotland, in return for supplying a reliable block of MPs to support the government of the day. From 1828, responsibility for the provision of Scottish administration was formally rested in the Home Secretary while the actual business of administration was undertaken by the burgh and, later, county councils and a variety of *ad hoc* boards.

It was the growing volume of complaints at the inefficiency of this system and the lack of adequate ministerial control over Scottish government, as well as an awakening nationalism, which led, in the nineteenth century, to calls for a Scottish Office. In 1884 Gladstone agreed to appoint a Scottish minister and the first Secretary for Scotland took office under the Conservative Government of 1885. It was a long time, however, before the Scottish Office established control of Scottish administration. Many of the old boards continued in existence under the somewhat vague supervision of the Secretary for Scotland and only in 1939, following the report of the Gilmour Committee, were the remaining boards absorbed as departments of the Scottish Office, with the Secretary bearing full ministerial responsibility for them. At the same time, the bulk of the Scottish Office was transferred from London to St. Andrew's House in Edinburgh, with only a small liaison staff remaining behind. Up to this point, the development of the Scottish Office had represented, not the fragmentation of British functional administration but the unification of a fragmented Scottish administration. Since then, the Office has gradually accumulated further functions where strict uniformity throughout the UK was not considered essential or in response to pressure from Scottish interests.

The period of governmental reform and expansion during the Second World War and the post-war Labour Government saw the Scottish Office assume responsibility for hydro-electricity, assistance to agriculture, the National Health Service, town and country planning, forestry, civil defence, and child care though not without some fights with the large Whitehall departments. In 1954 electricity was added and, following the Balfour Commission, set up in an effort to defuse the Covenant movement for a Scottish Parliament, roads and bridges and the appointment of Justices of the Peace. Transfers in the opposite direction have been few. Roads were transferred to the Ministry of Transport in 1911 but back again in 1956 and pensions and national insurance were lost in 1948.

The next period of expansion came in the 1960s when concern began to be felt about the performance of the Scottish economy and the need to improve physical and economic planning. The Scottish Development Department (SDD), set up in 1962, was an early attempt to bring together the major environmental, planning and local government responsibilities. The model was later to be followed in England with the giant Department of the Environment. In 1964 the Labour Government introduced new planning machinery for Scotland, Wales and the English regions. A Scottish Economic Planning Board was set up, bringing together representatives of the major economic departments in Scotland under a Scottish Office chairman. A Scottish Economic Council, including representatives of local government, business, trade union and other interests in Scotland, was set up to advise the Secretary of State on economic plans for Scotland. Significantly, in 1979, when the corresponding Regional Economic Planning Councils in England were abolished, the Scottish Economic Council was retained. In 1973, a Scottish Economic Planning Department (SEPD) was set up in the Scottish Office, taking over the 'economic' responsibilities of the SDD including the Economic Council. This rendered the Economic Planning Board redundant and it fell into desuetude. In 1975, SEPD took over responsibility for some selective assistance to industry and the new Scottish Development Agency.

The Scottish Office now comprises five departments as follows:

- Department of Agriculture and Fisheries for Scotland (DAFS), responsible for most agricultural and fisheries matters;
- Scottish Development Department (SDD), responsible for planning, housing, roads, transport and local government;
- Scottish Economic Planning Department (SEPD), responsible for regional economic development, electricity, selective aid to industry, new towns and the Scottish Development Agency;
- Scottish Education Department (SED), responsible for education outside the universities and social work services;
- Scottish Home and Health Department (SHHD), responsible for police, prisons, criminal justice, fire and the National Health Service.

In addition, there is a Central Services unit responsible for personnel and finance and the Liaison Division in London.

As the Scottish Office has expanded the number and status of its ministers has increased. In 1926 the Secretary for Scotland became a full Secretary of State and, by tradition, he is guaranteed a seat in the Cabinet. There have been up to four parliamentary under-secretaries and, since 1951, a Minister of State in the Lords and, under Labour Governments a second one in the Commons. At the time of writing (1982) there is a Minister of State in the Lords and three parliamentary under-secretaries in the Commons.

It is difficult to pin down any major distinctive features of Scottish

Office administration and research has shown that, in terms of structure, it is very much like other departments of government (Hood, *et al* 1980). However, it has been pointed out to us that any differences which can be measured by academics can also be measured by a suspicious Treasury and Civil Service Department so that the distinctive features of the Scottish Office are likely to be more subtle and related to behaviour rather than structure. Several suggestions have been made as to how these features might affect administration in the Scottish Office.

Some observers have commented that, by bringing together a wide range of functions under a single Minister, the Scottish Office is able to take a more 'corporate' view of policy and administration and to achieve a greater degree of co-ordination than is possible in England. Certainly, compared with the regions of England, Scotland has a more rational and cohesive system of government but it would be a mistake to see the Scottish Office as a monolith. Functions are divided amongst its departments, often in a curious way. So, while planners have for many years preached the necessity of bringing together land use/physical planning and economic/industrial planning, the Scottish Office has chosen to divide these between the SDD and the SEPD. The failure to co-ordinate these two areas of activity provoked criticism from the Select Committee on Scottish Affairs in 1972. Page (1978) has commented on complaints by local authorities that the Scottish Office does not speak to them with one voice, a question we explore below (Chapter Six). As Parry (1981) has shown, fragmentation and departmentalism has been a persistent managerial and structural problem which the Gilmour reforms did not resolve, and specialist interests maintained substantive policy autonomy in functional departments. The result was a largely 'symbolic', reactive role for the Secretary of State, rather than priority determination.

There has certainly been a trend in recent years towards strengthening the corporate existence of the Scottish Office. In 1969 common finance and establishment organisations were established and in 1975 these were absorbed into Central Services, effectively a sixth department under a Deputy Secretary. The introduction of the block financial allocation (see below) and the increased emphasis in the 1970s and 1980s on tight financial control has led to some strengthening of the centre within the Scottish Office, though the role of Central Services here is more that of a referee ensuring order in bids for finance than that of a Scottish 'mini-Treasury' bargaining with departments itself. Once spending plans are agreed, there are separate cash limits for each of the departments and, a unique feature of the Scottish Office, seven accounting officers. Since the early 1970s, corporate planning has been helped by a Management Group of heads of department, with a secretariat and regular meetings. However, the continued separate identity of departments is testified by the fact that representatives of interest groups almost never refer to the 'Scottish Office' rather than individual departments.

The change in economic environment to one of financial retrenchment has helped the centralisation process, and sharpened the arbitrative role of the Management Group in determining priorities. Departmental secretaries, however, retain considerable autonomy, and departmental interaction resembles the independence of Whitehall ministers. Advocates of corporateness regard the education and agricultural departments as "hopeless cases"! (Parry 1981). The Management Group's role is largely reactive. It has a leading role to play in the planning of Scottish public expenditure, seeking to shape a collective view of the package which emerges from functional departments. The emphasis, however, in Management Group, is on administrative rather than policy co-ordination, and it concentrates on internal management and inter-departmental issues. Agendas do not include current policy issues, which are pursued independently by departments in direct contact with Ministers (Parry 1982).

Another curious feature of the Scottish Office is the lack of correspondence between ministerial responsibilities and departmental boundaries. One minister might be responsible for education and industry and another for agriculture and housing. The reason for this is partly the fact that there are not enough ministers to provide one per department and partly the need to link the less sought-after jobs with the more glamorous ones. So, under Labour, the less attractive (to Labour MPs) agriculture portfolio has been linked to the politically central housing one. The small size of the Scottish Office and the close links within it can make these divisions manageable but problems do arise. For instance, ministerial responsibility for housing might be split from responsibility for infrastructure, making a unified assessment of development schemes difficult. At the civil service level, however, the responsibilities are kept together, giving the officials the key role in integration. Together with the absence of ministers for a large part of the time in London, this may weaken ministerial control in the Scottish Office.

Relations among ministers within the Scottish Office vary according to the character of the Secretary of State and his junior ministers, who are chosen not by him but by the Prime Minister. Most matters will come initially to a junior minister for a decision, with the papers being copied for the Secretary of State and other involved ministers. Some Secretaries of State have taken a relaxed view, delegating most matters to the junior ministers and only reading papers where the Private Office has indicated that the item is sufficiently important for their attention. Others have insisted on seeing all papers and have intervened frequently in decisions. However, any Secretary of State must delegate a great deal, given the breadth of his responsibilities, especially when he is preoccupied with a major decision or studying a lengthy report on one particular item.

Policy making and 'policy leadership'

We have seen how the Scottish Office has come to administer a wide range of functions. The next question to consider is how far it makes policy for itself and how far it merely follows policy lines laid down elsewhere. Parry (1981) argues that there are three policy dimensions, the British super-structure, the Scottish autonomous field (social policy) and areas of ambiguity, such as industry, agriculture, and law and order. This in itself is a sweeping generalisation which overlooks the complexity through which autonomy is possible in areas of social policy. To examine this question, we shall first look at the links between the Scottish Office and other parts of the central government, then consider the process of policy making and the place within it of the Scottish Office.

The Scottish Office is linked into the decision-making structure of UK central government at several levels. The Secretary of State is a member of the Cabinet and able to put the Scottish viewpoint on major matters of policy. However, the full Cabinet spends little time on the sort of matters dealt with by the Scottish Office. Of more importance is the network of Cabinet and ministerial committees. Although the very existence of these committees is still largely secret, we know that they cover all the major policy areas, in addition to 'one-off' issues which arise from time to time. The Scottish Office is represented, usually by a junior minister, on all the committees dealing with the matters for which it is responsible and it is within these committees, from which there is a limited right of appeal to the Cabinet, that interdepartmental policy matters are settled.

The civil service provides an important set of links between the Scottish Office and UK departments. Although St. Andrew's House is separated by some 400 miles from Whitehall, communications are fast and efficient and the basic homogeneity of the civil service makes for close contacts. Scottish officials are in weekly or daily contact with their opposite numbers in UK ministries, by telephone or on visits to London and advantage is usually taken of routine or casual contacts to discuss current policy issues. In this way conflicts can be smoothed over, ideas exchanged and advice to ministers brought into line. As in relationships amongst government departments generally, there are suspicions that on occasion this goes as far as briefing ministers in collusion to avoid unwelcome issues being raised!

Personal links between UK and Scottish ministers are surprisingly weak. Ministers are so absorbed in the work of their own offices that they have little time for general policy discussions with colleagues, apart from the odd brief exchange in the Commons tea-room. This leaves them reliant on civil service contacts, except where close personal or political links exist. In this connection, the convention of having a Scottish MP as one of the junior ministers in the Ministry of Agriculture, Fisheries and Food seems to help strengthen the important link between the MAFF and the Scottish Office. In recent years, a similar convention has developed, of having a Scottish MP as one of the Ministers in the Department of Energy, responsible for North Sea oil.

Thus the relations between the Scottish Office and the 'UK departments' are similar to the relationships amongst government departments generally. What distinguishes the Scottish Office, though (and also the Welsh and Northern Ireland Offices), is that it is responsible, within Scotland, for the same functions as are exercised, for the rest of Britain or for England alone, by the main 'functional' departments. This raises the question of where the policy input to these functions comes from and the extent to which the Scottish Office 'makes' its own policy or simply 'administers' policy made elsewhere.

The process for handling major policy initiatives is fairly standard. Proposals are formulated in the department which is to take the 'lead', with, normally, a considerable amount of outside consultation. Often, it is outside interest groups who have raised the issue in the first place and where the issue has been raised is the first factor determining which department is to take the lead. At a very early stage, other departments are sounded out through the civil service grapevine and the Treasury is consulted on any financial implications. Policy clearance will then be sought from the appropriate Cabinet committee, where bargaining and negotiation are likely. To clarify this, let us divide policy proposals into three types: Scottish Office proposals for Scotland alone; proposals from 'UK departments' for England and Wales; and proposals for the whole of the UK (or Britain), in which the initiative and lead will almost invariably be taken by a UK department. A purely Scottish or purely English proposal may be passed on the nod, with provision made only for the copying of the relevant papers to the other territorial departments. Alternatively, major objections, amounting to a veto, may be made and the initiating department forced to withdraw the proposal. More likely, the proposal will be the subject of negotiation and emerge from the committee in a modified form. If the proposal requires legislation, then this, too, will have to be approved by the committee, which will continue to monitor the passage of the bill and approve any amendments to it. So policy is agreed interdepartmentally and can be presented as the policy of the Government, no matter which department takes the lead. On the other hand, the amount of bargaining and the influence which departments can bring to bear will vary greatly. We can see the Scottish Office role in the policy process in terms of a spectrum ranging from, at one extreme, almost complete autonomy in policy making to, at the other extreme, complete dependence, following, more or less exactly, the line laid down by a UK lead department. Where an issue involves more than one department, the process by which that policy is forged depends on a complex interplay of forces, the principal ones of which we will now examine.

The first of these is the *statutory responsibilities* of the departments concerned. Where the Scottish Office has administrative responsibility for a function, it will have staff working on policy development and automatic membership of the appropriate interdepartmental committee. Its civil servants will be part of the grapevine. The degree of administrative responsibility for a function can vary greatly. In the case of education, it is almost total, allowing considerable autonomy. In the case of energy, the Scottish Office has responsibility only for electricity. However, this still gives it membership of committees on energy policy and allows the Secretary of State to maintain a small group of civil servants working on energy policy generally. While this group is too small to formulate much in the way of policy initiatives, it does enable the Scottish Office to keep abreast of policy development in the Department of Energy and to provide a Scottish input where appropriate. Similarly, the Secretary of State's rather ill-defined but official role as an economic and industrial minister and his limited range of economic responsibilities give him an entree into the industrial and economic policy network. A great deal of Scottish activity here is reactive, trying to modify proposals coming from a UK lead department, but, as far as possible, Scottish ministers and officials do try to contribute to the making of overall UK policy rather than just harping on the 'Scottish angle'. In this way they are able to maximise their impact.

The extent of *cross-border spillover* effects is, of course, of great importance in determining the degree of autonomy allowed to the Scottish Office. Where a matter has few repercussions for England, UK departments are often content to let the Scots go ahead on their own. Where Scottish actions would affect England or vice versa, on the other hand, there may be a need for a unified policy. Professional education provides two contrasting examples. Because the Scottish primary/secondary school system and its teaching profession are largely self-contained, teacher-training and teacher supply can be handled independently in Scotland. In social work, however, there is a UK-wide job market, so that qualifications and supply have to be co-ordinated closely. In housing, there is scope for some autonomy but it was not considered possible to exclude Scotland from the operation of the Housing (Homeless Persons) Act, as Scottish ministers wished, because of the possibility of homeless people migrating.

In many areas, UK departments are prepared to recognise the existence of a separate *Scottish tradition* providing for autonomy. Where such a tradition exists, with separate legislation and administrative structures, then it may be difficult in any case, to obtain uniformity of policy. On the other hand, this autonomy only exists within the constraints which we are examining.

The *public expenditure* implications of a policy proposal will largely determine the role of the Treasury. In the past, expenditure considerations were a major constraint on the autonomy of the Scottish Office, as its expenditure was allocated under the functional headings of the PESC system. Thus, any policy change involving expenditure required the approval of the Treasury, which was also involved in monitoring expenditure. Now most Scottish Office expenditure is expressed as a block allocation within which the Secretary of State has scope for virement. The Treasury has, consequently, retreated to a concern mainly with the Office's overall cash limits. However, the Scottish Office block allocation is built up functionally and based on the budgets of the corresponding UK departments. So the total of Scottish expenditure can only be influenced by the Secretary of State by his supporting UK functional ministers in their battles for more resources. Further, transfers can only be made from one Scottish Office function to another in the course of a financial year with the approval of Parliament. While such approval would presumably not be denied, the process of obtaining it could be time-consuming and perhaps, *politically* embarrassing. Just how much freedom the Secretary of State has gained as a result of the block allocation system will be impossible to judge until the system has been in operation for a number of years.

The need or otherwise for *legislation* will also affect the Scottish Office's freedom of manoeuvre. If the Office requires legislation for its own policy proposals, this will need the approval of the Cabinet, which rarely allows more than one major Scottish bill per parliamentary session. UK departments will also have to consider whether a change in Scottish law will affect them. Where a UK department proposes legislation, the Scottish Office will consider whether it wishes Scotland to be included or excluded and, if the former, will usually try to secure a separate Scottish bill which, as well as producing clearer law for Scotland, will give it greater control over the legislative process.

Party policy and the *political salience* of an issue are important factors. Though there are some variations in party policy on either side of the border, the basic ideological thrust is the same and, on partisan matters, there is a tendency to uniformity, even where Scottish ministers might try to resist it. So the last Labour Government's legislation on private beds in National Health Service hospitals, on which the lead was taken by DHSS, was applied to Scotland despite the objections of Scottish ministers, who believed that the conditions in Scotland were quite different and that the problem was being dealt with satisfactorily by other means. Generally, both civil servants and ministers try to minimise policy divergence on either side of the border to prevent the spectacle of a government apparently believing in two different policies for the same issue. This is particularly so where an issue has attracted a great deal of public attention, leading to pressure on government to 'do something'. For instance, following the Maria Colwell case, action was taken in DHSS leading to the Children Act of 1975. As it was considered politically intolerable to appear to provide different degrees of protection to children in England and Scotland, a UK bill was devised, with the DHSS leading and the Scottish Office contributing to the policy development and to the framing of Scottish clauses. (The actual drafting of Scottish clauses is the responsibility of the Lord Advocate's Department.) However, while the general clamour for action was felt equally in England and Scotland, detailed negotiations with COSLA and other interested parties revealed that Scottish priorities were rather different, so that the implementation and phasing-in of the legislation, under the Scottish Office, followed a different pattern.

Sometimes the political need for uniformity may prevent the introduction of a policy. So, in the 1970s, when English departments agreed on a proposal for compulsory fluoridation of water supplies through the appointed water authorities, they sought to have the legislation apply in Scotland. However, the Scottish Office raised the constitutional objection that the water authorities in Scotland are the elected regional councils who should not be instructed on such a matter. Given the emotive nature of the issue and the absence of any relevant difference between English and Scottish teeth, DHSS and DOE felt unable to go ahead for England alone.

Occasionally, surprising divergences in policy are allowed through the system, for instance the Criminal Justice Bill which originated under the 1974-9 Labour Government was taken over and modified by the Conservatives. The Bill stemmed from a separate Scottish working party and the preparation of the proposals took place in the Scottish Office but, in committee, the Home Office appears to have raised the objection that it would be wrong to have radically different police powers on either side of the border. The fact that the legislation was nevertheless approved seems to be due to the relative weakness of the Home Office in policy matters, a certain amount of ministerial log-rolling and a feeling that, if Scotland was allowed to go ahead, it might prove a useful experiment.

Where *finance* or *charges* for public services are involved, there are usually political objections to variations so that these tend to be uniform.

Where policy is, formally, made separately in Scotland and England, it may nevertheless develop on the same lines because of common *professional views* and fashions. Thus, developments in health care or the social services will be transmitted through UK-wide professional networks and suggested at the same time to both Scottish and English departments.

Leadership and the balance of influence are also affected by the *relative importance* of the issue for Scotland and England and the relative size of the corresponding sections of the Scottish and English departments. On most matters it is the UK or 'English' department which is the larger and more senior but, occasionally, Scotland is of equal weight, for example in fisheries, where it accounts for over half the UK industry, and in some aspects of agriculture. Here joint policy making is the rule, with the Scottish Office having equal weight and sometimes taking the lead. The balance of power here is partly a function of the size and staffing of departments. One Scottish official will usually face several specialised officials from the UK department and has great difficulty matching their expertise. Further, as the Secretary of State and the heads of the Scottish Office departments must delegate a great deal to junior ministers and officials, the latter will face UK 'opposite numbers' from specialised ministries who are a rank or two senior to them.

The policy process is, finally, influenced by *personal and political factors* which can vary from time to time. Ministers can smooth their way by personal friendships and log-rolling and an energetic and determined minister will be able to achieve more than one who sees his role in terms of keeping the department ticking over or following leads given elsewhere. The status of the Scottish Office depends, too, on the political rank of the Secretary of State and on the perceived importance of Scotland to the Government. In recent years, Labour governments have been much more dependent on their Scottish seats than have Conservative ones and this, combined with the threat to those seats from the SNP, gave Secretaries of State in the late 1960s and late 1970s added political weight.

Political influence can also arise from the Secretary of State's links with the Prime Minister. The close relationship between Churchill and James Stuart allowed the latter a considerable freedom of action. Similarly, under Wilson, William Ross was able to pursue many independent lines, to the extent of provoking Richard Crossman to comment on his incipient "separation" through his insistence on keeping Scottish business absolutely privy from English business (Crossman 1977). In turn, where a Secretary of State is seen to possess political 'weight', his civil servants gain added status in the interdepartmental bargaining game.

It is difficult to specify which areas of policy are controlled within the Scottish Office because of the variable impact of the factors we have looked at. However, in general terms, Scottish education policy is largely self-contained, as is policy on social work services. UK departments are kept informed of developments and ideas are exchanged but there is little joint policy making. However, because the perceived requirements of the economy and public and professional demands tend to be similar on both sides of the border, the practical differences in education have more to do with administrative structures and practices than with substantive issues of policy.

Policy on matters relating to local government is also handled separately with exchanges of information and ideas but little policy leadership on matters of local government structure and central-local relationships. On the issue of salaries for councillors, however, it is known that the Scottish Office would like to see a reform but are held back by Treasury and DOE opposition. On roads, transport (except railways) and infrastructure generally, the Scottish Office is quite independent with only 'cross-border' issues like speed limits and drivers' regulations decided jointly. In these areas, as in town and country planning legislation, professional views and fashions tend to produce a degree of uniformity. Similar considerations apply to health policy, where the Scottish Office's small size and lack of research capacity prevent it taking many major initiatives.

In agriculture and fisheries the need to agree policy within the EEC and internationally leaves little hope for a separate Scottish policy so joint policy making is the norm. Again, the administration of policy is quite separate, particularly in fishing where the Scottish fleet is of a different type to the English. (The Scottish fleet is predominantly 'inshore' while the English ports retain what is left of the 'deep water' fleet.) DAFS and the Ministry of Agriculture, Fisheries and Food both maintain agricultural research stations but they are distinguished by their field of research and not by the territory they serve as they all produce research which is used by all the fisheries departments (for Scotland, England, Wales and Northern Ireland) on a 'customer' basis. The allocation of work to the laboratories and research stations is done jointly by DAFS and MAFF.

Law reform, criminal justice and the administration of justice are areas where there is a need for separate Scottish policy making because of the existence of a separate legal system. So there are separate advisory committees and a Scottish Law Commission producing initiatives for the Scottish Office. Occasionally, this can lead to policy initiatives quite different from anything happening in England but, generally, governments have preferred uniformity in *policy* in criminal justice, while allowing scope for wide variations in administrative practice.

The Scottish lobby
The role of the Secretary of State and the Scottish Office in defending and advancing Scottish interests within government has long been recognised. This role extends well beyond the Secretary of State's statutory functions.

Already, by 1937, the Gilmour Committee was moved to remark on the 'increasing tendency to appeal to him on all matters that have a Scottish aspect, even if on a strict view they are outside the province of his duties as statutorily defined'. The Secretary of State's wide responsibilities as 'Scotland's Minister' have led to successive Secretaries seeking wider powers to discharge those responsibilities. This was an important factor in the expansion of the economic role of the Scottish Office, together with the growing expectation amongst Scottish opinion generally that he should do so. This led in 1964 to his being assigned more explicit responsibilities in the comprehensive machinery for economic planning which was introduced on the advent of a new administration (Select Committee on Scottish Affairs 1969). In recent years, Secretaries of State have been aware of the danger that a creeping expansion of their responsibilities could result in political and administrative overload and have not generally sought extra functions. Their role as the 'voice of Scotland' in Cabinet, however, has continued to be an important part of their duties.

The political weight of the Secretary of State as lobbyist will depend on a number of factors. We have already mentioned the strong position of a Secretary of State in a government dependent on a large block of Scottish seats. Behind every Secretary of State is the implicit threat to the Government of Scottish nationalism and, at least since the wartime tenure of Tom Johnston, widely considered the greatest holder of the office, Secretaries of State have used this as a bargaining lever.

In 1976, the Secretary of State played a vital role in the decision to rescue the Chrysler motor manufacturing operation in Britain, the closure of which would have had drastic consequences for Linwood in Renfrewshire. This was at a time when the SNP appeared to be threatening Labour dominance in Scotland and the fall of the Government was feared. However, the failure to secure the implementation of the Scotland Act and the lack of any immediate popular resistance to its repeal may have damaged the credibility of the nationalist card and thus the bargaining power of the Secretary of State. In 1980, the Linwood factory was closed by its new French owners.

Parry (1982) argues that the Secretary of State is not a central actor in most of the business discussed by the full Cabinet. But the Scottish Office remains securely established within the policy networks concerned with its own function and able, at least, to defend its interests, as was shown in the 1982 battle over the future of the Ravenscraig steel works.

Recent research (Keating and Midwinter 1981, Parry 1982) has demonstrated that the structural differences in Scottish Office administrative arrangements have not resulted in substantive policy autonomy. The British political system is a unitary one, and the pressures for alignment of policy within the Whitehall network are considerable.

Greater degrees of autonomy are likely over organisational issues (local government reform) or administrative process (regional reports, financial planning) than in functional policies. The Scottish Office itself emerges as a federal department unlike the English super departments (such as Environment) which are designed to facilitate internal priority determination. Ministers can be an important integrating force (e.g. over social work reorganisation) in such areas where autonomy exists, but they are part of a United Kingdom policy, and a British Cabinet system, which results in considerable policy uniformity, the diversity of Scottish social and economic conditions notwithstanding.

The Lord Advocate's Department

The Office of the Lord Advocate for Scotland is quite separate from that of the Secretary of State. He is responsible for the Crown Office, which deals with prosecutions and the procurator fiscal service (there are no police or private prosecutions in Scotland); the Lord Advocate's Department; and he shares with the Secretary of State responsibility for the Scottish Courts Administration.

The Lord Advocate's Department, which is based in London, act as Scottish legal advisers to a variety of government departments, a task they share with the Scottish Office. This includes following EEC rulings as they affect Scottish law and passing on matters of Scottish legal interest to departments; as well as keeping under review general questions of law, as the Lord Chancellor's Department does for England and Wales. Their main responsibility, however, is the drafting of Scottish legislation. The Lord Advocate is responsible for the drafting of all Scottish bills and Scottish parts of UK bills and, indeed, tends to take a personal interest in the details of drafting.

There was a certain amount of rationalisation of the legal functions of the Secretary of State and the Lord Advocate in the 1970s, with the latter taking over responsibility for the laws relating to certain aspects of the administration of justice, tribunals and the Scottish Law Commission. The position was summarised in a parliamentary answer of 1979:

> The Lord Advocate is the principal Scottish Law Officer. His responsibilities include the provision of advice to Ministers on Scots law and, with the other Law Officers, advice on matters of constitutional and international law, including EEC issues. He is also responsible for the Scottish parliamentary draftsmen, for the Scottish Law Commission, for certain matters relating to tribunals and consolidation of the law in Scotland, and for certain branches of the law of Scotland, such as the jurisdiction

and procedure of the civil courts, the law of evidence, and the law relating to the prescription and limitations of actions. Prosecutions in Scotland are in the hands of the Lord Advocate and others. The Lord Advocate is also master of the instance and, as such, controls the flow of cases in criminal courts (*Hansard*, 12.3.79, col. 6).

CHAPTER THREE

PUBLIC AGENCIES AND 'QUANGOS'

A GREAT deal of public administration in Scotland, as in other areas of the United Kingdom, is undertaken not by central government departments or local authorities but by special purpose or *ad hoc* agencies and 'quangos'. This whole subject is a varied and complex one and most attempts to classify these bodies and discover general rules underlying their structure and operations have either lapsed into over-simplification and polemic or been given up in despair.

Hogwood (1979) has classified the historical origins of agencies in Scotland under seven headings: 'hived-off' sections of government departments such as the Property Services Agency; specially appointed boards, commissions etc. such as the Scottish Development Agency; previously private or municipal organisations brought into public ownership such as the Scottish Transport Group; formally private organisations carrying out tasks on behalf of government such as housing associations; local authority joint boards; local authority fringe bodies and enterprises; and European and other international bodies. The list ranges from bodies which are clearly part of government, through intermediate bodies to those in the private sector with certain public responsibilities.

Classifying the reasons for the establishment of *ad hoc* agencies and the roles they perform is even more difficult. In some cases, *ad hoc* machinery has been established because there is no suitably sized unit of central or local government to perform the task in question; for example regional planning in Scotland before local government reform. In other cases, an *ad hoc* agency will be established because of the need to enlist the co-operation of important producer groups who can be given representation in the agency; for example the medical professions are so involved in the administration of the National Health Service. It is often thought that, in some policy areas, technical, professional or commercial criteria are more important than political judgment and that therefore the matter should be entrusted to an agency standing outside government and able to co-opt expert help from non-governmental sources; for example the NHS or the nationalised industries.

Some bodies are carefully established as quasi-governmental or quasi-non-governmental organisations (the origin of the term 'quango') in order to provide a neutral meeting place for government and private interests or to allow a measure of government intervention or subsidy without direct government control; for example the Arts Councils or the Scottish Development Agency. In these cases, a special agency in which they are represented might be demanded by the private sector as the price of co-operation; or it may be preferred by government which can then distance itself from direct political responsibility and allow the agency to take risks which would not be acceptable in a ministerial department. Setting up *ad hoc* agencies also allows government to satisfy the demands of vociferous lobby groups without upsetting its main programmes and may even allow it to pursue contradictory policy objectives; an oft-quoted example of the latter are the activities of the Industrial Reorganisation Corporation promoting mergers and the Monopolies Commission discouraging them in the 1960s; or the contradictory briefs given to successive bodies set up to administer incomes policies. The demands which agencies are set up to meet may be territorial as well as client-based. Both are important in the Scottish context.

We have already noted the Scottish tradition of government by 'boards' though, by the Second World War, most of these had been absorbed into the Scottish Office. Since then, there has been a new proliferation of special agencies. While the development of the Scottish Office and the reform of local government has largely eliminated the need for the plethora of bodies standing between central and local government which are found in England (Hogwood and Keating 1982), government has still felt the need for agencies to stand between it and the private sector and for bodies to satisfy distinctive Scottish demands. The other reasons we have given for setting up *ad hoc* agencies also apply in Scotland.

There is a complex pattern of inter-relationships amongst Scottish agencies and between these and the Scottish Office and UK departments and agencies. In some cases, there is a symmetrical structure for the UK or Britain and its constituent parts, for instance in tourism, where there are boards for Scotland, England and Wales and a British Tourist Authority. In other cases, a Scottish body has been set up as a special additional measure without an English equivalent. Thus, although the Scottish Development Agency and the National Enterprise Board have some similar functions, the latter is a UK body which operates in Scotland and there is no equivalent special agency for England. Although we have seen a similar asymmetry in the organisation of government departments, with functional and territorial departments existing side by side, the potential for overlap is greater in *ad hoc* agencies which lack the co-ordinating mechanisms and unity of purpose found in government. Practical arrangements must thus be worked out between the agencies themselves.

By and large, the Secretary of State for Scotland has responsibility for appointments to, and general oversight of, those purely Scottish agencies operating within the Scottish Office's field of functions. This includes most of the purely Scottish agencies though some, for example the Scottish Consumer Council, come under UK departments. In some cases, for example, the Scottish Transport Group, Scottish Office responsibility was only conceded after a battle within government. Apparent anomalies remain as a result of past battles, so that the Scottish Office has responsibility for the two Scottish electricity boards while the rest of the energy industry comes within the purview of the Department of Energy. Where a UK agency operates in fields which are the responsibility of the Scottish Office, the practice is to give the Secretary of State a voice in appointments and, in some cases, to provide for joint supervision. Finally, there are a few bodies whose responsibilities are British or UK-wide which are sponsored by the Scottish Office. These are agencies the bulk of whose work is in Scotland, such as the Herring Industry Board and some agricultural research institutions. Appointments are made jointly by the Scottish Office and non-Scottish departments.

We can now look at some of the more important quangos, illustrating different types of status and styles of operation.

The Scottish Development Agency
The Scottish Development Agency, founded by the Labour Government in 1975, is one of the most important of Scottish 'quangos'. Like many such bodies, it has a variety of aims, as we can see from its initial remit to further the economic development of Scotland, to promote efficiency and international competitiveness in Scottish industry, and to support environmental improvement, especially in areas of industrial and urban dereliction. To some extent these objectives complemented those of the National Enterprise Board, set up at UK level at the same time to extend state participation in industrial regeneration without resorting to wholesale nationalisation. But the SDA should also be seen as a response to specifically Scottish demands for special treatment within the framework of a unified economy.

Three existing bodies were absorbed into the new agency, the Scottish Industrial Estates Corporation, the Small Industries Council for the Rural Areas of Scotland and the section of the Scottish Development Department responsible for administering grants to local authorities for derelict land clearance. To these inherited tasks were added those of investment in industry in the form of money and of management services; industrial promotion, particularly the encouragement of investment from overseas; and the co-ordination of major comprehensive urban development schemes which in the early years effectively meant the Glasgow Eastern Area Renewal (GEAR) project. A borrowing limit of £200 million was set, with provision for an additional £100 million by parliamentary order, if required. Sponsorship of the Agency rests with the Secretary of State through the Scottish Economic Planning Department; he has the duty of laying down guidelines and the power to issue directions of a specific or general character.

Criticisms immediately abounded from right and left as well as the nationalist quarter. Some pointed to the scale of the agency's resources measured against the task of regenerating the Scottish economy and dismissed it as mere tokenism. On the right, there were allegations of 'backdoor nationalisation' and predictions that the agency would merely prop up 'lame duck' industries with no future. The Government's response was to point to the guidelines which laid down a specified rate of return and limited investment to firms which could expect to move into profit. In turn, this was criticised from both right and left on the grounds that profitable firms should be able to raise capital in the market without recourse to public funds. The question came to hinge on the existence or otherwise of an 'equity gap', an area of business finance in which potentially viable enterprises were unable to obtain capital because of their size, the absence of securities or lack of access to the main financial markets. By concentrating on this and on selected sectors such as high technology and by a stern policy towards 'lame ducks', the agency was able to fend off much criticism and controversy had to a large extent died down by 1979. The environmental improvement functions aroused no serious opposition and even local authorities which might have regarded this as a trespass on their own 'turf' welcomed the prospect of agency support and finance.

Despite earlier threats to clip its wings and a hostile attitude from the new team at the Department of Industry, the incoming Conservative Government of 1979 moved slowly with regard to the SDA. A new Industry Act symbolically reversed Labour's decision to increase its borrowing limit to £800 million. As there was never any prospect of the agency being able to spend that amount both Labour and Conservative decisions must be seen as political gestures. Proposals were floated to hive off the controversial investment function to a new institution to be financed jointly with the banks, so defusing the 'backdoor nationalisation' charge and bringing the agency's operations into the market. These came to naught when the banks declared, in effect, that they did not believe in the 'equity gap'. Instead, a new body, Scottish Development Finance Ltd., was created *within* the agency to involve private businessmen in the investment decisions; in effect it is little more than an advisory committee. New guidelines were issued removing the requirement to create jobs and substituting that of providing 'stable and productive employment'. Finally, the chairman, a former Labour Lord Provost of Glasgow, was replaced by a businessman. More serious controversy took place over the promotion of 'inward investment' from abroad. As we shall see in Chapter Nine this led eventually to the function being partially hived off to another new body, Locate in Scotland, housed within the SDA but headed by a Scottish Office civil servant.

AGENCY STRUCTURE

Initially, the SDA's organisation reflected that of the agencies from which it had been formed. Gradually it has sought to integrate its functions and forge a common identity and policy. There are now seven directorates:

Finance and Industry Service responsible for dealing with larger Scottish companies and internal finance;

Small Business and Electronics with divisions for each;

Estates and Environment responsible for factory building and land renewal;

Planning and Projects, responsible for corporate planning, industrial programme development, area programme development, and initiatives in research and the health care industries;

Area Development, set up in 1982 to co-ordinate the agency's area projects (see below);

Investment (Scottish Development Finance Ltd.), responsible for involving the private sector in industrial development;

Marketing, responsible for industrial promotion, public relations and advertising.

In addition there is a Secretariat and Locate in Scotland, officially an 'associate organisation'.

It is Planning and Projects which has the task of formulating Agency policy, drawing together the work of the operational directorates and devising new initiatives. The three-year rolling Corporate Plan which is drawn up here goes for approval to the Board appointed in turn by the Secretary of State for Scotland. The Secretary of State sets guidelines for the agency's work covering matters such as the required rate of return on investments and must approve certain types of decision. In practice, there are close day-to-day links between the agency and SEPD to clear issues before formal decisions are made.

To get an idea of the allocation of resources within the agency let us look at the pattern of expenditure in the year to March 1982. Of a total expenditure of just over £104 million some £61 million went on acquisition and maintenance of factories and industrial estates; some £12 million to new investment and managing existing investments; and £21 million to land reclamation and environmental improvement. The remainder went on promotion, research and advice. About £25 million was recovered, mainly from property rentals and sales and from investment income (SDA 1982).

AGENCY POLICY

As we have seen, the SDA was given a very general remit and had therefore to forge an identity and purpose in a difficult political climate. This took time to develop and, in its early years, the agency's role was largely reactive, responding to approaches by firms and local authorities, as well as carrying on its inherited commitments. It was able to avoid becoming a collector of 'lame ducks' by resisting pressure to a degree which might have been impossible for an elected body; by June 1977 it had accepted only four out of 38 rescue proposals (Radice 1978). However, it had, in 1976, been given by the Scottish Office the task of organising GEAR, the Glasgow Eastern Area Renewal.

This is an ambitious urban renewal project for the east end of Glasgow, involving a co-ordinated approach by the SDA, Glasgow District Council, Strathclyde Regional Council, the Scottish Office, the Scottish Special Housing Association, the Housing Corporation, the Greater Glasgow Health Board and the Manpower Services Commission and linking industrial, environmental and social policies. The establishment of GEAR was linked with the decision to cancel the proposed Stonehouse new town, representing a switch of resources from dispersal back into the inner city. There has been a great deal of criticism of GEAR on the grounds of the vagueness of its six key objectives and the failure to secure genuine inter-agency co-ordination. Some observers (Booth *et al* 1982) have claimed that little has been achieved which would not have happened anyway though others (Boyle and Wannop 1982) have maintained that the programme, by binding the participants to some degree, has safeguarded commitments which otherwise might have been cut back. Although in 1982 a review of GEAR concluded that it should continue for another five years the agency was already seeking gradually to disengage itself from the commitment, which was absorbing a large part of its resources, in order to branch out into new initiatives. These had emerged from the SDA's experiences over the years and from its search for a more 'pro-active' as opposed to 'reactive' role and are of two types, area projects and sectoral initiatives.

Area projects grew out of the experiences of GEAR and of two 'fire brigade' operations into which the agency had been led by the Scottish Office. In 1979, a Scottish Office-led working party produced an SDA-led task force to cope with the problems raised by the closure of the Glengarnock steel works. In 1980, the agency was pressed to take the lead in another task force at Clydebank, following the closure of the Singer factory. It later took on the responsibility for organising and managing the Clydebank 'Enterprise Zone'. Originally billed as an experiment in non-intervention, the Enterprise Zone thus became the focus of intense interventionist activity! (Keating 1981). But all this was largely reactive and the SDA was in danger of becoming an agency for distressed areas rather than a force for growth and regeneration; it was also in danger of being branded as a purely West of Scotland operation.

So a more structured approach to area initiatives was decided on in the form of Area Projects, multi-agency programmes focused on small areas but, unlike GEAR, confined to the SDA's major economic and environmental activities. Leith was chosen as the site of the first of these projects, having been identified by Planning and Projects as an area threatened with industrial decline which could be 'pulled back' by some positive action; it also had the political advantage of being on the East Coast. An Area Development Directorate was set up to absorb the former directorate of Urban Renewal — until then preoccupied almost exclusively with GEAR — and parts of Estates and Environment. Area Development is essentially a co-ordinating rather than an operational directorate but the commitment to the area-based approach was affirmed by a Board decision to aim to spend 60% of 'targetable' agency resources in the Project areas.

Since then, Projects have been drawn up for other areas. While the content of these varies considerably according to local conditions, the basic format is an Agreement devised in Planning and Projects committing the agency and its partners to decisions and financial commitments over the period specified. These differ from many of the multi-agency approaches to urban renewal which have been so generally criticised in recent years in several respects.

First, the agency is able, despite the political pressures we have noted, to choose most of its own locations. The policy is to go not simply for the areas with the worst problems but for those with the greatest potential for improvement. If agreement is not forthcoming from the local authorities it can refuse to proceed. Further, the agency is able to offer, as a reward for co-operation, considerable investment funds and entrepreneurial skills. This gives a potentially strong leadership role in making co-operative arrangements work. On the other hand, some of the early Project Agreements committed the agency to a very precise programme of factory provision and environmental improvement but gave only generalised or non-timetabled objectives to the local authorities. There is, in any case, a limit to the number of leadership roles which the the SDA can take on at any one time. Some of the smaller projects give the district council the lead role, with the agency choosing to take a back seat. With all these reservations, however, the Area Projects do provide a promising Scottish contribution to the problem of co-ordinated urban renewal.

The agency's 'sectoral' work in industry has similarly developed from a reactive to a pro-active role. Research on the Scottish economy identified opportunities in electronics, health care industries, energy related industries and advanced production engineering. Further studies identified specific gaps and requirements in these sectors and policies were devised, through investment, attraction of overseas capital and advice, to meet these. A number of 'science parks' are being established in collaboration with universities and industry.

Given the agency's limited resources, it has been unable to cope with the growth of unemployment in Scotland or the consequences of major industrial collapses. Indeed, where possible, it has avoided taking on responsibility for the latter except in a limited role. Again despite political pressures, it has sought to make the creation of internationally competitive industry and not the creation or maintenance of jobs the criterion for action — in the modern world the two do not necessarily mean the same thing. This has undoubtedly helped it to survive the change of government in 1979 and emerge as an ally of the Scottish Office in securing for Scotland as large a share as possible of modern industrial developments.

The link between the agency's area and sectoral programmes appears rather tenuous. Although there are connections, the sectoral work is orientated to Scotland as a whole, choosing optimum locations according to industrial needs. So while environmental improvement and, to a lesser extent, factory building, have been steered into the Project Areas, most of the investment and overseas attraction work is considered 'non-targetable' within Scotland. So, although the agency would maintain that sectoral and area approaches are two essential and complementary ways of getting at Scotland's industrial and economic problems, there is a certain amount of tension between them. This emerged in the proposal for an ambitious Area Project for Dundee, based on a consultant's report which had identified sectoral possibilities in electronics and health care within the area. This aroused some suspicion that the sectoral work might have to be subordinated to area considerations though in the event the two have tended to remain separate.

A SUCCESS?

Has the SDA been a success? Perhaps not, measured against the promise of Labour's 1974 election manifesto to make it 'the main instrument for the regeneration of the Scottish economy'. Such a regeneration would require measures at a UK and international level to increase the demand for Scottish goods and services. If, however, one adopts a more realistic view of what such an agency can achieve, the record is more positive. It has established an entrepreneurial role in Scotland's economic and physical development, intervening selectively and *seeking* out opportunities, such as those in high technology industry and area redevelopment. At a time when 'quangos' have come under sharp criticism for their cost and lack of accountability, it might be argued that much of the SDA's success is attributable precisely to the fact that, free of direct democratic control and partially insulated from political pressure, it is able to act in an entrepreneurial way, to compete for industry with other parts of the UK, and to take risks and unpopular decisions. It has thus come a little way to filling the gap left by the collapse of Scottish indigenous enterprise since the First World War.

The Highlands and Islands Development Board

The Highlands and Islands of Scotland have long been recognised as an area presenting special problems. Before 1745, they presented a military problem. In the nineteenth century they presented a social and economic problem as overcrowding and evictions led large numbers of Highlanders to emigrate. By the late nineteenth century, they presented a political problem as the crofters, organised into a disciplined and effective movement, succeeded in electing five MPs to Westminster and securing favourable legislation on crofting rights. In the twentieth century, however, population continued to decline, unemployment was consistently high and the traditional occupations of farming, fishing and home industries continued to run down while few of the newer, expanding industries came to the region. Even the Highland whisky industry suffered a severe recession in the 1930s. The causes of these difficulties were seen by reformers as partly to do with the physical environment and its remoteness from markets and centres of population but also as social and political. The system of land-ownership by large estates was seen as a major problem as was the absence of development capital; hence a long series of proposals for special agencies to tacke these problems directly.

In 1928 the Liberal Party proposed a Highland board and from the 1950s the Labour Party and the Scottish Trades Union Congress advocated variations on a type of new town development corporation to supersede or work with local authorities in the Highlands. For many people, the Highlands were a stain on Scotland's conscience and the parties of the left had inherited a long tradition of opposition to the interests of Highland landowners. Special measures were seen as necessary to overcome centuries of neglect and the area's natural disadvantages, but the dominance of landlord and Conservative interests meant that any such initiative would have to come from outside. The structure of local government in the Highlands was in any case unfitted for undertaking major regional development and planning initiatives. For the Labour Party, success could, further, pay electoral dividends in an area where it had, despite considerable effort, failed to make a major breakthrough, to the rural and small town working class. The Liberals' interest in the Highlands was strengthened by their electoral successes there in the 1960s.

So Labour's return to office led to the creation, in 1965, of a Highland and Islands Development Board with the general task of 'preparing, concerting, promoting, assisting and undertaking measures for the economic and social development of the Highlands and Islands', defined as the seven crofting counties and any adjacent areas which the Secretary of State by order might designate. In more detail, its duties were (a) to keep under review everything relating to the economic and social well-being of the area; (b) after consultation with local authorities and other bodies, submit proposals to the Secretary of State; (c) undertake, or assist in the implementation of any proposals approved; (d) advise the Secretary of State and prepare an annual report (Williams 1973). Its powers are considerable. It can, with the approval of the Secretary of State, compulsorily acquire land, hold, manage and dispose of it. With the approval of the Secretary of State and the Treasury, it can set up and carry on any business. It can provide training, management, accountancy and other services; promote the publicising of the Highlands and Islands; and, in accordance with arrangements approved by the Secretary of State and the Treasury, give grants and loans. It can engage in other activities to promote industrial, commercial and other enterprises, carry out or commission research and charge for services; and, again with the consent of the Secretary of State and the Treasury, can borrow money. It does not require local planning permission for its own developments but the Secretary of State must consult the local authority before approving developments. (In practice, the HIDB has worked within local planning policies.) The status of the HIDB was emphasised in its constitution. Four of the seven board members, including the Chairman, are full time, appointed by the Secretary of State for Scotland for five-year terms. They are advised by the Highlands and Islands Development Consultative Council, comprising nominees from local authorities and other interests.

So the Board has a wide remit and was surrounded by high hopes on its establishment. However, it was hampered by its limited resources and by a series of dilemmas as to the strategy it should employ for using these resources. While the objective of promoting the economic and social development of the Highlands might appear to be a relatively straight-forward one, it in fact concealed an important strategic policy choice, namely: was the HIDB to go for an 'assimilationist' strategy, linking the Highlands into the national economy and producing economic and social conditions similar to those of the rest of the country? or was it to try and preserve traditional ways of life and the distinctive character of the Highlands?

At the outset, this dilemma presented itself in the form of a choice between a strategy of industrialisation, based on the fashionable idea of 'growth centres', particularly around the Moray Firth; or a dispersed effort to hold population and preserve traditional activities in the periphery of the west and the islands. In the 1960s, under the impetus of the first chairman, Sir Robert Grieve, prominence was given to the growth centre policy (Carter 1975). This reflected the mood of the times, the push for growth and the assumption of a continually expanding population. There was a widespread belief that only manufacturing industry could provide the numbers of jobs required for the future; and there was a great deal of pressure on the Board to 'think big'. Major industrial projects could only realistically be sited in the most favoured locations in the Highlands, so strengthening the arguments for growth centres. The most dramatic expression of this strategy was the 'Jack Holmes plan' for a city of half a million people on the Moray Firth, though this should be seen as a projection of ways in which such growth could be accommodated rather than a firm Board objective.

At the same time, the HIDB did not lose sight of its other goals and, indeed, its first report stated 'No matter what success is achieved in the eastern or central Highlands . . . the Board will be judged by its ability to hold population in the true crofting areas' (HIDB 1981). In practice, the Board's resources have gone increasingly into these areas as it has pulled back from the grand plans of the 1960s to concentrate on small projects on a case-by-case basis. This is partly in recognition of the fact that the HIDB's resources are not sufficient to undertake very large projects; and partly in recognition of the inherent limitations of planning in a mixed economy. An interventionist agency like the HIDB can anticipate market trends and encourage innovation, as it has done, for instance, in establishing a fish processing plant at Beasclete or building hotels on the islands. It cannot, however, go directly counter to market trends, as it needs private sector involvement in its projects and they need to be viable in the long run. At the same time, population projections for the UK as a whole have been revised sharply downwards and large-scale planning has gone out of fashion. Manufacturing industry as a whole has gone into decline and is no longer universally recognised as the most promising source of jobs. So the Board has adopted more of a 'reactive' strategy, backing likely developments, whether in manufacturing, tourism, agriculture or fisheries, wherever they appear. Although it still favours industrial development around the Moray Firth, its encouragement is primarily non-financial.

This change of emphasis also owes a great deal to the entry onto the scene of other agencies, notably the Highlands Regional Council, the Scottish Economic Planning Department and the Scottish Development Agency. Local government reform meant that the HIDB was no longer the only agency with the ability to draw up large-scale plans for the Highlands and it has handed over most of its planning function to the regional and islands councils, while retaining membership of appropriate working parties and commenting on plans. It supported Highland Region's Structure Plan at the Examination in Public but criticised Strathclyde Region's in respect of the proposals for Argyll, the only part of Strathclyde to fall within the HIDB area.

Transport responsibilities, too, have been redefined. In the 1960s, the Board was officially recognised as the Secretary of State's principal adviser on Highland transport. Since then, the new local authorities have assumed major transport responsibilities, through the Transport Policies and Programmes System. So the Board has withdrawn from detailed work on transport investment priorities; but it continues to concern itself with those matters receiving little attention in TPPs, notably air services and freight movement. It has also taken a particular interest in ferry services, promoting the idea of the Road Equivalent Tariff.

With the Scottish Development Agency, the Board has concluded a 'concordat' governing their respective responsibilities. The HIDB looks after industrial estates and small businesses (the SDA's Small Business and Scottish Industrial Estates divisions do not operate in the Highlands). Large-scale projects will be the subject of discussions involving the SDA, HIDB and SEPD and could receive help in various forms from any of them; the HIDB in the form of grant, the SDA in the form of equity and the SEPD in the form of selective assistance. In practice, it is very rare for any enterprise to be funded from more than one of these sources but it can happen. In general, as we have seen, the HIDB has concentrated aid on small projects in the western Highlands, leaving the major developments around the Moray Firth to other agencies.

In tourist promotion, the Board has an agreement with the Scottish Tourist Board whereby it is responsible for the promotion of the Highlands at home and overseas. Under the Board are sixteen Area Tourist Organisations responsible for local promotion and dealing with visitors. Tourist promotion is thus linked with the Board's development function, under which it provides grants and loans for investment in tourist facilities.

Outside the field of development, the HIDB undertakes a wide variety of tasks. It commissions and undertakes research, makes representations to central and local government on Highland problems, seeks out development opportunities and engages in overseas promotion and educational work, its activities responding to the perceived needs of the time. It has been criticised for its 'reactive' stance and for not making more use of its statutory powers. In particular, it has come under attack on the vexed question of land. The HIDB was on its establishment given powers of compulsory purchase and it was widely hoped that it would be able to take radical measures to tackle alleged land under-utilisation and misuse. However, legal opinion held that it would be extremely difficult for the Board to use these powers effectively, given resistance by landlords and lengthy court actions. So little happened until Sir Kenneth Alexander, the Board's third chairman, launched a new initiative in the 1970s. Alexander produced a scheme for action short of compulsory purchase whereby local committees could examine problems of land under-utilisation and work out voluntary schemes in conjunction with landowners. The ultimate sanction would be the power to put in a 'designated tenant' to work the land. This scheme was put to government in 1978 but no response came until after the Conservatives had returned to office. The the Secretary of State declared that he was not persuaded that the Board's existing powers were inadequate. So, if there has been a lack of action on land problems in the Highlands, it would appear that lack of political will on the part of governments is as much to blame as timidity by the HIDB.

Controversies have also broken out over HIDB-backed developments where differing Highland interests have clashed. In 1981, a proposal for expanded skiing facilities in the Cairngorms, backed by the Board, aroused considerable opposition from conservationists and mountaineers, wishing to preserve the natural environment. The consequent public inquiry revealed deep conflicts over the use of the Highland environment and the form which development should take.

Over the years, then, the HIDB has retreated from the brave visions of some of its early backers, as a vehicle for the radical transformation of the Highland economy. Its role was described by its second chairman, Sir Andrew Gilchrist, as 'a merchant bank with a social purpose'. An idea of its operating priorities can be gained from the distribution of Board assistance by sector. From 1971-81, taking grants, loans and equity purchases together, some 13% went to land development; 24% to fisheries; 23% to manufacturing and processing; 4% to construction; 30% to tourism; and 6% to other service industries (HIDB 1981). This allocation is to a large extent 'demand led' in that, although budgets are allocated to these headings in advance, they reflect past experience and take-up rates. So the large allocation for tourism reflects the expansion of that industry in the 1970s and allocations for individual projects can reflect the increasing need for the Board, like other interventionist agencies, to mount rescue operations for troubled firms. In terms of the geographical distribution of aid in the same period, there was a definite bias towards the more remote areas and islands (HIDB 1981).

An assessment of the success of the Board is extremely difficult, given its multiple objectives and all the other factors which are working to influence the Highland economy. For instance, oil development has had a major impact in parts of the Board's area out of all proportion to any Board activity. Particularly in the better-favoured areas like the Moray Firth, major developments have been proposed of a scale larger than that which the Board can handle. However, the Board's own figures give a total of 60,465 jobs created or retained over the decade 1971-81, and by 1980, while unemployment had increased everywhere, the rise in the Highlands and Islands had been less severe than for Scotland or the UK as a whole. Population figures for the Highlands as a whole had stabilised by 1971 and during the 1970s showed a gradual increase. However, the increase has tended to be in the more favoured areas around Inverness and, during the 1970s, the oil-affected areas. In the more peripheral rural areas there has been continued decline or, at best, no change, though even in the latter case there has often been a movement from country to small town. Thus, on the criteria laid down by its first chairman, to hold population in the true crofting areas, the Board has not been an unqualified success. However, it is almost certain that, without the Board's intervention, matters would have been considerably worse.

The Scottish Council (Development and Industry)

The Scottish Council (D & I), a unique Scottish institution, almost exactly fits the original definition of a 'quango'—'a formally private organisation . . . carrying out public policy functions, normally on a contractual basis, on behalf of government' (Hogwood 1979). It was founded in the 1930s as the Scottish Development Council by a group of industrialists concerned about Scotland's industrial decline. In 1942, Secretary of State Tom Johnston set up the Scottish Council on Industry to bring government and industrialists together. The two bodies later amalgamated to form the present Scottish Council (Development and Industry), hence its rather cumbersome name. Since the war, the Council's membership and tasks have expanded. It now comprises representatives of large and small firms, chambers of commerce, banks, trade unions and local authorities, with the bulk of its finance coming from large firms and regional councils.

While the Council would maintain that its basic objective, to promote economic and industrial development in Scotland, has not altered over the years, the tasks which it undertakes have changed in response to developments in industry and the machinery of government. Many of these developments, in turn, have been in response to proposals emanating from the Council itself. The Council's quasi-governmental role expanded considerably in the post-war years when the machinery of industrial and economic planning in Scotland was weak and the Scottish Office still felt inhibited by its status as a department of central government in openly lobbying private and overseas investors to give Scotland preference over other parts of the UK. Attraction of such inward investment, funded both by government grants and from its own resources, accounted, by the mid-1970s, for some three-quarters of the Council's work. In addition, trade missions were undertaken with the backing of the British Overseas Trade Board. Policy developments included the production, with government backing, of the 1961 Toothill Report on the Scottish economy and, in the early 1970s, the Oceanspan and Eurospan plans. In 1974 the policy side of the Council was strengthened by the establishment of the Scottish Council Research Institute which looks at general policy issues as well as providing data services for members.

During the 1970s the increasing economic role of the Scottish Office and its associated agencies (see Chapter Nine), in particular the creation of the Scottish Economic Planning Department and the Scottish Development Agency, led to a reduction in the Council's workload. In part, it was the victim of its own success as it had itself campaigned for the creation of these specialised agencies. For a time, the Council acted as agent for the SDA in attracting inward investment but in 1979 the Agency took over the task itself; at the same time, the export promotion role, as agent for the British Overseas Trade Board, began to shrink under the impact of expenditure cuts.

The Council has consequently become less of a 'quango' and more of a private body providing services for its members and lobbying government for favourable policies. For its members, it provides the services of the Research Institute and a meeting place for the exchange of advice, ideas and information. There is an annual International Forum at Aviemore and committees and working parties produce a steady stream of papers on a variety of industrial subjects. Though these committees tend to be staffed by people from the larger firms, who can afford to release them, by and large, the Council's services are probably of most use to small firms who lack the resources for their own research or export promotion drives. Co-operation is thus a strong theme in the Council's work and this extends to its relationships with government. As a broadly representative body including both sides of industry as well as local authorities of diverse political complexions, it carries some weight with government but the corollary of this is a considerable difficulty in reaching consensus on major contentious questions of economic and industrial policy. In matters where Scottish interests appear clearly in opposition to those of other regions, for instance in UK or EEC regional policy or competition for overseas investment, agreement is easier. On the other hand, as the wider question of the proper degree of government intervention in industry has aroused deepening controversy in recent years, the Scottish Council has been unable to take a definite line on it. So, while it called for the creation of the SDA to unite the tasks of land clearance and industrial attraction, it was silent on the Agency's investment role. Similarly, while the Council has always campaigned against centralisation and for the recognition of Scotland's distinctive needs, it had to take a cautious line on devolution, once this had become an issue between the Conservative and Labour parties in the mid-1970s. Its submission to government in response to the 1974 consultative paper on devolution largely avoided the question of a Scottish Assembly calling, instead, for the dispersal of UK government departments to Scotland. The quasi-independent Research Institute, however, took a bolder line shortly after its establishment in 1974, producing a report which advocated a very radical measure of economic devolution (SCRI 1974).

The Scottish Council maintains extremely close links with government, both through politicians and through civil servants. While some contacts do exist with UK departments, it is the Scottish Office which provides its main route into both UK and EEC centres of decision-making. Regular meetings with ministers and informal exchanges with civil servants cover all matters relating to Scottish industry and development, allowing the Scottish Office to use information from the Council in contributing to UK and Scottish policy making on all questions where there is a distinctive Scottish aspect. In addition, some direct contacts have been made with the EEC, using the services of Scots retired diplomats to bring influence to bear on the creation of the Regional Fund and sending staff members on secondment to the European Coal and Steel Community, to learn about the workings of the system and how it can be used to the advantage of Scottish industry.

The loss of its quasi-governmental role and rumours of financial crisis combined with the resignation of the Director in 1981 to place a question mark over the future of the Scottish Council. At a time of sharp political conflict, whether over devolution, government intervention in industry or public expenditure cuts, such a broadly based body concerned with public policy is bound to come under strain. However, it is likely to survive as a comtinuing direct channel to government for the economic community in Scotland and a means whereby industrialists, trade unionists and others can come together to promote common Scottish interests without prejudicing their wider political or industrial loyalties.

The Manpower Services Commission

The Manpower Services Commission (MSC) was set up in the early 1970s to take over the Department of Employment's employment and training services and the Government's special employment creation programmes. Its extremely complex national, regional and local structure can only be described in outline. The Commission itself consists of nominated members representing government, employers, trade unions and other interests and is responsible for broad MSC policy. There are separate structures of line management for three divisions — employment services, training services and special programmes, reaching down to the local level. Cutting across these is a regional structure, including the Scottish region. The Scottish director has line responsibility for the special programmes division but, for the other two divisions, he has only a co-ordinating role. There is also an MSC advisory committee for Scotland and, a feature unique to Scotland and Wales, a Manpower Research Unit. The latter is responsible to the Scottish Director, as is the Manpower Intelligence Unit.

Although MSC is sponsored by the Department of Employment and its employees are officially part of the DE group of the civil service, the Secretary of State for Scotland does have a role here in guiding its activities. His existing responsibilities for the Scottish economy, the calls for 'economic' devolution in the 1970s and the decision, following the proposed establishment of a Scottish Assembly, to give the Secretary of State an enhanced economic role, led to his formal involvement in manpower policy. He is consulted by the Secretary of State for Employment before the MSC's corporate plan is approved. Then, within the framework of this plan and in consultation with the Scottish advisory committee, a plan for Scotland is drawn up. This is in turn subject to approval by the Secretary of State for Scotland, in consultation with the national chairman of the MSC and, where appropriate, the Secretary of State for Employment. Most of the work of the MSC in Scotland is funded through the Scottish Office vote, though this is not part of the expenditure block over which the Secretary of State has unlimited powers of virement.

There is thus an intricate meshing of Scottish and UK elements in policy making for the MSC in Scotland. Within the overall framework of UK policy on matters such as the total budget for training or employment centres, there is scope for some variations in Scotland. However, this is tightly constrained by the line structure of the MSC's own divisions, with their direct links to London, and by the existence of a UK-wide labour market which requires uniformity on matters like rates of allowance and minimum ages for those on training courses. There is more scope for variation in operational matters, such as responding to the needs of local labour markets within Scotland or deciding, in consultation with the MSC nationally, on the mix of different types of training. On the Special Programmes side, there is a large measure of decentralisation to local offices but this does not imply a distinct Scottish-level policy.

The MSC in Scotland maintains close links with other bodies in the economic and industrial policy network, at both Scottish and UK levels. It helps the Scottish Economic Planning Department with advice, assessments of employment and parliamentary questions. It consults with the Scottish Education Department on training matters and co-operates with the Scottish Development Agency on industrial concerns, seeking a common assessment of the employment needs of Scotland which can be incorporated in its national and Scottish policy. It is also able to draw together resources to deal with major crises, such as large-scale redundancies, taking the lead in assembling packages of measures, involving both UK and Scottish agencies.

The MSC in Scotland is less clearly a Scottish entity than the SDA or the HIDB, being an integral part of its UK parent organisation. It does have the ability to operate in both UK and Scottish networks and to make some allowances for the distinctive Scottish environment in which it works. However, supporters of devolution have claimed that there is scope and need for a more distinctive Scottish manpower policy and that this could be one of the principal economic powers of a Scottish Assembly.

The Scottish Consumer Council

We include the Scottish Consumer Council (SCC) in our survey of 'quangos' as an example of an officially sponsored pressure-body created to give a Scottish dimension to a UK-wide function. The SCC is part of the National Consumer Council (NCC) set up and funded by the Department of Trade to act as a watchdog for consumer interests, particularly in relation to legislation and the operation of public authorities. Councils were set up for Scotland and Wales (though not for England) as subcommittees of the NCC. Appointments are made by ministers through the grapevine of consultation of interested organisations and there is a small full-time staff.

The Scottish Consumer Council tends to focus on peculiarly Scottish issues, leaving UK affairs to the NCC. From time to time, however, it is able to bring a viewpoint based on Scottish experience to UK discussions, for instance on Sunday trading laws, which do not exist in Scotland or on milk supply, where pricing policies and the delivery system are rather different. In other cases, it takes the lead over the NCC where it has acquired a particular expertise. For instance, it was brought into the field of civil aviation from its involvement with flights to the Highlands and Islands. From there, it went on to consider Scotland-England flights. With the experience thus built up, it was able to act on behalf of the NCC in negotiations at the EEC level. Similarly, the SCC has become particularly involved in insurance matters because of the large numbers of insurance companies which have their headquarters in Scotland.

Although sponsored and financed by the Department of Trade, the SCC has close links with the departments of the Scottish Office. Their informal contacts enable SCC staff to learn what is happening or about to happen in the field of consumer policy and to take appropriate action. This can on occasion involve supporting the Scottish Office in presenting a united Scottish front in battles with Whitehall departments, though it is always necessary for the SCC to be looking over its shoulder at its sponsoring department.

Links with the parent body, the National Consumer Council, are of course very close with daily contact on matters of policy. Although the SCC does make its own policy on Scottish matters, it tries to avoid contradicting the NCC policy line, and generally goes along with the latter on matters which it has chosen to investigate. There are also links with local authorities and a wide range of voluntary organisations in Scotland, concerned with consumer affairs, transport, housing and other public services. So the SCC represents a form of decentralisation or 'administrative devolution' analogous to that of the Scottish Office itself — a separate organisation able to respond flexibly to Scottish conditions while at the same time remaining a part of its UK parent and operating within a remit set at the UK level. Its success will thus depend on its skill in operating in the UK and Scottish networks and managing the links between the two.

The National Health Service
ORGANISATION AND MANAGEMENT

The National Health Service in Scotland is organised on the same principles as that in England — that is, as a separate organisation distinct from central government departments and from local authorities but financed entirely by central government. Such a structure has been defended on grounds of the uniqueness of the service and the need to preserve the independence of clinical judgment from political pressure. It has been criticised, on the other hand, as giving too much power over resource allocation to the medical professions and as artificially separating health questions from the social and environmental policies of local government.

When the NHS was created in 1948, a decision was taken to allocate responsibility for it to the Secretary of State for Scotland. A number of reasons lay behind this. The Scottish Office had traditionally looked after health matters in Scotland and during the war had pioneered several initiatives. The development of medical services in Scotland presented several distinctive features. For example, the four Scottish medical schools provided about a third of all medical graduates in the United Kingdom. As a result of the presence of the teaching hospitals, the cities were relatively well endowed with medical services but on the other hand general practitioners often faced financial problems and in some areas were in very short supply. Finally, the participation of local authorities in some areas of health policy provided another reason for bringing health services under the control of the Scottish Office though in the event integration of NHS and local government services has been no greater than in England.

The National Health Service (Scotland) Act, 1947, created a tripartite administrative system within a national framework under the Secretary of State. The *hospital and specialist services* were administered by five Regional Hospital Boards, decentralised into sixty-five Boards of Management for hospitals or groups of hospitals. *Family practitioner services* were administered by twenty-five executive councils. In Scotland, in contrast to England, the Secretary of State assumed responsibility for the provision and finance of health centres, to allow central planning to meet the needs of areas of inadequate supply. Finally, *community and environmental services* were provided by fifty-five local health authorities. Ambulances and blood transfusion were provided on a national basis by the Secretary of State.

By the 1960s, there was a strong belief in Scotland, as in England and Wales, that the system was in need of reform. This was a time when administrative reform was much in fashion and the arguments for reform of the NHS were strikingly similar to the arguments used to justify local government reform (see Chapter Five). As expenditure grew in the 1960s, it was felt that there were too many units, leading to fragmentation (Brown 1978). This resulted in problems of planning and co-ordination, and ineffective use of resources (English and Martin 1979). At the same time, changes in technology were seen as pointing to bigger and more cost-effective units. One report published in 1965, *Administrative practices of Hospital Boards in Scotland*, whilst acknowledging the existence of *ad hoc* arrangements between service sectors in some areas, argued that there was a need to ensure more effective integration of service provision to specific client groups (e.g. elderly or handicapped) than the existing structure provided. The creation of unified Social Work departments in 1969 gave a further boost to reform and a review of health service provision was set in motion.

Arguments in favour of a rationalisation of the administrative structure had been circulating for some ten years or so, and a Green Paper, *Administrative Reorganisation of the Scottish Health Services*, was published within a year. This largely reflected the views of 'insiders' and in particular the medical profession's opposition to making the reformed health services a function of local government. The Green Paper contained a number of proposals for a unified service, which formed the basis for consultation and negotiation between central departments and the professions, leading to a 1971 White Paper, *Reorganisation of the Scottish Health Services.*

The principles of reform were to provide unified units for organisation and management of health services, funded by central government. At national level, centralised planning would be provided by a Scottish Health Service Planning Council. Locally, there would be single health authority responsible for service provision, supplemented by a professional advisory system and a system of local health councils. The new system became effective from 1974.

HEALTH BOARDS

The fifteen Health Boards took over most of the functions of the Regional Hospital Boards, Local Health Authorities and Executive Councils. They are responsible to the Secretary of State for Scotland for the planning and provision of integrated health services, and as such concentrate on strategic policy issues such as the allocation of resources. Board chairmen are appointed by the Secretary of State, and Board members are drawn from local authorities, trades and other organisations.

The management and administration of the service is delegated to an Area Executive Group, who also service the Boards at their meetings. This group comprises four senior officers, the Chief Administrative Medical Officer, the Chief Area Nursing Officer, the Treasurer and the Secretary. They are joined by the Chief Administrative Dental Officer and the Chief Pharmacist for the discussion of items relevant to their responsibilities. They are the Health Service equivalent of the local authority Management Team, and present advice and information to the Board to help it establish policy and priorities. Health Boards were encouraged to set up area programme planning committees, and we shall discuss their effectiveness in the next section.

For operational management, ten of the fifteen Boards have decentralised into districts. English and Martin (1979) argued that in the creation of districts primary account was taken of the distribution of existing health care resources and patterns of use, and that "continuity of interest" was achieved in part by reference to the district units of the new local authorities. A District Executive Group, composed of a District Administrator, District Nursing Officer, District Medical Officer and District Finance Officer, are jointly accountable to the Area Executive Group for a number of functions but have considerable autonomy over day-to-day management issues within the framework of Health Board policy.

Fig. 3.1

ADMINISTRATIVE STRUCTURE OF NHS IN SCOTLAND

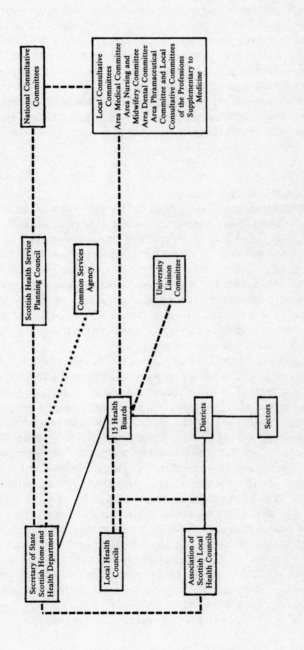

National Consultative Committees

Local Consultative Committees
Area Medical Committee
Area Nursing and Midwifery Committee
Area Dental Committee
Area Phramaceutical Committee and Local Consultative Committees of the Professions Supplementary to Medicine

Scottish Health Service Planning Council

Common Services Agency

University Liaison Committee

15 Health Boards

Districts

Sectors

Secretary of State Scottish Home and Health Department

Local Health Councils

Association of Scottish Local Health Councils

Management relationship
Service relationship
Advisory relationship

THE PROFESSIONAL ADVISORY COMMITTEES

Whilst the medical professionals were present on the Health Boards, this membership was seen not as 'interest representation' but as reflecting 'management ability'. In practice, of course, the stress of role conflict on the part of participants asked to wear 'two hats' (professional/ managerial) cannot always be coped with by neutral disinterest. The White Paper insisted that a separate machinery be created for the articulation of professional views and advice, and professional advisory committees were created, at each tier in the administrative structure, area, district, and also at national level where the chairmen of all national professional advisory committees attend meetings of the Scottish Health Services Planning Council.

LOCAL HEALTH COUNCILS

Having made provision for professional interests, the 1972 Act created a new mechanism for the 'consumer' of the service to make their views known. Unlike local government, where the policy-makers are directly elected and accountable for their actions, democratic control of the service is theoretically through the Secretary of State's accountability to Parliament. Many of the complaints of the electorate about local government services are channelled through local councillors, and also the community councils. This aspect of democratic accountability over the *detail* of service provision has no real counterpart in the health service, and this was an issue of some concern.

Bochel and Maclaran (1979) argue that before reorganisation, there was substantial participation by lay members. They saw the creation of health councils as a gesture to those concerned about democratic scrutiny and participation, and also to assuage fears of centralisation. (The parallels to the creation of community councils in local government are very close.) Members are appointed by local authorities, and also by the Health Board from voluntary organisations and trade unions. There are forty-eight councils, who must be consulted by Health Boards on any major development in the pattern service provision (e.g. hospital closure). According to English and Martin, these councils have had mixed fortunes, and found it difficult to establish a community identity. Further, they argue that unlike professional advisory committees, they do not have the experience, understanding or expertise about the operation of the National Health Service which would enable them to make timely and effective interjections in the decision-making process. With minor exceptions they have failed to make much impact and been given little attention by most Health Boards (English and Martin, 1979, p. 68).

There is a major question of principle here, about the relative importance to be given to professional or technical judgments and political considerations. Bochel and Maclaran (1979) point to the stress on consensus and the dislike of politics within the health services while the former Secretary of State for Scotland, William Ross, claimed that 'the medical profession hold up their hands in horror when they hear about public participation'. On the other hand, the Health Councils are there to provide the 'lay' or 'community' input into decision-making, an essentially political (though not in the party sense) role. Given their lack of executive power and the conflict of values involved, with Councils, for instance, advocating decentralised provision on 'community' grounds, while the professionals insist on centralised provision for reasons of technical efficiency, the role can often be a deeply frustrating one.

THE SCOTTISH HEALTH SERVICES PLANNING COUNCIL

The Planning Council was created in 1972 to ensure that effective strategies could be devised and implemented to improve Scottish health service provision on an integrated basis, in a context of limited available resources, with the fullest participation from the health authorities.

The chairman is appointed by the Secretary of State, there is one representative from each Health Board, one from each university medical school, and six civil servants from SHHD. The chairmen from all national professional advisory committees attend, and the Council has the power to co-opt onto its planning groups. The Council provides a meeting place for central government and the Health Service. There is also a Health Service Planning Unit in SHHD, which provides information and advice to the Council. Wide participation of administrators and professionals in the planning process is therefore possible. The Planning Council operates through a series of programme planning groups, each of which is concerned either with one specific aspect of the services, or with the needs of one client group.

THE COMMON SERVICES AGENCY

This central mechanism provides support services (ambulance, blood transfusion, major capital projects, common administrative training, the legal service and health education) so that Health Boards would not have to duplicate these functions. A Management Committee supervises an amalgam of agencies which provide different services, under the chairmanship of a Health Board chairman. The other members are from the Health Boards (three) and civil servants from SHHD (five).

The organisational charts of any administrative system provide a static rather than dynamic description of how things actually happen. Like many administrative developments of the 'seventies, reorganisation of health was imbued with the planning philosophy which dominated thinking about how the business of government could be improved. All this took place in a political context. It is to the interplay between the planning philosophy and the reality of day-to-day politics that we now turn.

PLANNING, POLITICS AND RESOURCE ALLOCATION

The Scottish Health Service fared well in the era of public expenditure growth. In the period 1964-75 there was an annual average growth rate in real terms of 4.5% per annum, while the annual growth in total population has been only 0.1%.

By 1975, the total revenue expenditure had reached £462.5 million and capital expenditure £32.7 million. Within these totals, the share consumed by Hospital Services grew from 66% to 72%, whilst the share of family practitioner services had fallen from 22% to 16%. 1975-76, however, marked a turning point in the pattern of expenditure development, with the publication of the SHHD statement of priorities, *"The Health Service in Scotland: The Way Ahead"*.

This marked the recognition that the past practice of confining discussion of policy options to the use of the new resources represented by the regular growth of expenditure was unsatisfactory, and that if new developments were sought, then savings would have to be generated from within existing services. *The Way Ahead* attempted to draw up a national framework of policy priorities for service development. The details of expenditure, however, remained the preserve of the Health Boards, who accounted for 90% of revenue expenditure. The emphasis in *The Way Ahead* was on the need for the Health Boards to make the most effective use of existing resources by taking account of six main principles.

1. The need to operate the services within the budgets available which allow for a limited measure of growth.
2. The need to promote health care in the community through the progressive improvement of primary care services and community health services.
3. More positive development of health services for families in areas of multiple deprivation.
4. Lessening the growth rate of the acute sector of the hospital service in order to finance essential developments in other sectors.
5. Continued improvements in hospital and community health services for the elderly, the mentally ill, the mentally handicapped and the physically handicapped.

6.   Encouragement of preventive measures and the development of a fully responsible attitude to health on the part of the individual and the community.

This quite clearly demanded a change in emphasis from hospital based institutional care to that of community care, what Hunter (1980) calls the 'cinderella' services, and also reallocation of resources *between* geographic areas, to ensure that allocations reflected need rather than the historic pattern of expenditure. Such policies necessarily challenged traditional interests and disturbed the power-relationships within the health policy network, particularly the medical profession.

The Way Ahead was seen only as a first step towards the development of a strategic planning cycle, reflecting the fashion for increased rationality in decision-making within which central policy documents would play a key role. One Government paper saw the system developing thus:

"It would be based on three yearly reviews, and would involve lengthy consultations with all interested parties — the Department taking an overview, with the views of the Scottish Health Service Planning Council and its advisory structure, and area planning statements produced by each Board on the basis of national guidelines derived from all central review. Ultimately, the Department would produce a composite area planning statement for the whole of Scotland. The Secretary of State could reject or modify the recommendations. *It is unlikely though that there would be at this stage any wide divergence of views within the health service in Scotland,* (our emphasis) since the proposals would have had considerable prior informal exposure."

(Royal Commission of the NHS, Research Paper No. 2, April 1978)

In 1980, the SHAPE (*Scottish Health Authorities: Priorities for the Eighties*) report was produced and Health Boards required to draw up a parallel set of their own priorities. These should correspond to the priority categories in the SHAPE report 'unless there are good reasons for departing from them in the light of local circumstances' (Milne 1982). The problem with such a rationalistic approach is that it rests upon a consensual view of inter and intra organisational relations, and ignores the inbuilt tension between central control and local autonomy. Local priorities may *not* accord with the view from the centre. Within health service organisations, different groups will pursue their interests, and given resource limitations, the exercise of choice becomes a necessity. The interplay between party and organisational politics is unlikely to produce the hierarchical, orderly, rational pattern of resource allocation assumed in central government's approach.

How then, are such conflicts of interest reconciled within the pursuit of rational planning? To answer that question we shall analyse three dimensions, the financing of the health service, the development of planning arrangements, and the politics of decision-making.

Hunter's (1980) study paints a picture of strong central control by SHHD, who provided finance, guided Health Boards in the implementation of government policy, and greatly influenced health service priorities. As we have seen, the bulk of expenditure is directly carried out by Health Boards, and, while this is also true in England and Wales, there are important differences from English arrangements. First of all, the *cash limit* system is not applied to individual Health Boards, but managed on a national basis by SHHD. Boards send in regular expenditure returns, which facilitate this. Secondly, greater leverage is offered by a more 'liberal' interpretation of the definition of capital, which allows possible underspend in capital programmes to be taken up by conventional revenue expenditure when necessary. Thirdly, some leeway is provided through the 'tolerance' of up to 1% of revenue expenditure, which means that a revenue *underspend* of 1% can be carried forward into the next financial year, whilst any overspend is reduced in the next year's budget. Finally, there is the SHHD's role of 'broker', which allows unspent funds to be 'deposited' with the department, and drawn upon in future years. Similarly, Boards who have a shortfall may borrow and repay in future years.

With regard to capital expenditure, it is necessary to distinguish between the 'national' programme and the 'ordinary' programme. The 'national' programme is approved by SHHD, who determine when the specific schemes will take place. The 'ordinary' programmes are funded by block allocation from SHHD, but larger projects (over £0.5 million) must be approved individually. There is no 'tolerance' agreement as with local authority capital funding (see Chapter Seven) and any slippage on large schemes will usually be taken up by bringing forward smaller projects.

Health expenditure has been treated favourably in recent years, and relatively protected from government cutback. Total current and capital in 1980-81 was £847 million from a total Scottish Office spending programme of £3,740 million, compared to only £757 million from a total budget of £3,886 million in 1975-76 (all at 1979 Survey prices).

The two strands in national policy in the 1970s were, as we have seen, a reorientation of expenditure by geographic area and by service development. This required the development of sophisticated planning systems for identifying the key decisions whereby the centre can control the general direction and development of the organisation while delegating as much operational decision-making as possible to the subsidiary units who can act both in the light of centrally determined general policy and in their awareness of local conditions and circumstances (Barnard and Lee 1977).

Wiseman (1979) argued that at national level, the existing process was an incremental one of administering and managing existing services, with new policies resulting from reaction to outside stimuli rather than research and analysis. The major planning innovation to counter this, and foster systematic corporate planning, was the establishment of Programme Planning Groups, which looked at, for example, the case of the elderly, mental disorder, child health, and cardiac surgery (Wiseman 1980). These developments were also taking place at local level, indeed this occurred as early as 1974 in the Greater Glasgow Health Board, which aimed to analyse major options facing the Board in a rational manner. A Programme was defined as an 'organised NHS response to reduce or eliminate one or more health problems. This response should be based on one or more objectives which should create targets against which performance can be measured. The setting of objectives, the planning of services and the evaluation of results should be seen as closely related processes'. The six PPCs established were maternity, child health, dental health, mental health, geriatric and primary care services. Related to this was the development of policy statements derived from a review of Scottish priorities or, as with *The Way Ahead* following DHHS leadership in producing its own strategic document, and because of the need to give guidance to Health Boards in the new era of economic stringency.

At Board level, reorganisation resulted in a slimmed down administrative structure, and the creation of policy and resources committees in Health Boards similar to those advocated by the Paterson report for local government (see Chapter Six). Lay representation was considerably reduced (Hunter 1980) and there was extensive decentralisation of operational management to area and district executive groups, leaving Boards free to deal with strategic policy making and the broad allocation of resources. However, the early research evidence suggests that little progress towards rational planning has been achieved, for four main reasons; problems of measuring need and output, inter-agency politics, organisational politics, and community politics.

Wiseman (1980) points out that little cross comparison of priorities has taken place, and indeed, that no consistent or coherent basis for setting priorities exists. The lack of objective data was commented on by Hunter, who asked, "How do decision-makers compare providing care for an elderly person with undertaking cardiac surgery for a middle-aged man suffering from heart disease?" (Hunter 1980). The Research for the Royal Commission on the NHS concluded that a striking feature of the decision-making process is its reliance on 'professional' judgment and the absence of formal criteria for the evaluation of capital developments. They quoted one major investment, a body scanner costing £0.4 million which was approved in a 72-hour period in order to avoid a large underspend in a budget! The main criteria was 'ability' rather than 'need' to spend (Royal Commission of the NHS Research Paper 2, April 1978). One review of ways of overcoming these problems suggested the use of "health status indices" whereby an individual's state of health would be measured, but rejected because the 'problem of measurement was insurmountable', and a more limited 'criteria' approach advocated. This latter approach would utilise 'explicit specification of a list of criteria which are relevant to the case study for priority attention', but relying on political processes and judgment in the determination of such criteria (Wiseman 1980).

Inter-agency politics was also a major constraint. In spite of oft recited views of the 'corporateness' of the Scottish Office, Wiseman concluded that 'departmentalism' made a corporate response difficult to achieve, with the Social Work Services Group and SHHD each pursuing multiple and often conflicting objectives. Relations with local authorities have often been marked by mutual incomprehension and lack of a common approach to problems. This stems partly from their differing environments and composition. The health service operates in accordance with an apolitical model in which the involvement of practitioners and professionals is of major significance, whereas local authorities are democratically elected bodies (Wiseman 1980).

Similar problems were found at Health Board level by Hunter, where decisions taken by the local authority affected the Health Board and vice versa. The policy of fostering community care is dependent upon home-help facilities offered by local authorities, but these were being reduced because of cuts in local government expenditure. Similar problems were encountered with SHHD, where conflicting advice hindered the development of this policy. Boards were asked in 1976 to give priority to schemes with no running costs, in contradiction to the policy of shifting the balance of health care provision towards deprived areas and community care. Such inconsistency makes rational planning very difficult.

Organisational politics also prevent the achievement of the corporate ideal. Within Health Boards for example, there are numerous competing interests, by sector, area and district, between members, officers and professionals, often resulting in role conflict for the various participants in Area/District Executive Groups. Boddy (1979) noted that a substantial degree of potential conflict existed within the programme planning committees, themselves reflecting the diverse interests within them.

Finally, there is the interaction of community politics. Hunter, Boddy, and Bochel and Maclaren are all pessimistic about the influence of lay representatives in health service bodies. Pressure from outside may be more effective. Successful campaigns of public resistance have been mounted against technically rational schemes for closures for example of acute beds scattered in small hospitals.

These factors together present a major hindrance to the attempt to rationalise provision and reallocate resources in the health service. The impression is one of only minimal change. Even the SHARE exercise (Scottish Health Authorities Resources Equalisation) intended to equalise resources between areas by 1988, was to do this only by utilising the increment of growth to cope with the political problem of achieving 'cuts' in the base.

Given the failure to achieve a rationalist consensus or develop purely technical criteria for judging health policies, political conflict remains a feature of the NHS. The politics of health are as pervasive as the politics of housing or education. At the moment, the evidence strongly suggests that the democratic element is much weaker than the bureaucratic or the professional, but as Barnard (1977) argues, "expert solutions always evade or conceal the underlying problem of politics". Hunter (1980) suggests that the 1974 reorganisation had only a minimal effect on the 'cultural milieu' of the NHS.

The basic dilemmas remain, between the need for long-term planning and the short-term pressures on ministers, administrators and professionals; between the need for purposive policy making and the weight of the status quo. We have suggested that the structure of the NHS makes for an incremental style of policy making and militates against radical initiatives. It also gives particular weight to certain types of criteria and downgrades others which may be of importance in the 'political' arenas of central and local government. Some of the questions of control and accountability in the policy process which this presents are discussed in our final chapter.

CHAPTER FOUR

CHANNELS OF INFLUENCE

A MAJOR theme of this book is that of the United Kingdom and Scottish policy networks and the links between them. This chapter considers some of the channels of influence through these networks whereby demands are made and pressures brought to bear on decision-makers. A common feature of most of our channels is that they belong both to UK and to Scottish networks, so that actors can operate at both levels as appropriate. A further dimension is added by the links to European Community decision-making. Another common theme is the importance of the Scottish Office itself as a channel of influence for Scottish demands to UK and EC levels of decision. Indeed, it is the existence of a distinct Scottish administrative system that has called into being some of the distinctive Scottish party-political and interest group channels while, in turn, the existence of these channels may encourage specifically Scottish demands in addition to those which arise spontaneously.

There is a variety of types and styles of influence and pressure in Scottish policy making. Partisan and class politics are played out in Scotland as in the rest of the UK and major industrial interest groups seek to defend their traditional interests. At the same time, there is a 'Scottish dimension' to these sometimes giving them a different form in Scotland. Occasionally, a purely 'Scottish' interest can emerge in which regular opponents can come together and make common cause with each other and with the Scottish Office to promote a common interest, but without sacrificing their basic partisan or class identities. An obvious example would be public expenditure in Scotland. Labour and Conservatives, unions and employers, civil servants and citizens might disagree on how high total public expenditure should be but could all agree that, for a given UK total, the Scottish share should be as high as possible. Similarly, there would be wide agreement on the desirability of encouraging overseas investors to come to Scotland or on exploiting to the maximum any European available funds. In other cases, the balance of Scottish opinion may differ from that in other parts of the UK so that, for instance, there seems to be less dogmatic opposition to state intervention in industry.

We consider first the role of political parties in Scotland, then that of interest groups. Next, we examine Scottish representation in Parliament and the role of the Scottish MP. Finally, we look at Scottish links with the decision-making process in the European Communities.

Political Parties

Political parties perform a central role in liberal-democratic political systems, recruiting politicians and political activists, formulating policies, channelling demands to government and presenting choices to the voters at election time. With the exception of the Scottish National Party (SNP), the parties in Scotland are British parties and fulfil these tasks at both UK and Scottish levels, providing an important link between these two arenas of politics. We shall, therefore, examine the structure of the major political parties in Scotland and their links between the UK and Scottish structures.

THE LABOUR PARTY

Labour is a British party, organised in England, Scotland and Wales and, despite the 'democratic' nature of its constitution, with power flowing from the grass roots to the top, it has a relatively centralised structure. Although the organised labour movement started separately in Scotland and developed an early attachment to the ideal of Scottish Home Rule, its political organisation was weak and under the 1918 constitution of the Labour Party Scotland became a region, with the same status as the regions of England. There is a Scottish Council of the Labour Party, with an annual conference representing constituency Labour parties (CLPs), trade unions and affiliated organisations such as the Young Socialists and the Fabian Society. In turn, the conference elects a Scottish Executive. CLPs, trade unions and affiliated organisations also send delegates to the (British) National Conference. CLPs themselves are organised on an affiliate basis, with delegates representing branches, trade unions and affiliated organisations. In addition, there are regional and district parties representing CLPs and concerned with local government matters.

The professional side of the Labour Party in Scotland is centred on Keir Hardie House in Glasgow, headquarters of the Scottish Council. There is a Scottish Secretary, concerned with political work, a Scottish Organiser, and a research officer but these are appointed and employed by the National Executive Committee in London, although working closely with the Scottish Executive. Despite the strong Labour tradition, especially in the West, Labour Party organisation has never been strong on the ground in Scotland. Before 1932 most of the local organisation consisted of ILP branches and after the disaffiliation of the ILP had to be built up from scratch. Since the war, Scotland has had a disproportionate number of CLPs with a very low membership, many of them in solid Labour seats and there are only two or three full-time constituency agents in the whole country.

Selection of parliamentary candidates in the Labour Party is the responsibility of constituency parties, with a national list of approved potential candidates being kept by the National Executive in London. Although approved candidates can seek nomination in any part of Britain, there has been a strong tendency in recent years for candidates for Scottish seats to be chosen among Scottish residents. Under recent constitutional changes, candidates, including sitting MPs, must be reselected for each General Election.

Policy making on all matters, whether Scottish or UK, is the sole prerogative of the National Conference, with the Scottish Council acting only in an advisory capacity. In practice, the Scottish Council is able to contribute to policy making by passing resolutions on both Scotland and UK affairs at its annual conference and through the work of study groups and working parties which report to the Scottish Executive. These have on occasion produced ideas which have gone on to form the basis of action in government — for instance, the Scottish Development Agency owed its origins to the work of a Scottish Council study group. On matters of special concern to Scotland, the views of the Scottish Council will carry weight in the party as was shown over the change of policy on devolution in 1974. The parliamentary leadership, having determined on the need for a new policy, persuaded the party in Scotland to come into line before making a manifesto commitment. It was not until two years later, when plans for devolution were well advanced, that the matter was brought before National Conference for endorsement. On matters which only concern Scotland, the Scottish Council is generally allowed to go its own way, within the limits set by national party policy and since 1974 it has issued a separate Scottish election manifesto including Scottish items not featured in the British version.

However, the impact of Scottish members on policy, even on matters like devolution, is reduced by the sheer physical problem of contributing to deliberations and research activities under the aegis of the National Executive (NEC) in London. This was illustrated by the row which broke out when, by an oversight, the NEC's interim manifesto of 1980 failed to make any mention of the party's commitment to Scottish devolution. Efforts, in the 1970s and 1980s, to gain more independence for the Scottish Council, in line with the party's commitment to devolution, have been strongly resisted by the NEC, which insists on the Scottish Council retaining the same status as that of other 'regional' arms of the party.

In Parliament, there is a Scottish group of Labour MPs with the same standing as other 'regional' groups. It elects its own officers and maintains working parties on major items of current policy. This keeps the Scottish group busier than the other regional groups, given the need to keep up with developments in Scottish administration and legislation. There are links between the Scottish group and Keir Hardie House but, given the problems of distance and scale, it is impossible for the latter to produce as much research and information on matters like local government as does Labour Party headquarters in London. So, again, the Scottish wing of the party is able to exert only a limited influence on policy and can face severe difficulties in handling even Scottish legislative matters.

The Labour Party in Scotland

One reason for the Labour Party failing to develop a distinctive image in Scotland may be the lack of an identifiable leadership in an age of personalised politics. When Labour is in office, there is a Secretary of State but he owes his position to prime ministerial patronage and not to having a power base in Scotland. In opposition, the shadow Secretary of State may or may not be a member of the elected Parliamentary Committee and, either way, will owe his position to the votes of the PLP as a whole or to the party Leader rather than to the Scottish MPs or the party in Scotland. There is the additional problem that many of the ablest Scots in the party will sit for English seats or, if they represent Scottish seats, will choose to operate in the UK arena rather than building a career in Scottish politics.

At the Labour Party Conference and in the NEC, there is no Scottish 'bloc'. Scottish delegates and members operate as individuals or members of ideological or union-based factions but never as a territorial interest. This, together with the willingness of Conference and NEC to leave purely Scottish issues to the Scottish Council, means that there is no recognisably Scottish input to national policy making. On the other hand, the left-right balance in Scotland may, from time to time, differ from that of the rest of the party. There has been a myth in Labour circles in Scotland that it was more left-wing than in England. While, in practical terms, this is historically very dubious, the leftward swing since the early 1970s has perhaps placed Scotland among the more left-leaning regions of the party. In the 1981 Deputy Leadership election, for example, Tony Benn gained 86% of Scottish constituency party votes, as against 81% nationally, while Benn also achieved a majority among Scottish MPs, though scoring only 34% among MPs as a whole. On the other hand, this shows Labour in Scotland distinctly less left-wing than the party in Greater London.

Since 1974, Labour has been committed to the creation of a Scottish Assembly with legislative powers. The 1974-79 government's proposals were frustrated by the '40% rule' inserted by Parliament for the 1979

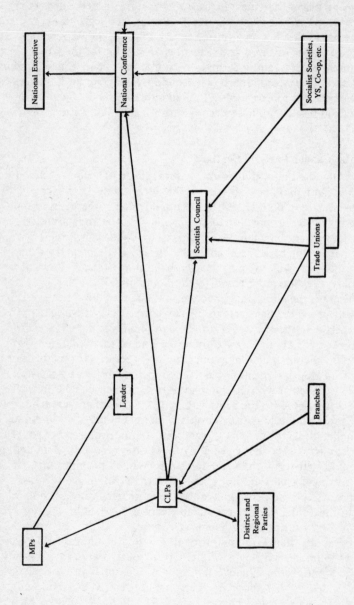

Fig. 4.1   THE LABOUR PARTY IN SCOTLAND

referendum which meant that the 52% popular vote, comprising less than 40% of the electorate, was insufficient to guarantee implementation of the Act. Shortly afterwards, the Conservatives won the 1979 General Election while Labour slightly improved its electoral position in Scotland. This might have given rise to a change in Scottish Labour's perception of its role in the political system to a questioning of the legitimacy of a Conservative government in a minority in Scotland and administering Scottish domestic affairs in defiance of a referendum result at least as clear as the Conservatives' own electoral mandate. Yet, this did not happen and Labour in Scotland has continued to play its traditional role as an element of the UK political system, viewing most issues in a UK perspective, though able to operate at the Scottish level of politics as well.

THE CONSERVATIVE PARTY

Strictly speaking, the Conservative Party consists only of Conservative Members of Parliament. As such, it is an autonomous body, choosing its own leader and making its own rules; Scottish Conservative MPs are members of this body on the same terms as the others. On a looser definition, however, the Conservative Party is much larger than this, embracing grass roots activists as well as a substantial professional organisation. For a long time, the voluntary and professional side of the party in Scotland was separate from that in England. The party, known until 1965 as the Scottish Unionist Party, was less well organised than in England, especially at constituency level where there were few full-time agents, and in local government, where Conservatives tended to stand under such labels as Independent, Progressive or Moderate. A series of reforms in 1965 strengthened organisation at the Scottish level, with a Scottish Central Office under the Scottish chairman to run the professional side. The voluntary side was represented by the Scottish Conservative and Unionist Association (SCUA) which was independent of the (English) National Union of Conservatives and Unionist Associations, although it sent representatives to the latter. Scottish constituency parties affiliated to SCUA but not directly to the National Union.

In 1977, following the 'Fairgrieve Report', there was a further series of reforms tending to merge the party in Scotland with that of England. This was seen as desirable because of the financial and organisational weakness of the Scottish party but, because of the prevailing political climate, it was not considered desirable to extinguish the Scottish party altogether. The Scottish Central Office was merged with the London one. All finances were centralised and all staff henceforth employed by London. A Scottish Director continues to co-ordinate the work of the Edinburgh office, with research and press officers responsible jointly to him and to their functional directors in London. The chairman of the Scottish party, appointed by the Leader, now has a co-ordinating and policy role but, unlike the national chairman, no executive responsibilities.

The voluntary arm continues to be SCUA, to which constituency parties affiliate but now Scottish constituencies are automatically, and without payment of any extra fee, affiliated to the National Union as well. Under SCUA are a series of advisory committees for interests such as local government, women, young Conservatives and trade unionists. Constituency parties, which are autonomous organisations, are responsible for the selection of candidates and, unlike constituency parties in England, employ and pay their own agents. Central influence over candidate selection is maintained by the need, as in the Labour Party, for would-be parliamentary candidates to be on an approved list. In the Conservative Party, however, there are separate lists for England and Scotland (though an individual can be on both).

While there are annual conferences of both the National Union and SCUA, policy in the Conservative Party is made by the Leader. The party in Scotland certainly advises and helps in the development of policy and can at times be influential. For instance, the leadership under Heath had great difficulty in holding the line in favour of devolution in the early 1970s. Generally, though, the voluntary wing of the Conservative Party is more interested in support than in control of the leadership and activists do not take an intense interest in policy matters.

Conservatism in Scotland has had great difficulty in preserving its identity in recent years. One of the reasons for the merger of the Scottish and English party organisations was that the decline of Scottish-owned and controlled private industry had led to a drying-up of financial contributions. Conservatism in the urban and industrial areas is reflected in a steady loss of seats over the twenty years 1959-79 and the virtual disappearance of the self-made industrialist-MP. By the late 1960s, this had reinforced the 'grouse-moor' image of Scottish Conservatism and was causing widespread concern in the party. In the early 1970s, the rural strongholds in their turn came under threat, from the SNP. Hence the efforts to update and de-Anglicise the party's image and to recruit a new type of candidate. By 1979, this had changed the composition of Scottish Conservative representation in Parliament but had failed notably to revive the party's electoral fortunes.

Like Labour, the Conservative Party in Scotland has never been able to produce an identifiable leader or to form itself into a bloc within the party. The Secretary of State or shadow Secretary of State is dependent on prime ministerial or leadership patronage and none has ever sought to build a power base within Scotland. His is a difficult role when, as has happened in recent years, he is in office while Labour is dominant in Scotland. Then he

Fig. 4.2

THE CONSERVATIVE PARTY IN SCOTLAND

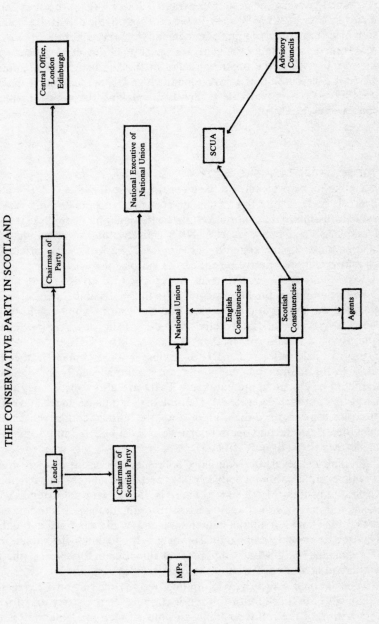

is trapped between the need to conciliate Labour local authorities and the majority of Scottish MPs and, on the other hand, the demands of his own supporters who expect him to implement Conservatism in Scotland. The role is made tenable by the general respect by all involved, including the Labour Party, for the unwritten rules of the Scottish political game, in which it is accepted that a government with a UK parliamentary majority does have the right to rule in Scotland, making the necessary limited concessions in return.

THE SCOTTISH NATIONAL PARTY

Unlike the two parties we have considered so far, the SNP is a purely Scottish body. While this makes its structure and functioning easier to explain, its internal organisation is nevertheless quite complex. It is also variable as, in recent years, the SNP has rarely stood still for long. It has always been either expanding or contracting and this has affected its structure and the relative power of the various elements.

Like the Labour Party's but unlike the Conservatives', the SNP's constitution places the ultimate power in the hands of the members and is founded on democratic principles. The basic unit is the branch, formed where there are sufficient activists and centring on communities and groups of members rather than, as in the other parties, on electoral divisions. This reflects the SNP's origins as a 'movement' rather than simply an electoral machine and the lack, until recently, of significant numbers of elected representatives. There are also constituency parties made up of branch delegates and, although the emphasis in recent years on elections has enhanced their importance, the branch remains the centre of activities. Regional and district parties also exist but are important mainly at election time (Brand, 1977).

At national level, the Annual Conference, made up of constituency delegates, is the supreme body in policy and other matters. In particular, it elects the officers of the party. There is also a National Council which meets quarterly and is largely chosen from the branches. It is concerned with policy between annual conferences and, while the division of labour between Conference and Council is not clearly laid down, the latter is more of a working body, while Conference is an occasion for social gatherings and creating an impression in the mass media.

The National Executive Committee, elected by National Council, is responsible for the month-to-month running of the party and for the supervision of the full-time staff. An unusual feature of the SNP is that policy matter are not generally handled by the NEC but by a body known as the National Assembly, elected from constituents, which receives reports from specialised policy committees, considers them and passes them on to National Council or Conference.

The officers of the party are elected at Conference. There is a president and three vice-presidents whose positions are largely honorific and a chairman who is effectively the head of the party. A number of executive vice-chairmen are responsible for specific matters such as Policy or Administration. These offices have in recent years been hotly contested among the various factions and tendencies in the party.

In 1974, with the election of seven, then eleven SNP MPs to Westminster, it was necessary to choose a parliamentary leader but he has never attained the status of the leaders of the other parties. Indeed, the SNP is almost unique among modern parties in having no clearly identifiable leader. Nor does the parliamentary party have the special position which its equivalents enjoy in other parties. This is explicable in a number of ways. The SNP has never had a major commitment to Westminster and, of course, has never sought to attain power there. So the Scottish end of its activities will inevitably be of more importance. Because of the small number of seats held by the party, some of its major figures do not sit in Parliament. However, in terms of finance and organisation, the SNP is fairly centralised. Candidate selection is a matter for constituency parties but, as in the other parties, a list of approved candidates is kept nationally.

As a political party, the SNP is, of course, a channel of influence in the policy process. However, its primary commitment is to changing the political system itself and this is bound to affect the manner of its participation in day-to-day politics before its goal of independence is achieved. Some nationalist purists hold that no other issues should be allowed to distract attention from the fight for independence and that the party should take no line on social and economic questions. Others believe that independence can only be 'sold' by relating it to bread-and-butter concerns and that the SNP should involve itself in government wherever possible to show its fitness for office. The latter strategy was tried in the 1960s when the party made considerable advances in local government but in many cases SNP councillors showed themselves politically divided. In the 1970s, the emphasis was on parliamentary activity, with eleven seats won in 1974 and the long saga of Labour's devolution legislation. The failure of this led to a bitter debate in the party and the formation of the '79 group', committed to independence and socialism by breaking Labour's control in industrial Scotland.

The SNP's influence in the policy system is perhaps less a question of its proposals being accepted by government, still less itself being in a position to implement them, as of other parties reacting to the 'danger' represented by the Nationalists. As early as the 1940s, Tom Johnston was said to have gained substantial concessions as Secretary of State by pointing to the electoral threat posed by the SNP. In the 1960s and 1970s, SNP election victories were widely seen as due to economic dissatisfaction and to be combatted by the other parties through special measures for Scotland. In 1974, it was the rise of the SNP which finally convinced Labour that it should return to a policy of devolution.

Yet, while producing such concessions can objectively be interpreted as the SNP's *function* in the political system, its *role* as seen by itself is very different, to provide a vehicle for the achievement of Scottish independence. It may be that each concession to Scottish particularities strengthens the political identity of Scotland and thus brings independence nearer. On the other hand, such concessions are generally intended by the other parties to defuse the case for independence and strengthen the United Kingdom. The clearest example of this was the 1978 Scotland Act, supported by Labour as a means of keeping the UK united and by the SNP as a step to breaking it up. It is not surprising that the question of whether to support any future measure of devolution falling short of independence sharply divides the SNP.

If the SNP were to decide not to be a one-issue party but to become simply a 'Scottish party' representing the territorial interest in the way other parties represent class or ideological interests, this might force the Labour, Conservative and Alliance parties in Scotland to compete more on distinctively Scottish issues. In turn, this would create more of a Scottish input into the party-political process which, as we have seen, is now tied closely to UK patterns. By emphasising the independence issue, however, the SNP excludes itself from widespread participation in the existing political system which thus retains its 'UK' character.

THE LIBERAL PARTY

As a result of the rifts in the Liberal Party between the wars, the Scottish Liberal Party is quite separate from the Liberal Party in England, though in Parliament Scottish, English and Welsh Liberals form a single group. The Scottish Liberal Conference makes policy for the party in Scotland, though the Scottish Liberals do attend the Liberal Assembly in England. In 1961 and 1968 joint Assemblies of the two parties were held in Edinburgh.

The existence of three quite separate Liberal parties could potentially give rise to considerable problems in policy making but in practice the Liberals' distance from government in the post-war period has meant that policy, though often produced in vast quantities, has been of less immediate importance than to the other British parties. One issue which has given rise to some tension is that of devolution. The Scottish Liberals have long been committed to a federal United Kingdom in which Scotland

and England would be individual units. English Liberals, on the other hand, have favoured a system of regional assemblies for England, implying a non-federal arrangement. Disagreement about this and vagueness about policy generally partly explains the lack of impact of the Liberals on the devolution debate of the 1960s and 1970s, in spite of their longstanding commitment to Home Rule.

Another vexed issue was the alliance with the Social Democratic Party. In 1982 the Scottish Liberals, claiming that they were not bound by the terms of the electoral agreement with the SDP, refused to accept the candidature of J. Dickson Mabon, a Labour defector and long-time enemy of local Liberals, as Alliance candidate in Greenock and Port Glasgow. In the event, the issue was resolved by Dr Mabon's stepping aside but not before a determined show of independence by the Scottish Liberals. The SDP alliance has, more generally, forced the Liberals into the necessity of hammering out agreed policy and among the other strains in the alliance tension between Scottish and English Liberals could well figure.

The Liberal parliamentary party, however, is not divided among English, Scots and Welsh. Although in 1974 Russell Johnston, MP, was appointed as Leader of the Scottish Liberal Party, there is only one parliamentary leader. While the Liberals have not been notably successful in breaking into the major-party vote in Scotland, they have been relatively successful in winning and holding seats and it is partly due to this that two of the last three party leaders have been Scottish MPs. However, a parliamentary party of a hundred MPs would be a very different body to manage to a party of a dozen or so and any electoral breakthrough for the party would so transform its structure and power balance as to make inferences from its present position almost impossible.

THE SOCIAL DEMOCRATIC PARTY

At the time of writing (1982), the organisation of the Social Democratic Party (SDP) is still evolving, but the main lines are clear. The base unit of organisation is the Area Party, covering between two and six parliamentary constituencies. It chooses election candidates, decides major issues by ballot of all its members and may, if it chooses, delegate matters such as the selection of local election candidates to smaller district branches. Between meetings of the full Area Party, business is handled by an elected Executive Committee.

At UK level, the policy-making body is the Council for Social Democracy elected from the Area Parties. It is this body which holds the conference equivalent to the national conferences of the other parties. Organisation is the responsibility of the National Committee, comprising representatives from the Council for Social Democracy, four MPs, councillors, the Young Social Democrats and the membership at large. Finance is centralised, with all membership subscriptions going to London, though there is now provision for a proportion of the subscription of those members paying in the higher bracket of the variable rate to be sent back to Area Parties. Otherwise, money for local activities must be raised locally.

At Scottish level there is a Regional Committee set up under a permissive clause in the constitution, comprising delegates from Area Parties. While this does not have any formal policy-making role, it is expected that it will influence the deliberations of the Council for Social Democracy. It is also likely that, as in the other parties, informal understandings will emerge that purely Scottish policy should be left to the Scottish end of the party, acting within the limits set by national decisions. There is a Scottish organiser, appointed and paid by the National Committee; his precise relationship with the Scottish Committee, which considers both policy and organisational matters, will perhaps become clear in time.

Scottish Interest Groups

The pattern of interest group activity in Scotland, as elsewhere, is a complex one. Interest groups are formed for a variety of purposes — to protect their members, to promote worthy causes, to lobby government on behalf of their own members or others. In the pursuit of these purposes they employ a range of different means — publicity, demonstrations, pressure, industrial action and persuasion. As we are interested particularly in the role of interest groups in the policy making process and in the distinctive features in this respect of Scotland, we can divide interest groups into three types — UK-wide groups operating in a unified manner with no special provision for Scotland; UK groups with a Scottish organisation which has some autonomy; and independent Scottish groups. Which types of group have developed will reflect, in part, the structure of government itself. So the existence of a Scottish Office in Edinburgh provides the opportunity for groups to form in order to use it as a pressure point and a means of access to government. In part, the pattern of group activity is the product of distinctive Scottish demands or needs calling for separate treatment. Finally, a great deal is due simply to tradition or historical chance. So the Scottish Trades Union Congress was originally founded not to press special demands but because trades councils, which were important in Scotland, had been barred from affiliation to the TUC.

In general, the main producer interest groups are UK-wide, reflecting the existence of a UK economic and industrial system. In the course of this century, independent Scottish trades unions have gradually disappeared while the control of industry has been increasingly concentrated. There are

Fig. 4.3

THE SOCIAL DEMOCRATIC PARTY IN SCOTLAND

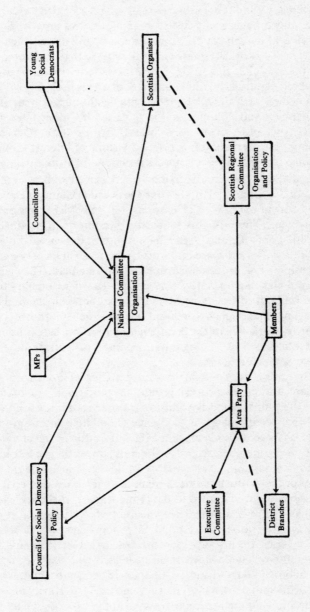

exceptions, though. Farming and fishing interests, which differ significantly from those in England, are separately organised, as are the teaching and legal professions concerned with the separate education and legal systems. Within those groups organised on a British or UK basis, the existence and influence of Scottish branches varies greatly. Some trade unions have a Scottish council, committee or conference which is able to express views on Scottish issues. This is the case with the National Union of Mineworkers, which has a highly decentralised structure reflecting its origins as a federation. In other unions, Scotland is itself divided into areas which may then be dealt with together with neighbouring areas of England or Northern Ireland. The position is as varied for other interest groups.

The existence of Scottish-based interest groups or Scottish sections of UK groups cuts across the functional divisions of interest group activity just as the Scottish Office cuts across functional divisions in government. Occasionally, this can give rise to joint or concerted lobbying on behalf of Scotland under the aegis of bodies like the Scottish Council (Development and Industry) or the STUC-sponsored Scottish Assemblies on unemployment. There is also a Scottish version of 'tripartitism' in the Scottish Economic Council (see Chapter Nine). In general, however, the functional loyalties are more important, with close links between Scottish and English interest groups operating in the same field. They will usually try to avoid clashing on policy matters for fear of weakening their joint influence and will often agree to share tasks between them. This often means letting the English organisation do much of the research and investigative work where the Scottish organisation lacks the necessary resources; or the Scottish organisation may concentrate its efforts on distinctive Scottish matters.

Interest groups in Scotland have a number of points of access to government. For purely Scottish groups, the most important of these is the Scottish Office and the most promising approach is usually to convince the latter of their case and get it to pursue the matter within government. Given the absence of ministers and MPs in London for most of the week, interest group contacts, except for the most powerful groups, tend to be limited to civil servants. The presence of the latter in Edinburgh and the small size of the Scottish political arena further means that civil servants are accessible and well known to the group leaders. However, even where the Scottish Office has formal responsibility for a function, it does not always have the power to respond to group demands. In the case of teachers' salaries, for instance, Scottish teachers' better organisation and greater militancy have availed them little in recent years as, despite the separate Scottish salary structure, final decisions on this matter are taken inter-departmentally, with the Treasury and the Department of Education and Science having the predominant say. In the case of agriculture, joint responsibility is officially recognised and negotiations involve all three territorial farmers' unions and all four agricultural departments.

For Scottish groups which are affiliates or branches of UK groups, there is an additional point of access, via the parent group and the UK departments. It is unusual for a purely Scottish group to approach a UK department, given the Scottish Office's wide responsibilities but sometimes an approach will be made at both Scottish and UK levels, the latter through the parent group. In fact, pressure groups will seek to exert pressure at every point available to them.

Another channel of influence is the Scottish media. The independent broadcasting companies and BBC Scotland as well as the Scottish press provide coverage for Scottish political issues and are used extensively by interest groups to publicise their general concerns as well as specifically Scottish ones.

The power and influence of interest groups, of course, varies greatly. In some cases, as with the major producer groups, government needs the organised interests to provide information, to negotiate with and to mobilise support for, and acceptance of, its own policies. In these cases, there will be close and frequent contact and the groups will gain 'insider' status in government. Given the small and cohesive nature of the Scottish political and industrial elite, this insider network is particularly close and informal. In other cases, the group will be making demands which are unacceptable to government or will be asking for favourable treatment from government but unable to provide anything in return. In this case, it may have to rely on mobilising public and party support through open campaigning in the media.

To illustrate the structure and operation of Scottish interest groups, we shall examine two examples, the Confederation of British Industry (CBI), the main employers' organisation, and the Scottish Trades Union Congress (STUC).

The CBI represents 14,000 firms in the UK and has a large professional staff at its London headquarters engaged in work on economic, industrial, trade, legal and industrial relations affairs. Its National Council is elected from the thirteen regional councils, one of which covers Scotland and has an office in Glasgow. About 1,300 of the CBI's members are in Scotland, of which around 400 are indigenous firms and the rest subsidiaries. The functions of the CBI are to represent the interests of industry in the policy making process of government; to provide a service to individual members, though in general it tries to avoid taking up individual cases except where there is a major principle involved; and to engage in publicity and educational work to 'create the right climate' for industry.

In pursuance of the first function, the CBI has a network of very close contacts in government at both UK and Scottish levels. Where a matter concerns a UK department, the Glasgow office passes it to headquarters. Where it concerns a Scottish Office function, it pursues it itself. To maintain its network, for pursuing matters like this and for furthering its 'climate creating' role, the CBI keeps in contact with all the Scottish Office ministers, the secretaries of all the departments and the main officials of SEPD, SDD and the Finance Division, as well as MPs and leading local government figures. Even where specific matters are not being pursued, informal meetings are convened to keep contacts alive.

The CBI thus has very close links with government at both UK and Scottish levels. This is partly a matter of resources and professional organisation — the CBI must be the wealthiest pressure group in this country. More important, however, is the need for government to be able to talk to representatives of industry, to gain information and test the acceptability of their policies. For the Scottish Office, the links with the CBI in Scotland not only help it in planning and monitoring industrial trends in Scotland but also provide information and support in contributing to the making of UK industrial policy. They thus help the Secretary of State fill out his role as Scotland's economic and industrial minister. At the same time, the degree of consensus within the CBI on industrial policy means that the Scottish input will be on matters of degree or emphasis, or on the need for special measures in Scotland over and above UK policies. Similarly, the close links between the CBI and government, its 'insider' status, mean that, by and large, consensus has prevailed between it and government. Where major differences have arisen within the CBI or between it and government, these have concerned ideological and general economic policy matters and not territorial issues.

The Scottish Trades Union Congress (STUC) is a body quite separate constitutionally from the United Kingdom TUC. It originated in the late nineteenth century, not in response to nationalist pressures but because of the exclusion of trades councils from the TUC. The latter continue to affiliate to the STUC, in addition to trades unions. Following the decline and amalgamation of independent Scottish unions, most STUC affiliates are UK unions which are also members of the TUC. With the exception of the AUEW, these large UK unions have a 'regional' structure for Scotland though, apart from the National Union of Mineworkers, they do not have a Scottish policy conference. Affiliation and policy lines thus usually come from the UK level to the STUC which has an Annual Congress to make policy and elect its General Council. This operates through two major committees, the General Purposes Committee and the Economic Committee and the permanent paid secretariat. In addition, there are committees and subcommittees to formulate policy and monitor progress on important industrial, social and educational matters. These feed back ideas and information to the General Council and work on the implications of resolutions passed by Congress.

Because, by and large, it represents UK unions, the STUC cannot be seen as the voice of an independent Scottish trades unionism. However, there are important differences in emphasis and style between it and the TUC. The Scottish Annual Congress has traditionally been to the left of the TUC because it contains more workers from the shop floor or shop steward level and less full-time officials, because of the presence of trades council delegates and because of the influence of the Communist Party which has been able to channel its localised industrial strength in some parts of Scotland into the trades councils and the STUC. For a long time, while the TUC was under the dominance of right-wing leaders believing in a centralised trade unionism, this produced some very chilly relationships between the two bodies. In recent years, the advent of a new generation of leaders, the swing to the left in the UK unions and their common concerns in dealing with government have led to a greater degree of co-operation. The enhanced status of the STUC is marked by the attendance at its Annual Congress of some of the major UK union leaders.

By and large, the STUC leaves negotiation on major matters like prices and incomes policies or industrial relations legislation to the TUC though it does pass resolutions on these matters and make its views known. Purely Scottish matters it deals with on its own. On the third type of issue which we have discerned in our analysis of the Scottish policy process, where there is a distinct Scottish interest in a UK policy matter, the STUC works with the Scottish Office and, increasingly, in co-operation with the TUC. Thus the STUC's long interest in and experience of regional policy enables it to present ideas to the Scottish Office which can then, where it thinks fit, carry them further in government. The TUC has sought advice from the STUC, for instance, on devolution or on the 1981 Local Government (Miscellaneous Provisions) (Scotland) Act which gave the Secretary of State added powers over local government and which the TUC feared could be extended to England.

There is a great deal of informal and formal contact between the STUC and the Scottish Office, as well as Scottish arms of UK departments and *ad hoc* agencies like the SDA and the MSC. Where trade union nominations are sought for Scottish committees and 'quangos', it is the STUC who are approached. However, relations both with government and with employers' organisations like the CBI are very dependent on the prevailing political climate. Under a Labour Government, STUC access to the Scottish Office is easier than under the Conservatives while, when the latter are in power, the CBI are reluctant to criticise government too openly. Where the STUC criticises Labour governments, on the other hand, it is usually from a left-wing perspective, precluding co-operation with the

CBI. However, some discreet co-ordination of lobbying does happen and, generally, tripartite relations in Scotland are closer and more informal than those in England, with none of the total breakdowns in dialogue that occur from time to time at the UK level. This reflects the existence of a common Scottish interest, for example, in retaining development area status for the whole of Scotland as well, perhaps, as a greater consensus on the role of the state in industrial matters. On the other hand, in co-operating on a Scottish basis, the three sides are not abandoning their primary loyalties. Like the other actors in the policy process which we have examined, interest groups retain the ability to operate at both levels of politics.

Scotland in Parliament
The United Kingdom is unique among modern states in possessing a variety of legal systems but a single legislature. This means that Westminster must pass several different types of legislation; legislation applying to the whole of the UK; to Britain; to England and Wales; to Scotland. In addition, there is a very small amount of English legislation and Welsh legislation and there are special procedures, after the abolition of Stormont, for Northern Ireland legislation. The need to deal with Scottish legislation has led to the creation of a number of distinctively Scottish institutions and procedures in Parliament which, in turn, have influenced the role of the Scottish MP.

Scotland's representation in Parliament has always been determined on a different basis to that of England and Wales. At the Union, Scotland was allocated forty-five members, a number based on her share of Britain's wealth with some allowance for population. In the course of the nineteenth century, this was raised by steps to seventy-two, a figure in proportion to population. Since then, with the departure of most of the Irish members, the total size of the House of Commons has shrunk and Scotland's population relative to that of England has fallen but the number of Scottish MPs has remained by convention the same for many years, save for the University members, finally abolished in 1950. So Scotland now has seventy-one MPs though in proportion to population she should have about fifty-seven. The 1982 Boundary Commission recommendations have proposed increasing this to seventy-two.

The party composition of the Scottish contingent of MPs has often differed from that of Parliament as a whole, particularly since 1959. This is attributable both to swings in popular opinion and to the workings of the electoral system. In 1945, the Conservatives were stronger in Scotland than in England but from 1950 though they advanced across the UK, their advance was slower in Scotland than in England. In 1955 they achieved a bare majority of Scottish votes and seats but then began to decline (see Chapter One). In October 1974, they won just sixteen seats and in 1979, the year of their UK victory, they won only twenty-two. Labour's strength among Scottish MPs increased steadily from 1959 reaching a high point of forty-six in 1966. In 1979, they held forty-four. In the late 1970s the SNP held eleven seats but by 1979 they were down to two. The Liberals, who showed considerable electoral strength in the 1960s, have since 1970 held three seats. As a result of these trends the Conservative governments of 1959-64, 1970-74 and from 1979 have been faced with a Labour majority among the Scottish MPs, with effects which we explore below.

The backgrounds of Scottish MPs during the post-war period have tended to distinguish them as a group from MPs as a whole. On the Labour side, manual workers have been more in evidence in Scotland than in England, with a lower proportion of graduates. Also notable among Scottish Labour MPs is the high proportion of former councillors. On the Conservative side, the pattern has changed with the party's changing electoral fortunes. At one time there were a number of self-made businessmen in its parliamentary contingent but the decline of urban Conservatism in Scotland has meant their virtual disappearance. In the rural areas, representation was dominated by the aristocracy, landowners and retired military officers, usually products of English public schools and often graduates of Oxford and Cambridge. By 1970, over 80% of Scottish Conservative MPs were educated at public schools and 65% at Oxbridge, giving Scottish Conservatism a distinctly 'anglicised' image (Keating 1975b). Defeats at the hands of the SNP in the rural areas and the subsequent emergence of a new generation of MPs has led since 1974 to a further change, with an increase in the number of members educated in Scotland. In both parties, there has been a growing unwillingness to select candidates from outside Scotland, though this may reflect a growing localism among MPs throughout the UK.

The machinery for dealing with Scottish affairs in the House of Commons has been developed steadily over the years, in response to demands for devolution, the growing volume of Scottish business and the congestion of the House. Of course, the existence of Scottish committees in Parliament does not itself represent devolution, as ultimate control is maintained by the whole House in which Scottish members are a minority. The committees represent, rather, a division of labour within Parliament and a pragmatic response to the need to deal with the large volume of Scottish legislation.

Scottish legislation is necessary because of the existence of a separate Scottish legal system and because of the separate policy initiatives which, from time to time, come out of the Scottish Office. Where a UK bill extends to Scotland, there is consultation between the Parliamentary Counsel and the Lord Advocate's Department on whether Scottish clauses, Scottish sections or a separate Scottish bill are necessary. There are no fixed rules here but, in general, Scottish clauses will be needed where legislation amends existing Scottish 'enactments', i.e. Acts of Parliament or 'rules of law', i.e. common law. This means that there is a tendency for Scottish clauses to be more necessary in UK legislation on traditional matters like patents and contract than on 'new' policy areas like race relations, industrial relations or consumer affairs. In addition, separate Scottish bills are commonly brought forward to deal with those matters where the Scottish Office has the major administrative responsibility in Scotland, such as town and country planning or housing, even in cases where the policy content is similar to that of corresponding English and Welsh legislation. Since the report of the Renton (1975) Committee, there has been a deliberate policy of using separate Scottish parts or clauses in UK legislation rather than cumbersome adaptation clauses to be read in conjunction with the relevant England and Wales clauses. So the legislative separation of Scottish and non-Scottish affairs has gradually increased over the years.

The earliest Scottish committees in Parliament were the Grand Committees set up in the sessions of 1894 and 1895 in response to demands for more time to debate Scottish affairs. In 1907 the Scottish Grand Committee became a permanent institution consisting of all members for Scottish constituencies, plus ten to fifteen non-Scottish members, added to maintain the party balance prevailing in the House. The original function was to take the committee stages of Scottish bills and, on occasion, to debate matters of concern to Scotland.

In 1945, the first suggestion was made that second readings of Scottish bills might also be taken in the Grand Committee but this, at the same time, was widely considered to be a threat to the unity of Parliament. The Government argued that Scottish members would resent their bills being put in an inferior class and that English members would resent being debarred from debating Scottish affairs. The idea was rejected by the Select Committee on Procedure.

By 1948, attitudes had changed as a result of growing pressure for devolution and, from the Government's point of view, parliamentary congestion. A White Paper on Scottish Affairs proposed that three categories of bill be eligible for referral to the Grand Committee for second reading: bills of a technical character relating only to Scotland which, though debatable, are not controversial in the party sense; certain bills which make for Scotland provision similar to that already made or proposed for England and Wales; certain bills of purely Scottish interest for which time could not be found under existing arrangements. Where a bill was certified by the Speaker as applying exclusively to Scotland, a minister could move that it be referred to the Scottish Grand Committee for consideration of principle. The motion could be rejected by ten members objecting. On its return, the bill could, on the motion of a minister, be 'deemed' to have been read a second time unless six members at that stage put down an amendment, in which case a full second reading debate on the floor of the House would take place. It was also proposed that the Committee should debate estimates on six days per session, in addition to the two days in the House already devoted to Scottish estimates. Opinions on the schemes varied. Sir Thomas Moore found the whole scheme 'futile . . . a meaningless sop to the Scottish Nationalists' but others thought it too timid and criticised the exclusion of controversial matters. The Secretary of State, Arthur Woodburn, modestly commented that the proposals were in no way revolutionary, nor did they create a new Parliament. They merely gave more time for Scotland to discuss and control its own affairs (H.C. Deb. Vol. 450, Col. 416). Since that time, most bills eligible for referral have been sent to the Grand Committee for second reading.

The next major reform of the Scottish parliamentary machinery came in 1957 and again the principal reason given by the Government concerned parliamentary congestion, in this case, the burden on Scottish members imposed by attendance in the Grand Committee and their consequent inability to play their full part in UK affairs. In the 1955 session, indeed, the Scottish committee had been exceptionally busy and Scottish participation in the UK standing committees had, in consequence, been very low (Keating 1975b). The Labour Opposition were against any reduction in the size of the Scottish Committee and charged that Government back-benchers were less worried about their inability to take part in UK affairs than by their inability to pursue their extra-parliamentary careers but the Government's proposals were adopted. A Scottish Standing Committee was established with a minimum membership of thirty members representing Scottish constituencies and up to twenty other members added to reflect the party balance in the House. The Grand Committee was to continue to debate second readings and estimates and, in addition, could now debate 'matters' on two days per session. Later, provision was made for the Grand Committee to take the Report Stage of Bills which had had their second reading debate in the Grand Committee but this procedure has never been used. Complaints about the lack of facilities for Scottish private members' bills led in 1963 to the establishment of a second Scottish Standing Committee.

In 1971, in accordance with a recommendation of the Select Committee on Procedure, the size of the Scottish Standing Committee was reduced. Labour members charged that the real motive was to be found in the difficulty of finding sufficient Conservatives to man the committee, the special position of which was being downgraded. Nostalgic references were made to the old committee, which had included all Scottish members. The First Scottish Standing Committee now consists of between sixteen and fifty members, of whom sixteen must represent Scottish constituencies. In practice, the latter requirement is superfluous, as the 'added' non-Scottish member is now unknown.

In the session 1968-69, as part of the parliamentary reforms of that period, a Select Committee on Scottish affairs was established. An investigative committee, with power to call witnesses and take evidence, in Scotland as well as in London, it was intended to complement the deliberative and legislative functions, respectively, of the Grand and Standing Committees. Despite the difficulties of the new Conservative Government in finding enough backbenchers to form a majority on it, the committee was re-established for the session 1971-2 but then lapsed until a new committee was set up in 1979 (see below).

For the next few years, attention was concentrated on proposals for devolution but, in 1979, following the repeal of the Scotland Act, inter-party talks were launched on ways of improving parliamentary procedures for dealing with Scottish affairs. These produced little beyond the recommendation subsequently enacted that the 'added' English members should be removed from the Grand Committee, a reform of little practical effect as, even with the added members, the 1979 Government did not have a majority on the committee. This Grand Committee has also been given the right to sit in Edinburgh. Before the inter-party talks had begun, the Government had conceded the case for a new Select Committee on Scottish Affairs, which was set up in 1979.

As the volume of legislation has increased over the years, so has the workload of the Scottish committees. The easing of the burden on Scottish MPs by the creation of the standing committees was balanced by the increase in the number of bills, leaving Scottish MPs with a much heavier load of committee work than other members and maintaining the boundary between Scottish matters and UK matters. We shall therefore consider the role of the Scottish MP first of all at the 'Scottish level', then at the 'UK level'.

Some observers have described the Scottish committee system, and the Grand Committee in particular, as 'Scotland's Parliament'. Given the role of Parliament as a means of publicising Government and Opposition policies, of bringing pressure to bear on ministers through MPs, of probing into the implications of proposed legislation and bringing to light examples of ministerial incompetence, there is something to be said for this view. The establishment and development of the Scottish committees have not altered the balance of power as between the executive and the legislature; what they have done is altered the allocation of functions within the legislature, so that it is now Scottish MPs who have the task of scrutinising the Scottish Office. Proceedings in the Scottish committee are reported in the Scottish press alongside proceedings in the House and often make the front page. Not all the Scottish members are happy about being left to deal with Scottish business in their own committees. MPs have complained that the Scottish committees are 'inward-looking' and prevent members giving the necessary time to UK business. There is always some resistance to proposals to transfer business from the Chamber to the Scottish committees as Scottish members value highly their time on the floor of the House. Conversely, some English members regard the Scottish committees as the only proper place for Scottish business.

Scottish members are often jealous of the rights of their committees and time on the floor of the House and resentful of intrusions by English members. Thus, Richard Crossman felt obliged in 1968 to stay away from the second reading debate on the Social Work (Scotland) Bill, fearing that 'the Scots would suspect some poisonous English conspiracy, so we would have to keep out, come what may' (Crossman 1976). The real influence of Scottish MPs, however, is difficult to judge and is likely to vary from one issue to another. We will consider now their role in Government legislation, private members legislation and the scrutiny of administration.

Overwhelmingly, Scottish MPs react to Government Bills on party lines. Rebellions are no more common than among non-Scottish MPs and where the Government is defeated at the committee stage of a Scottish bill it can, as with other bills, use its majority in the whole House to reverse the defeat. The sharper the party division on the issue in question, the less willing the Government is to loosen its control. Often on partisan issues, the Opposition will bring out a distinctive Scottish line of attack to add to its ideological onslaught. Thus, opposing the Financial Provisions (Scotland) Bill in 1971, William Ross accused the Secretary of State of neglecting his Scottish duties:

> "One of the great responsibilities of a Secretary of State for Scotland is to convince his Cabinet colleagues that the Scottish housing position is very much worse than the English one and that the whole position is different. . . . The whole tradition of Scottish housing finance which it should have been (the Secretary of State's) responsibility to safeguard, has gone."
> (H.C. Deb. Vol. 827, 16 Dec. 1971)

Conservatives have on occasion taken a similar line against Labour governments, particularly in 1945-50, when their own position was stronger in Scotland than in England. Walter Elliot then attacked

Labour's nationalisation programme, claiming that 'for Scotland, nationalisation means denationalisation'. However, in these cases, the Scottish argument is simply an additional weapon in the partisan armoury and does not represent the main thrust of attack.

Where the issue does not raise sharp partisan differences or the Government lacks a clear commitment, however, Scottish MPs may be able to influence policy, just as MPs as a whole can sometimes influence policy on United Kingdom matters. Pressure may be brought to bear in the Grand Committee where in 1977 the Labour Government was defeated on the issue of teacher training. More commonly, defeats take place in the Scottish Standing Committee. Where these votes appear to reflect strongly held views in Scotland or among Scottish MPs, the Government may accept the decision. Thus, after a defeat in the Standing Committee on the bill to reform local Scottish government in 1973, the Secretary of State announced that the Government did not intend to take the initiative to reverse the decision unless pressed to do so by a majority of the Scottish Members of Parliament (First Scottish Standing Committee, 6 March 1973, Col. 868-9). This echoes the sentiment of Lord Advocate Balfour in 1886 that the custom of the House was for the government of the day to come to an understanding with Scottish members (Pottinger 1979). In modern times, however, partisan loyalties have usually overridden any tendency to a Scottish consensus.

On matters dealt with through private members' legislation, notably in the area of social reform, Scottish MPs, free of party doctrine and discipline, have often produced distinctive laws. Thus, for nearly ten years after the divorce law in England had been reformed, opponents were able to block attempts to extend the reform to Scotland. In this, they were reflecting the stronger opposition to reform in Scotland, as well as exploiting the difficulties in the way of successful private members' legislation. So the first attempt failed when it was opposed by a majority of Scottish MPs and the Government refused to give parliamentary time for the bill to complete its stages. The second attempt failed because its supporters could not secure the necessary 100 votes for the closure motion. This, of course, required the support of English MPs whose intervention was condemned by opponents of reform including at least one staunch opponent of Scottish devolution, on the grounds that Scots alone should decide the matter (Cook 1978). Reform was not finally achieved until a broad consensus of Scottish opinion and Scottish MPs had come to favour it. Similarly, reform of the law on homosexuality was delayed in Scotland for a number of years by the opposition of a majority of Scottish MPs (Keating 1975b).

On less controversial matters, there is a great deal of Scottish private members' legislation. Indeed, the need to revise and update Scottish private law means that Scottish MPs are responsible for about a third of all private members' bills enacted (Keating 1975b). Many of these are inspired by the Scottish Office or the Scottish Law Commission and are passed without opposition.

Scrutiny of the Scottish Office presents a particular problem for MPs because of the breadth of its responsibilities. It is said that this forces Scottish MPs to become 'generalists', rather than specialising in a particular policy area. It has, further, been said that, because of the presence of the Scottish Office bureaucracy in Edinburgh, close to its clients but remote from Parliament, MPs play a less important role in pressurising and pursuing complaints against the administration. On the other hand, the small scale of the Scottish political world means that ministers, civil servants and MPs are more likely to know one another personally and informal contacts are easier than in the large Whitehall departments. The formal means by which MPs can scrutinise the work of the Scottish Office are through Parliamentary Questions, Matters and Estimates Days in the Grand Committee and the work of the Select Committee on Scottish Affairs. Parliamentary Questions to the Secretary of State come up approximately every six weeks and, as with Question Time generally, the occasion is typically used for scoring party points rather than for unearthing the secrets of government. Suggestions have been made that Question Time could be extended and taken in the Grand Committee but this has always been rejected as a threat to Scottish members' time on the floor of the House.

Matters and Estimates days in the Grand Committee allow Scottish members to debate topics chosen by the Government or the Opposition, usually without a vote being taken. This allows MPs to make their views known and such days are valued by Scottish members but an increase in their number has generally been opposed as, again, it would divert attention and members' energies away from the floor of the House.

The Select Committee on Scottish Affairs was established in 1979 to scrutinise the work of government in Scotland, not merely the Scottish Office. Its composition reflects that of the House of Commons as a whole but, after a lengthy wrangle, Opposition MPs have chaired it. It has powers to summon ministers and take evidence from civil servants and private individuals, to examine written evidence and to travel. To date, it has divided its time between major, full-scale investigations on issues such as civil service dispersal and one-day sessions interviewing ministers and civil servants on matters such as public expenditure. Like the other Select Committees, it has to steer a careful course between the natural tendency of MPs to see issues in partisan terms and the desire by some supporters of the Select Committee system for a cross-bench approach, pitting Parliament against the Government. In addition, some observers have seen the Scottish Committee as a potential voice of 'Scotland' and have wanted to promote consensus within it to maximise the power of that voice. As, on its establishment, the Opposition held the majority of Scottish seats, such a claim could be embarrassing to both Government and Opposition. Consequently, the committee started on a low key, despite the expectations of some sections of the Scottish press. Its initial strategy was gradually to acquire influence with government by constructive work in areas largely free from acute party controversy and to avoid being seen as a substitute for a Scottish Assembly. Later, it launched into more controversial areas, such as the battle between central and local government.

Fig. 4.4

Grand Committee—all Scottish MPs.
 (i)   Second reading debate of most Scottish bills.
 (ii) Report stage of bills considered in committee at second reading stage (never used).
(iii) Scottish Estimates—six days per session.
(iv)   Scottish Matters—two days per session.

First Scottish Standing Committee—16-50 MPs. At least sixteen must be Scottish MPs. Usually all are Scottish MPs.
Committee stage of Scottish bills.

Second Scottish Standing Committee
Committee stage of Scottish (usually) private members' bills.

Select Committee on Scottish Affairs
Investigative.

Floor of House
Second reading debate on some Scottish bills.
Report stage debate on Scottish bills.
Third reading of Scottish bills.
Questions to Secretary of State.

Fig. 4.5

PROCEDURE FOR SCOTTISH LEGISLATION

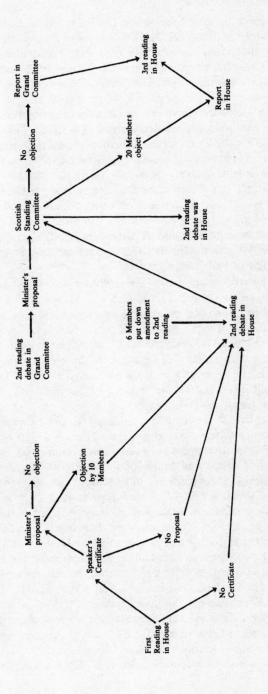

The procedure for taking Report stage in the Grand Committee has never been used.

As well as operating at the Scottish level of politics, the Scottish MP is a channel of influence to the UK level. This gives him a double burden of responsibility not shared by other MPs and most Scottish members face an early choice of whether to remain simply as 'Scottish MPs' or to strike out for the UK arena. Keating (1975b) has analysed the behaviour of Scottish MPs over a twenty-five-year period, looking at participation in standing committees and select committees, sponsorship of private members' bills and early day motions, parliamentary questions, promotion to government office, media impact and members' own perceptions of their role. A clear typology emerged. Most Scottish MPs were 'Scottish oriented', concentrating overwhelmingly on matters falling within the Scottish political arena. Where they did venture into the UK arena it was usually in pursuit of a distinctly Scottish interest within a wider question. So they showed great interest in economic and industrial legislation with an immediate impact on Scotland but little concern with general financial, foreign or defence affairs. On fisheries legislation, as we would expect, there was a high rate of Scottish activity.

In sharp contrast was a group of 'UK-oriented' members who showed a consistent pattern of interest in UK-wide or foreign affairs in all their activities. Many of these had at some time served in UK departments and, significantly, they had very low rates of participation in purely Scottish affairs. Most of these UK-oriented MPs had made a conscious decision early in their parliamentary careers not to become trapped into the Scottish system but to make a name in some wider field of policy.

It is difficult to measure the success of Scottish MPs in gaining promotion to posts in 'Whitehall' departments (to use our earlier terminology) as before they can be considered for these there is a specific number of Scottish Office posts to be filled. There is no bar on a Scottish MP serving in any department, nor even a convention as powerful as that which makes a Secretary of State for Scotland sitting for an English constituency almost inconceivable. In practice, however, Scots MPs are rarely found in overwhelmingly English departments, such as the Home Office or the Department of Education and Science; though they do serve from time to time in the Department of Transport, a mainly English department. In the Department of Energy and the Ministry of Agriculture, Fisheries and Food there is a convention that there should be at least one Scottish junior minister, despite the fact that the latter has virtually no responsibilities in Scotland. The reason given is the importance of North Sea oil and of Scottish agriculture and fisheries and the need to protect these at the highest UK and international levels — though in neither case is the minister concerned given a specifically 'Scottish' brief or expected, like the Secretary of State, to lobby for Scottish interests.

Given this pattern, the number of Scottish MPs finding themselves in other non-Scottish departments is relatively low. There have been few Scottish Cabinet ministers since the war, apart from the Secretaries of State for Scotland. In that time, the city of Glasgow has produced only one Cabinet minister, a Secretary of State for Scotland. On the other hand, many Scots have risen to the highest positions in politics from English constituencies, suggesting that it is the political environment of Scotland itself which makes for the relatively weak impact.

So the roles of Scottish MPs reflect the three types of policy concern which have recurred in earlier chapters — purely Scottish matters; UK matters with a specific Scottish 'angle'; and UK matters with no distinctive Scottish aspects. While MPs are able to operate at all these levels, they do tend to specialise, with most of them opting for largely Scottish concerns. At the same time, however, they retain their partisan attachments and, in the case of the major parties, are no less Labour or Conservative for being Scottish MPs. Occasionally, the Scottish party groups are able to act as blocs demanding specific policy measures for Scotland but rarely indeed does this extend to the threat of rebellion over a Scottish issue. The Scottish role is played out within a system in which partisan attachments are taken for granted as party loyalty and Scottish loyalty and seen not as competing but as complementary. For Labour or Conservative MPs, a government of their own at Westminster is seen as necessary both on ideological grounds and to have a body capable of responding at the other end of the parliamentary channel.

It is the peculiar role of the Scottish MPs which explains many of the ambiguous reactions among them to proposals for devolution. If anything, it was the Scottish-oriented members who in the early 1970s were most hostile to the idea of a Scottish Assembly which would have taken over most of their purely Scottish work and potentially rivalled them as a channel to the UK level. It is a problem to which we shall return later (Chapter Nine).

Scotland and the European Communities

Since 1973, there has been an added dimension to the policy process in the UK as major areas of government activity have come under the purview of the European Communities. In some areas, notably agriculture, policy making is almost exclusively a European function. In others, such as transport, EC responsibilities impinge only indirectly, while in the case of fisheries, the years since UK entry have been spent trying to agree on the framework for a common policy. As far as Scotland is concerned, the most important areas of European policy are the Common Agricultural Policy, which accounts for some three-quarters of the communities' budget, fisheries, industrial policy, finance and the special funds such as the Social Fund, the Regional Fund and the European Investment Bank.

The main policy making institutions of the EC are:

The Commission, appointed by member governments but whose members once appointed owe their loyalties to the Communities. It is responsible for the presentation of policy proposals to the Council of Ministers and has a major role in policy implementation.

The Council (of Ministers) consisting of representatives of national governments. Its membership changes according to the agenda of individual meetings, so that member governments may send along whichever ministers they choose. The Council takes decisions on the proposals of the Commission and makes Community law.

The European Council. A body unknown to the Treaty of Rome (the EC's constitution); this brings together the heads of governments of member states to discuss major issues.

The European Parliament, directly elected since 1979 which has few powers except the drastic ones of rejecting the budget and dismissing the Commission. Its functions are mainly deliberative.

While the Treaty of Rome and the aspirations of its founders contained a strong implicit commitment to 'supranationalism' — the creation of a European government able to reach down past national governments — in practice the EC's operations have been characterised by bargaining among national governments. The Council of Ministers and the European Council have come to dominate the policy process relegating the Commission to a secondary role. For Scotland, therefore, the Scottish Office, as part of the national government, is the principal avenue to Brussels. It is involved in EC policy making in the same way as it is in domestic policy making. The lead, in formulating policy and in negotiating at Brussels is usually taken by the appropriate UK department, with the Scottish Office contributing through the interdepartmental network we have already examined; most matters will be thrashed out in the main functional Cabinet committees but there is, in addition, a European Affairs committee for unusual or multifunctional items. As it is necessary to allow ministers involved in negotiations a certain amount of leeway at Brussels, there is a need to ensure that Scottish interests continue to be represented during the bargaining sessions. This is done in a variety of ways. Where there is an important Scottish interest, a junior Scottish Office minister will form part of the negotiating team. If the matter is more marginal, there may simply be Scottish Office civil servants attached to the entourage of the UK minister, with provision for them to refer back to Edinburgh for guidance, where necessary. Where Scotland has the largest interest in a matter, for instance on fisheries, hill farming or sheep meat, the Secretary of State for Scotland may take the lead in policy making and at negotiations, though this is unusual given the intense interest taken by Ministers of Agriculture in EC matters. While, generally speaking, relationships between Scottish and UK departments are harmonious, frictions do occur here. Brussels negotiations are complex enough matters without the addition of intragovernmental negotiations within the UK delegation and it is rumoured that UK civil servants occasionally get impatient with the Scots.

For Scottish interest groups, therefore, the best way of approaching the EC is through the Scottish Office and close relations are maintained by the principal economic interest groups, particularly the National Farmers' Union of Scotland. There is an element of mutual support here, as the Scottish Office is able to use pressure and information from interest groups in its battles within government; and having persuaded the Scottish Office of their case, the interest groups gain a vital channel of access into government. This gives Scotland (with Wales) an advantage not enjoyed by other 'regions' of the EC, even those with their own devolved governments.

The second channel of access to the EC for Scottish interest is through UK and European interest groupings. At the UK level, pressure can be put on UK departments for matters in which Scotland is not asking for special treatment. At the EC level, there is an extensive network of consultative committees and interest groups, encouraged by the Commission as an expression of supranationality. The most important of these is the Economic and Social Committee, on which Scottish interest groups are represented as part of the UK contingent. In addition, there are specialised consultative committees and 'private' federations of national interest groups, such as COPA, representing national farmers' organisations, and Europeche, for the fishermen's organisations. In both these cases, the appropriate Scottish group is independently represented. In other cases, such as that of the CBI, where there is not a separate Scottish interest group, Scotland is represented via a UK organisation. These channels, however, are mainly useful for *communication and information* gathering, as are the offices maintained in Brussels by the CBI and jointly by the UK farming organisations. Policy *influence* is exerted mainly through national governments though, of course, information is an essential prerequisite for policy making.

There are some direct links between Scottish interest groups and Community institutions where the Scottish group feels that a useful Commission initiative is unlikely to gain the backing of the UK government. The Commission can then be encouraged to put the proposals forward to the Council, and the interest group can keep up pressure through the Scottish Office to accept it. This, however, is exceptional and only possible for the best organised groups. Contacts are also made through UKREP, the UK permanent representation in Brussels but, again, this is largely for the purposes of communication and information gathering.

In the European Parliament, Scotland has eight members. While, according to population shares, this is a fair proportion of the UK's eighty-one members, Scottish nationalists complain that it compares unfavourably with the fifteen members representing the smaller population of the Republic of Ireland. In pursuance of the supranational ideal, Members of the European Parliament (MEPs) sit according to party rather than national groupings but, like Westminster MPs, also have the role of representing constituency interests. Scottish MEPs are thus able to raise those matters of particular concern to Scotland but, given the limited powers of the European Parliament, this does not comprise a major contribution to the policy making process.

Scotland and Wales have a further link with the EC in that Edinburgh and Cardiff together with West Berlin, are the only cities other than the seats of national governments where the Commission has established offices (though there are proposals to establish them elsewhere). This is a recognition of the special political and constitutional position of Scotland and Wales — as well as the Commission's worries about the level of support for EC membership there. The role of the Edinburgh Office is essentially an information one. A great deal of its time is spent defending the EC in the media and correcting alleged misrepresentations of its work. It also helps interested parties through the maze of EC regulations and grants and has very close links with the Scottish Office bureaucracy. However, it would be wrong to see it as a channel of influence to Brussels, for the way to Brussels lies through national governments and the major interest groups.

Where the *implementation* of EC policy is concerned, the network becomes more complex involving the Commission, national governments, local authorities, interest groups and individual enterprises. To illustrate this, we shall examine the establishment and operation of the Regional Development Fund. The RDF was set up in 1975 in response to complaints that the effect of European economic integration was to favour those areas already well-off. In principle, the RDF should thus redistribute resources to the needy areas of the Community according to an agreed set of criteria.

In practice, matters are complicated by the vexed questions of 'quotas' and 'non-additionality'. The former means that each member state of the EC is allocated a fixed proportion of the fund — though, since 1979, five per cent has been held back as a 'non-quota' sum available for projects anywhere in the Community. The non-additionality principle means that national governments — and particularly the British government — use RDF funds to replace either moneys they would have otherwise paid out in grants or capital sanctions to local authorities. In the former case, the recipient gains nothing, merely receiving EC instead of national money. In the latter case, a local authority will save on interest charges by receiving the money as grant rather than have to borrow, though the saving will be deducted from its Rate Support Grant calculation.

In all cases, the handling of the grant is in the hands of the central government, which submits its list of projects to the Commission, which in turn passes them to the Fund Management Committee, on which all member states are represented. Grants awarded by the committee are then administered by national authorities.

Within the UK, there is an understanding that Scotland will receive a predetermined proportion of RDF funds, and while the lead department in dealing with Brussels is the Department of Industry, SEPD is responsible for eliciting and administering Scottish applications. Given the existence of effective quotas at both EC and UK levels, there is not in practice a great deal of territorial competition for grants. Most effort is devoted to ensuring that enough applications are forthcoming to spend the money that is available. SEPD has a particularly good record here. Because of the multifunctional nature of the Scottish Office and the close links with local authorities and firms, it is able very rapidly to produce lists of schemes. In this way, by spending the money when it is available, it has been able to safeguard its nation allocation although the only money actually coming into Scotland is the rate-borne element of the interest charges on local authority projects. Money 'awarded' to Scottish firms or the Scottish Office's own programmes (e.g. for trunk roads) remains in the Treasury in London.

In the case of the Social Fund, applications are handled through the Department of Employment. These funds for areas suffering from structural employment problems, are genuinely 'additional' and go directly to the bodies to which they are awarded. Scottish local authorities have been particularly active in using this in recent years.

Around this process, there is a great deal of informal contact and lobbying. When the RDF was being designed, the Scottish Council (Development and Industry) organised a mission under a former ambassador to the EC to make sure that the Scottish case was heard at all levels. In order to foster contacts and learn their way around the EC, the

Scottish Council later seconded one of their staff to the European Coal and Steel Community (which allocates funds for the restructuring of the coal and steel industries and to help areas affected by closures). Contacts with Brussels can be used to find out what types of project are likely to be favoured under the RDF and other funds, such as the Social Fund, coal and steel funds, the Agricultural and Fisheries Fund and the European Investment Bank. In the case of the Bank, which loans money to local authorities, direct contacts are actually encouraged by central government (Jordan 1980). This seems to be regarded by government as 'harmless' because the relationship here is of a commercial rather than a political nature. In general, however, it remains true that central government jealously guards the right of access to Europe for the purposes of influencing and contributing to the policy process. So the European channel of influence, like the others we have examined, must pass through London. Scottish pressure can be exercised but on an essentially centralised system.

Within Scotland, a great deal of prominence is given to the operation of the various Funds. Their impact, however, is marginal and Scottish influence in Europe is much more important in the sphere of policy making on major EC questions such as fisheries.

Part Three:

LOCAL GOVERNMENT

CHAPTER FIVE

THE LOCAL GOVERNMENT SYSTEM

The reorganisation of local government

Traditionally, local government in Scotland, as elsewhere in the United Kingdom, was based upon the division between town and country, represented by the burghs and counties. Counties were first established in early Stuart times, mainly for purposes of law enforcement, while burgh charters, granted by the sovereign, nobility or church, date as far back as the twelfth century; after 1833, it was open to any community of 2,000 or more inhabitants to apply for a charter. Within the counties were parishes, reflecting the organisation of the church.

Reforms in 1889 and 1929 sought to reflect modern needs by transferring powers to larger units. In 1889 county councils were established, followed shortly after by the raising of the four cities of Edinburgh, Glasgow, Dundee and Aberdeen into 'counties of cities', single-tier authorities with all local government powers. Outside the cities, counties shared powers with districts, burghs and parishes. In 1929 the parishes were abolished and the small burghs lost most of their functions to the counties. The large burghs retained most functions except education, sending delegates to the county council only when education and other county matters were on the agenda.

By the 1960s, opinion in the Scottish Office, as in England and Wales, moved towards the need for radical reform. The old system was seen as out-dated, inefficient and ill-fitted to the social and economic patterns of contemporary Scotland. In particular, the division between town and country was seen as hampering much-needed economic and land-use planning, industrial and residential development and improved service provision. The planning theme was emphasised particularly strongly in the Scottish Development Department from its creation in 1962.

It is important to see the move to local government reform in its contemporary context. Planning for economic and population growth was the dominant concern and central government needed a structural framework to encourage and accommodate expansion. There was an emphasis on the capital investment programmes of the local authorities and their need to facilitate rather than frustrate economic and industrial development; the Scottish Office was particularly alarmed at the lack of co-ordinated provision for the vehicle plants which it had succeeded in bringing to Linwood and Bathgate. So a less fragmented structure, capable of strategic planning in co-operation with the centre and able to exploit economies of scale was sought. Underlying all this was a strong belief in consensus between central and local government so that strengthening the localities, far from posing a threat to the centre, would provide it with powerful allies in the pursuit of agreed strategies for growth and development.

The first attempt at reform, in 1963, however, respected existing boundaries, proposing a 'modernisation' of local government by creating a two-tier structure of about fifteen new counties, bringing in the counties of cities. Below these would be fifty-sixty smaller burgh and rural councils with only minor functions, not including housing. It was the change of government in 1964 which allowed those in the Scottish Office who favoured more radical reform their chance and, at the same time as the Redcliffe-Maud Commission in England, the Wheatley Royal Commission was established to examine local government in Scotland. Wheatley's main criticisms of the old system were as follows.

Structure	—the areas of local government no longer accorded with the facts of social and economic geography, with patterns of life and work.
Functions	—the areas of local government were too small to administer their responsibilities effectively and efficiently.
Finance	—the size of authorities in many cases led to heavy dependence upon central government grant, resulting in subservience to central government.
Membership and Internal Organisation	—the internal procedures of a local authority were hampered by an organisational structure which focussed on detail rather than wider policy issues.
Central-Local Relations	—the balance of power and responsibility between central and local government had gone wrong. There had been a movement of power towards the centre causing greater interference in administrative matters.

Four key objectives of any reform were identified: power, effectiveness, local democracy, and local involvement. Local government should be enabled to play a more important, responsible and positive part in the running of the country, to bring the reality of government nearer to the people. Therefore, local government should be equipped to provide services in the most satisfactory manner, particularly from the point of view of the people receiving the services. This necessitated democratic control, and thus power had to be exercised through elected representatives. Local democracy, however, needed a wider interpretation than traditional representative government, and public participation should bring the people into the process of reaching decisions as much as possible, and enable those decisions to be made intelligible to the people.

The evidence gathered by the Commission can be subdivided into two main groups, the Research Studies produced by the Intelligence Unit which supported the Commission's investigations, and the submissions of central departments, local authorities, local authority associations, professional associations, and other interested parties. The analytical studies examined community attitudes about local government, the shortages of local government manpower, and the administrative costs of local authorities. Whilst by no means comprehensive, what these studies did was to suggest that certain advantages would derive from the creation of larger units of local government. The submissions were more divided. Most evidence came from those within the system and, as Dearlove (1980) shows in the case of the English reform, reasoned professional judgment was sometimes not easily distinguishable from self-interested advocacy. Certainly the evidence which carried most weight was that of the central departments and professional associations urging economies of scale rather than that of the local authority associations and political parties arguing for smaller units. Most weight of all was given to the planners of the SDD whose concerns for strategic planning and the 'city-region' were closely reflected in the Commission's report.

The general conclusions reached were:

(a)   Very broad areas and large resources are required for *planning* and *associated services*, but some aspects of planning might be assigned to a more local level.

(b)   The *personal social services* require a minimum population of about 200,000 but do not necessarily require areas as big as planning.

(c)   *Housing* authorities must be strong in resources and fairly wide in area. Housing is bound up with planning and with the personal services. Certain ancillary functions might be discharged at a more local level.

(d)   The *protective services* require broad areas which would be as large as for planning.

(e)   The *environmental services* apart from water, sewerage and refuse disposal, would derive no advantage from being administered on a very large scale.

(f)   The *amenity services* are local in character. A minimum population of around 100,000 is normally required for the library services.

Some of these propositions may be, at least, questionable. The quest for uniform standards reflects the *centre's* concern and largely impressionistic statements about minimum population sizes for specific services often ignore the diversity of the social, demographic and economic environments in which local authorities operate. For instance, it may not be in the interests of efficiency, however defined, to group together sparsely populated areas to produce the 'required' population. Furthermore, much of the case for economies of scale in local government services has since been shown to rest on weak foundations (Dearlove 1980). Such criteria, however, did bolster the case for a few large authorities which would both simplify central government's links with the localities and permit a strategic planning role.

Wheatley linked this with the argument for strengthening local democracy and reversing the trend to centralisation. Here it parted company with Scottish Office officials who were concerned with the weakness and ineffectiveness of local government because it detracted from the performance of local government in implementing national policy and because it involved them in a great deal of detailed intervention —a time-consuming and ineffective means of control. A smaller number of councils with widened responsibilities could ease their own burden and make control of major policy items easier.

The Commission came down in favour of a system of seven strong regional councils, controlling all the major services including housing. It was certainly no coincidence that these corresponded to the seven regions which the SDD was already using for planning purposes. They were based on the major conurbations or potential conurbations in Scotland and took account of the principle that river estuaries are, in planning terms, a unifying feature and not, as in mediaeval times, a dividing one. So there were to be three great estuarial regions straddling the Clyde, the Forth and the Tay. In central Scotland, a region would be based on the Stirling-Falkirk-Grangemouth nexus while in the north-east, Aberdeen and its hinterland would be brought together. A Highland region, based in Inverness, would cover a vast land area plus the northern and western isles while in the south-west was a region which was recognised to be in reality only half a natural planning region, the rest being across the Solway in England. Given the size of the regions, the Commission felt the need for a second tier, nearer the localities. Here a dilemma presented itself. If they went for very small second-tier districts, these would not be able to assume any important functions and would not therefore (so it was assumed) attract members or staff. So they went for larger districts, with some significant functions of their own; but this presented the problem that most of these districts were too large to have a community base. Further, by dividing major functions between the tiers, they built in problems of co-ordination and conflict at a time when local government was trying to move towards greater co-ordination and corporate planning. A Note of Dissent by two members of the Commission, Russell Johnston, MP, and Betty Harvie Anderson, MP, proposed smaller districts at a very local level which would have no formal functional responsibilities but would have a 'general competence' to take up local issues and fill in gaps in regional services. In rejecting this option, the majority of the Commission insisted that regions and districts should have equal status, each dealing directly with central government and being responsible for its allotted functions. Most functions, including housing, were to go to the regions but the planning system was to be split between the two tiers and districts would have responsibilities in urban redevelopment, parks and recreation, museums and libraries, environmental health and licensing.

Proposed districts varied enormously in size, the largest being that of an enlarged Glasgow. Here was a practical illustration of the dilemma. If Glasgow was to exercise the functions recommended by Wheatley, then it could be argued that it would require a boundary extension, the last one having been before the war. On the other hand, the proposal to expand the city while reducing its functions was bound to arouse opposition.

The Wheatley recommendations were inherited by the incoming Conservative Government in 1970 and, in contrast to the rejection of the Redcliffe-Maud proposals for England, were accepted with minor modifications. An additional region was created in the Borders and separate all-purpose authorities proposed for Orkney, Shetland and the Western Isles. While the practical effect of these modifications was slight, however, they drove a coach and horses through Wheatley's logic of minimum population sizes and created a precedent which other areas were not slow to take advantage of. A very significant change made by the Conservatives was to allocate housing to the district level. This at once allowed potentially Conservative districts to escape the housing policies of Labour-controlled regions and gave an incentive to areas not designated as districts in the Wheatley scheme to claim district status.

As we have seen, the reform was the child of the SDD and the Conservative Government often gave the impression of disinterest in the whole business (Keating 1975a) relying on Labour support to carry the bill through its difficult parliamentary stages. Consequently, local pressure groups were able to score some important victories. A major campaign succeeded in getting Fife designated as a region while Bearsden, Milngavie, Bishopbriggs and Clydebank all succeeded in remaining outside the expanded Glasgow district. The latter is a good illustration of the clash between political interests and the administrative and planning rationality of the reform. Glasgow, as it expanded in the course of the nineteenth and twentieth centuries, had periodically extended its boundaries to include the newly built-up areas. The last such extension had been in 1939 to include land subsequently developed as the peripheral schemes of Castlemilk, Easterhouse, Drumchapel and Pollok. Lying between these areas but outside the star-shaped city boundary, were the middle-class suburbs of Bishopbriggs, Bearsden, Milngavie and Newton Mearns as well as the burgh of Rutherglen. Wheatley's analysis had shown these to be functionally a part of the city of Glasgow, with their residents using city services. However, these overwhelmingly owner-occupied areas showed no willingness to come into a city which had a correspondingly high proportion of council tenants. With housing becoming a district function, subsidies to council tenants would bear on the rates — while subsidies to owner-occupiers are met direct by the Treasury and escape local government control. So a vigorous campaign was launched in the Commons and the Lords. The result, which owed as much to chance and a great deal of confusion as to judgment, was that Bearsden, Milngavie, Bishopbriggs, Newton Mearns, along with Clydebank, stayed out of Glasgow while Rutherglen came in.

The confused outcome in Glasgow reflected the dilemma in Wheatley's analysis. The creation of Fife region was more serious, destroying the estuarial concept completely in the east of Scotland and leaving it intact only in Strathclyde. Other attempts to change the pattern, notably by breaking up the large region in the west, were unsuccessful so that, to a large extent, the new system is still recognisable as Wheatley. Certainly what remains is a much more radical reform than its English counterpart.

Criticisms of the new system have been prevalent, yet few have recognised the danger of attempting to compare it with its predecessors, given the lack of adequate comparative data, and more importantly, given the dramatic changes in the environment, from expenditure growth and low inflation, to economic stringency and high inflation. The performance of the new authorities has been kept in the public eye by the attention of the media, and the possibility of a Scottish Assembly for much of the period leading often to the assumption that the regions' existence would be short-lived. The severity of Britain's economic problems, and their resultant impact on local service provision, often went ignored in discussions of local government.

The first set of criticisms has evolved around the concept of size, and the view that the new authorities are remote, bureaucratic and costly, and that they have generated highly paid officials and increased staff. The second set of criticisms centre on the nature of the two-tier system, and the problem of duplication caused by concurrent functions, and of co-ordination of closely related services such as housing and social work.

Political parties are divided about the performance of the new system. The Scottish Nationalists and the Liberals have been most unhappy with the new system, and their diagnoses and remedies have been remarkably similar. Both advocate the transfer of powers such as strategic planning and water supply to a devolved Assembly, and the creation of a single-tier system of multi-purpose authorities. By contrast, the Conservative and Labour Parties have been divided over the issues, and each approached the matter by establishing working parties to review the system. Their reports, whilst rejecting several of the major criticisms of the new system, remained ambivalent, neither committing themselves to the status quo, nor saying major change was necessary.

The second group pressing for change are the city-district councils, where there is a concern for loss of status as a result of reorganisation, and with special emphasis on the concept of duplication and unnecessary cost. Thirdly, there is a loose collection of people who are unhappy with the present system, who in general would seek to go back to the 'old' system based on burghs and county councils. They are frequent letter writers to their local press, bemoaning the passing of the "toon cooncil". In this group there is much misunderstanding about the location of powers under the old system. Those who bemoan the disappearance of the 'Provost' often appear unaware of the limited powers which the small burghs possessed, and the problems of accountability inherent under the old system of county councils.

How relevant are these criticisms? The problem with the concept of remoteness, for instance, is its abstract nature. The tools of social science would find it very difficult to define and measure such an elusive and politically charged issue. As one major review of the local government system argued, such an issue would require a programme of research at least comparable to the surveys conducted for Wheatley, and to utilise data which could compare community attitudes *before* and after reorganisation (Page and Midwinter 1980).

The other two dimensions, bureaucracy and cost, are more amenable to evaluation. The conclusions of the above study demonstrate that reorganisation was not a factor which pushed manpower figures upwards, but continued a trend which began in 1971. Indeed, in 1976 and 1977, manpower actually fell. Whilst there has been a slight growth in administrative *manpower*, the paradox is that there has also been a fall in administrative *costs*. With regard to expenditure and rate levels, the findings suggest that the bulk of the increases can be attributed to inflation

(70% alone), inherited commitments stemming from the capital expenditure expansion of 1972-74 under the Heath Government, and the reductions in government grant in the immediate post-reorganisation period.

The second set of criticisms has been accepted as legitimate by the Conservative Government, which established the Stodart Committee to examine such issues. The terms of reference were restricted to reviewing the working relationships among the new authorities and recommending any rationalisation of functions which maintained the viability of the existing structure. Stodart (1981) ruled out major change as beyond its terms of reference and concentrated on tidying up overlapping and concurrent functions in planning, leisure, tourism, environmental health and industrial development. Its approach has been criticised (Keating and Midwinter 1983) for trying to take the Wheatley logic to extremes, separating out regional and district functions completely, rather than recognising the inevitable functional interdependencies in matters like housing and social services or the various aspects of planning. Most of the recommendations have been implemented by the Government but, as the report itself suggested, in the not too-distant future the arguments about a single-tier system are likely to resurface.

The Convention of Scottish Local Authorities

Any analysis of the new local government system in Scotland requires some elaboration of the role played by the Convention of Scottish Local Authorities (COSLA). As with many aspects of Scottish Government, however, there is an absence of serious academic research on which to base solid arguments and conclusions. Carol Craig's study of the politics of COSLA's constitutional crisis of 1978 is useful for understanding the development of political organisation and functions. The best study of COSLA, however, by Peter Daniels, remains unpublished (Daniels 1979). Much of the information in this section draws heavily on Daniels's work.

There is a further research problem in examining the role of COSLA in central-local relations. COSLA is, in effect, a sectional pressure group, whose raison d'etre is the promotion of local governments' interests. As such, it seeks mainly to influence the decisions and policies of central government, and an evaluation of its impact in that direction awaits more detailed research in the future. In the remainder of this section, we shall seek to suggest some tentative conclusions gleaned from the sparse academic literature and from our own research findings.

The objectives of the Convention are enshrined in its written constitution. They are:

—To watch over, protect and promote the respective interests, rights, powers and duties of its member authorities as these may be affected by legislation or proposed legislation or otherwise.

—To provide a forum for the discussion of matters of concern to its member authorities and to obtain, consider and disseminate information on matters of importance and interest to member authorities.

—To provide (in conjunction where appropriate with the other Local Authority Associations in the United Kingdom) such essential services for its member authorities as it may consider appropriate.

The creation of a single local authority association to represent Scotland's diverse local authorities has been interpreted as a "success" in its own right. There is no doubt that it is a unique development in British local government, as English local authority associations remain overtly partisan, in contrast to COSLA's task of representing region, district and island councils, urban/rural councils, and Tory/Labour/SNP/Liberal/Independent councils alike. The argument is that one association allows the presentation of a united front to central government. Yet those authorities' interests do not always coincide, particularly over the structure of local government, or the distribution of resources. This was reflected in COSLA declining to give evidence on the structure of local government to the Stodart Committee, which was seen by Carol Craig as 'a classic example of COSLA's weakness' (Craig 1980).

Craig's argument is that there are fundamental divisions *within* COSLA on the important local government issues, such as Stodart. Yet she offers little supporting evidence, apart from the constitutional crisis of '78 and the leadership elections. This question requires further probing, and we can begin by looking at how COSLA organises its business, how its decision-making processes operate, and how it seeks to advance the interests of local government.

COSLA operates from Edinburgh with a very small full-time Secretariat and budget. Most of the meetings are held in Edinburgh, but occasionally they meet elsewhere. The Convention itself is a general meeting of representatives of all sixty-five member authorities, but it has very limited powers, i.e. the election of the President and Vice-President, and the power to remit (*not overturn*) back to an executive committee any decision of that committee not previously acted upon. There are four meetings per annum, one of which is the Annual Meeting, and authority representation is based on population, and on a formula which is weighted in favour of the smaller authorities to avoid domination by a few large councils. (Financial contributions, however, are not weighted similarly.) The size of the full convention (about 150 members) is not conducive to it playing a central role in detailed decision-making, and it has also to be ensured that functions which are exclusive to one type of authority cannot be overturned by the full Convention where all authorities are represented. The solution has been the delegation of business to a system of executive committees, which are either 'policy' or 'functional' committees. The main Convention Policy Committee has the undernoted remit:

—To review in general the relationship between central and local government.

—To deal with matters concerning local government.

—To discuss matters of common concern to both regions and districts which are not considered appropriate for discussion in the functional committees.

—To consider international affairs and in particular, the effect on local government in Scotland of EEC policies.

—To monitor the operation of the Association, for example, the appointment of staff and the fixing of salaries.

There are also Regional, District and Islands Policy Committees, which meet only rarely, and whose remit is more limited to reviewing the relationships between the types of authorities they represent and central

government and to formulating separate viewpoints where disputes among them arise. Functional Committees, by contrast, deal with matters concerning particular services or subjects, such as housing or education.

The composition of such committees was a thorn in the flesh which provoked the constitutional crisis of 1978. It was brought to a head in 1977, when rural councils, who for some time had been becoming dissatisfied with the ability of COSLA to safeguard their interests, 'lost out' to urban authorities in the distribution of Rate Support Grant. Carol Craig has pointed out that this shift in resources also occurred in England and Wales, but instead of seeing this urban bias as part of a political choice made by a Labour Government, rural authorities in Scotland claimed COSLA was partly to blame. They argued that they were becoming the Cinderella of local government because they were under-represented on the COSLA subcommittee which negotiates with the Secretary of State on local government finance (Craig 1980).

The problem of lack of representation led to an amendment to the constitution which limited representatives on the committees to two per authority, effectively halving Strathclyde's representation. This led to an immediate threat of withdrawal from COSLA by Strathclyde, who paid one-third of the budget and, it was commonly agreed, had not wielded undue influence within the Convention. These amendments were reversed in 1978 (but by bringing forward the date of the AGM from June to January, Labour authorities were to lose the crucial votes for President and Vice-President in 1980, which they would have come by in June following Labour gains in the District elections). There has since been some compromise and Strathclyde's representation has been increased, whilst Borders are now represented on the Policy Committee and the Joint Working Party on Local Government Finance (for officers of the Scottish Office and local government).

Day-to-day administration of the Convention's affairs is the responsibility of the Secretary and Treasurer, who is its chief adviser. The Secretariat services the Convention and each of its fifteen committees; participates in meetings with outside bodies, particularly government; processes all correspondence; decides whether any matter is important enough to lay before the committees, and provides background notes or draft reports on any major proposals.

In the main, however, COSLA utilises part-time specialist advisers for the committee system, but they are nominated by their professional associations, not by the elected members. The Society of Local Authority Chief Executives (SOLACE) and the Chartered Institute of Public Finance and Accountancy (CIPFA) are represented on every committee, and specialist associations accordingly.

Decision-making in COSLA operates in the mode of local government, with agendas and reports prepared and circulated in advance by the Secretariat, including the views of the specialist advisers. The chairman leads the committee through the business, and often resolves the issue by stating "the feeling of the committee as he sees it". Divisions are unusual. As Daniels has shown, from April 1975 until September 1978, of 2,956 items considered by committees, votes were required only on ninety-one, of which forty-nine were simply votes on appointments to outside bodies. There is a qualitative difference, however, between the Convention Policy and the Functional Committees. The latter are relatively non-partisan, and a 'housing' or 'social work' consensus usually emerges. The meetings are held in private, and as a result there is less political points scoring and ideological posturing and more practical discussions of the problems than in council chambers. Members of the committee are themselves usually experienced chairmen of the appropriate service committees. Two or three personalities normally dominate discussion.

In the policy committee, however, membership is composed of the Council leaders from the major authorities. Although the four Presidents to date have adopted non-partisan approaches, the continued searching for public expenditure cuts, reinforced by the increased polarisation between the two major parties, makes debate more overtly partisan and strident. Nevertheless, there is still more unity than division. The Local Government (Miscellaneous Provisions) Scotland Bill was unanimously opposed at the Convention Policy Committee.

COSLA has nevertheless seen a growth of 'polarisation' from its inception, which became marked after 1978, with an influx of new councillors, and because of the way the Independents and the Conservatives organised themselves over the constitutional amendments, and the leadership elections. Whereas in 1975, three Labour leaders were nominated for the presidency, the more coherent operation of a group system will ensure a single nominee in future. Labour now hold regular 'pre-meeting' meetings, whereas the Conservatives limit these to the Convention Policy Committee and full Convention meetings. Time and geography make it easier for Labour to do so, but the Conservatives generally are more reluctant to utilise the group system, particularly rural Tories from a tradition of Independent politics.

It should not be assumed that such groups are homogenous. In Labour's case, the internal divisions mirror the political differences emerging nationally. 'Traditional moderates' continue to dominate in Strathclyde and Central Regions, and to argue in such meetings that they ought not to suffer unfairly from government cuts because of the 'high spenders' (e.g. Lothian). Similarly, urban Conservatives tend to be much more aware of the necessity of expenditure than their rural counterparts, who have been accustomed to minimal service provision in the past.

How then does COSLA carry out its role? Its main function is of influencing government and generally COSLA reacts to government requests for opinion/advice rather than initiates it. The main emphasis is on influencing the development of government policy and the framing of legislation, for once it goes before Parliament, the feeling is that it is too late to effect things, given government majorities and the use of the party whip.

Government consults COSLA over technical and administrative issues, as well as ideological. The former are more likely to be influenced by COSLA's representations than the latter, though even here minor changes of an administrative kind can be achieved whilst the principles of a proposal remain unaltered.

Interest articulation may be formal or informal. Ministerial meetings on finance are held on a regular basis, others are on *ad hoc* issues with some involving members, some only officers. In the period studied by Daniels, joint Scottish Office/COSLA working groups examined Medical Wastes, Pollution of Water, School Accommodation, and Alternatives to Corporal Punishment in Schools, as well as the regular Working Party on Local Government Finance.

Communication and influence can also be informal and again it would be difficult to measure. Scotland's governmental community is a small one, and discussions take place with civil servants (even ministers!) by telephone, over lunch, or at private meetings. In one such meeting a request was made by a Government minister to "get your lads to cool it" over spending cuts. For the academic analyst, such events are difficult to evaluate. But they are a feature of Scottish government and must be noted and appreciated.

Unlike the English local authority associations, COSLA is not well geared up to influencing Parliamentary legislation. Whereas detailed amendments were drafted by the English Associations to the financial clauses in the Local Government (Planning and Land) Bill and promoted in both Houses by their Honorary Vice-Presidents (ex-councillors), COSLA produced only a critical brief for Scottish MPs on the Local Government (Miscellaneous Provisions) (Scotland) Bill. Opposition was much fiercer and better orchestrated in England, and COSLA could in no way threaten the minister with "our friends in the Lords" in the way Tag Taylor, former Tory leader of the AMA, did at a seminar in London. The English Associations achieved considerable concessions on the controls over capital expenditure though these were rejected in Scotland by the Scottish Office.

However, COSLA does occasionally advocate legislative changes to the Scottish departments, and will establish machinery to monitor the passage of legislation through Parliament. Finally, there is evidence of some signs of COSLA seeking to play a more critical role in public debate over government policy, with the publication of the COSLA critique of Government Economic Strategy in 1981, which the new President of COSLA, Councillor John Sewel of Aberdeen, claimed marked COSLA's "coming of age".

Party politics in local government

The question of whether party politics ought to operate in local government has long divided both participants and electors. This is a question of political judgment to which no definitive answer can be given, but what is clear is that the political environment does affect the way in which councils operate.

Political parties bring different values and attitudes to the management of local government. Labour stand firmly by the *Party Government* view of local government. According to Bochel and Denver (1977) this view suggests that local issues are matters over which there is and should be overt partisan conflict. Thus candidates should stand as party representatives, and parties winning electoral majorities should exercise local political control to pursue their own policies. Parties are seen as simplifying and structuring the choices presented to the voters, and ensuring democratic control over administration. By contrast, the 'consensus' approach assumes that local candidates ought to be supported on the basis of their personal qualities and characteristics, and once elected should represent local communities, not a party viewpoint. This is a dominant view in rural authorities.

The Conservative Party falls between these two traditions, urban Conservatives leaning towards the party government view, and rural Conservatives being more pro-consensus. But both do take a political perspective in seeing the main role of the local authority as keeping expenditure down and efficiently administering existing services rather than developing new policies and programmes.

Reorganisation, however, resulted in several instances in combined urban and rural areas, and one significant result of this was growth of partisan at the expense of consensus local politics. Bochel and Denver's studies of local elections reveal this quite clearly (Bochel and Denver 1978, 1979 and 1981). Increased party participation in turn brought increased electoral competitiveness and increased voter turnout.

Table 5.1

ELECTORAL TURNOUT, REGIONAL AND DISTRICT ELECTIONS,
IN THE POST-REORGANISATION PERIOD

Year	Regions	Year	Districts
1974	50.6%	1974	51.4%
1978	44.6%	1977	48.3%
1982	43.0%	1980	45.4%

There has been a slight decline in turnout, but in some areas in fact it is over 60%. These figures are still much higher than pre-reorganisation voting. Moreover, political parties do not have unlimited resources, and the pattern of safe seats which emerged after the initial round of elections may well have resulted in parties selectively concentrating their canvassing on marginal or winnable seats, with a resultant effect on turnout.

A similar trend can be identified with regard to contested seats. From a very high level of contest in 1974, this has decreased somewhat but again remains much higher than pre-reorganisation, again the result of the decline of independent politics. Of the ninety-two seats won by Independents in 1978, forty-nine were uncontested (Bochel and Denver 1978).

Table 5.2

PERCENTAGE OF CONTESTED SEATS IN LOCAL ELECTIONS
SINCE REORGANISATION

Year	Regions	Year	Districts
1974	90.3%	1974	79.5%
1978	79.3%	1977	77.9%
1982	86.0%	1980	74.1%

Partisan systems in local government have been expanding. The Independent vote and share of seats has fallen consistently since 1974. In some cases, this resulted from former Independents standing as Conservatives. Others who lost in 1974 have retired from local politics. At the same time, both the Conservatives and the Scottish National Party have increased their involvement in local affairs. This does not mean, however, that the rural tradition disappears. Many Conservative councillors in urban/rural districts continue to behave as Independents, and Group discipline is weak. By contrast, urban Conservatives are dominant in Tayside and Grampian Region, and the group system, whilst fluid, still operates effectively.

Political control of the Regions has been more stable than the Districts. Of the regions, three remain Independent: Highland, Dumfries and Galloway, and Borders. In the latter, the Conservatives made a big push to gain control in 1978 and 1982, but on each occasion members elected as Conservatives refused to follow the Party Whip when offered convenerships. Independents themselves began to operate a more informal caucus system.

Labour has controlled Fife and Strathclyde since reorganisation, and Central since 1978. Lothian has moved from a minority Labour administration to a majority Labour administration, to a minority Conservative administration. The Conservatives have controlled Grampian since 1974, and increased participation in Tayside turned a minority Conservative administration into a majority in 1978. Partly, these changes merely reflect parties getting their local organisations into better shape and winning seats which they ought to have won in 1974. Mainly they reflect the changing fortunes nationally with few genuine local issues emerging apart, perhaps from the rates/expenditure battles which culminated in Labour losing control of Lothian Region in 1982.

In the Districts, things have been less stable, reflecting the instability of the national party system at the time of the 1977 district elections. Districts produced a wide variety of local political results in that year (see Bochel and Denver 1978), and some curious coalitions emerged (e.g. Lab/Con, Lab/Lib, and Lab/SNP). The minor parties, however, did very badly in 1980, with some signs of a return to two-party systems, though we should remember that third parties' poor share of seats did not always do justice to their share of the overall vote.

Table 5.3

POLITICAL CONTROL OF DISTRICT COUNCILS SINCE REORGANISATION

	1974	1978	1980
Labour	17	5	24
Conservative	5	8	5
SNP	1	4	Nil
No Control	11	17	5
Independents	19	19	19

The problem of analysing independent councils is the paucity of studies, and the fact that those which do exist are pre-reorganisation. Dyer (1978) captured some of the flavour in his study of Kincardineshire. The intrusion of democracy made little impact on the conduct of council business, as the social homogeneity of a rural, hierarchical society with traditional values ensured that elements of traditional social leadership (e.g. the laird) were dominant council leaders. Political accountability was weak, with only thirty-three electoral contests from a possible 273 contests between 1929 and 1970.

Councillors therefore, with few social divisions, could exercise their own judgment in decision-making. Strategic policies were absent, and committees and the council focussed on specific decisions, with issues being decided on their merits. This resulted in a lack of consistency. There was no guarantee that councillors would maintain a specific position even over as short a period as a committee cycle. Dyer notes that one county councillor in her dotage was once observed to second both the proposition and the opposing amendment to the same motion! The lack of party discipline meant that committee decisions could well be reversed in full council.

All of this raises problems for officers, particularly in some of the larger post-reorganisation authorities, where strategic decisions are needed. The same lack of consistency as in pre-reorganisation days can be noted. One Chief Executive referred to council meetings as "Lucky Dip Day" as the outcomes could not be predicted (Midwinter 1982). The former Chief Executive of Highland Regional Council has said it would have to 'go political' by 1982, as officials cannot do the necessary planning unless they get a sensible, consistent brief from an elected administration which they will stick to. Highland, however, remains independent, though there is some evidence of informal groups emerging to decide matters like the selection of council conveners. In one council, Independents now meet as a group to achieve what agreement they can before council meetings. In another, committee chairmen meet informally with the council convener before council meetings. Such groups are *not* as disciplined as party groups, but set out to seek consensus where it is possible, and agree to differ and let the council decide where it is not possible.

Where divisions occur, these are often the result of personality or parochial clashes. The search for spending cuts in one council led to a proposal to close several small rural schools to meet government spending targets (one of which had six pupils and was less than two miles from the nearest town school). This proposal was approved unanimously by the education and policy committees. Local pressure was then brought to bear on elected representatives, who then operated what the Americans call "log-rolling", i.e. they lobbied fellow councillors for support on this local issue with a promise to return the favour 'when a key issue arises in your ward'. At the budget meeting, the proposal was defeated overwhelmingly, with only the conveners of education and policy and resources voting in favour!

Political groups are seen as a means of providing consistency and coherence in the political process. Ideology serves as a unifying force, although divisions and factions *within* political groups do emerge. One result of group politics may well be the emergence of centralised political leadership (often referred to as the Gang of Three or Four nowadays). Their leadership is openly recognised though their recommendations are not always accepted. Some may be amended, or even rejected, during group discussion.

The group process has important implications for the reward system in local government. Ruling administrators will take all the key posts in council, the convenership and the committee chairmanships. Major issues will be discussed and a line adopted in advance so that in many cases the 'real' battles are fought in the political group. In some councils, group leaders even determine which items are placed on committee agendas. Party discipline, however, is mitigated by the conflicting pressures on councillors, whether as committee chairman, party member, or local representative.

Recent years have seen different types of challenge to the traditional committee-based political system in local government. One major critic is Councillor Ronald Young, Secretary of the Labour Group in Strathclyde. Young questions the thrust of democratic theory which regards the political system as the legitimate source of initiative. The reality as he sees it is that councillors more often than not are mere rubber stamps, and political groups adopt a managerial (maintaining an even keel on service provision) rather than a political (questioning the relevance of current practices) stance. Documents such as Transport Policies and Programmes and Structure Plans are written in a volume of jargon so daunting that few politicians even bother to read them. In a word, Young sees the current system as weighted in favour of professionals, at the expense of the political process (Young 1981).

A related view is that councillors have failed to deliver manifesto promises, and there is a need for party control of political groups. New militant activists in the Labour Party have been able to benefit from its demise as a mass party to obtain positions of power in constituency parties, and to put forward a new theory of activist democracy rather than traditional representative democracy. Calls for increased democracy and more accountability of councillors (and MPs) to the party are supported by allegations that they have shown in the past that they cannot be trusted (Geekie and Keating 1983).

In purely organisational terms, activist democracy faces formidable problems. In the latter part of 1981, Glasgow District and Strathclyde Regional Labour Parties, both of which claim considerable rights in the making of policy and the interpretation of the manifesto, attempted to arrange, respectively, a policy conference and a meeting to discuss the Region's policy options, the key stage in policy making for the forthcoming year. The policy conference collapsed because the arrangements were bungled and the policy options meeting was cancelled for lack of a quorum and rearranged for the following month. Nevertheless, by late 1982 the District Party had adopted a complex scheme for asserting its control over elected members.

Even where local parties have succeeded in formulating policy, there is little indication of willingness seriously to address the business of governing or its legal implications. In local government councillors are legally responsible for the actions they take and can be fined and surcharged for acting illegally. The fact that they may be taking illegal action at the bhest of a local party does not give them immunity. The activists of the local party, on the other hand, are beyond the reach of the law.

This policy of democratic control has some of the hallmarks of Lenin's democratic centralism. For example, the Labour Co-ordinating Committee (Scotland's) proposed standing orders for local council Labour groups include:

"In all matters of policy where the Labour Group feel they
have information which would make them wish to vote in

Council in a manner contrary to the expressed policy of the
(district/region) Labour Party, the Group Secretary shall
request a joint meeting of the full Labour Group and the
(district/region) General Committee to discuss the matter. No
contrary policy shall be supported by any group members
without the express permission of the General Committee of
the (district/region) Labour Party.

"Individual members of the Labour Group shall not submit
or move resolutions or motions or amendments (without) the
approval of the group meeting. . . .

"Members of the Labour Group are expected not to speak or
vote at meetings of the council in opposition to the decisions of
the Labour Group. . . .

"Members wishing to leave council meetings or Labour
Group meetings before close of business must obtain the
permission of the Group Whip."

Despite the Glasgow developments, such mechanisms of control have
not yet had a major impact on decision-making in local government.
Indeed, it is not clear how they can have a real impact. The 'realities of
power' may be a cliche, but local government has a limited margin of
discretion. The bureaucratic conspiracy theory model, which argues that
professionals 'control' local government, rests mainly on vague
generalities and innuendo. Very few studies demonstrate how political will
is usurped or what adverse impact this has. The reality of power is an
interplay between bureaucratic and political forces, in an environment
over which the local authority has only limited control. Policy change
requires skills, sophisticated knowledge and political will of an altogether
different order to the sloganising characteristic of many local Labour
Party meetings.

The evolution of party politics is gradual. Some councils remain
steeped in the traditions of pragmatism and consensus politics. Others are
making the transition to the party government approach. Others still are
seeking to render the party government approach more responsive to
political and community concerns. There is no 'one best way'. A wide
diversity of political traditions and values are reflected in the operations of
local government; and the increasing tendency to adversarial politics ought
not to blind us to the fact that much of the work of local government in
practice does not involve question of party ideology.

Reaching the grass roots: the role of community councils
Community councils were recommended by the Wheatley Commission,

which saw them as a means of filling the gap at 'parish' or 'locality' level created by the formation of bigger local authorities and as meeting the demand for participation voiced so widely in the 1960s and 1970s. Wheatley was insistent that community councils should be channels for the transmission of views to local authorities, not a 'third tier' of local government and this principle was carried into the Local Government Act. The Act laid on district councils the duty to produce schemes for community councils for their areas and to proceed with the formation of councils wherever twenty electors demanded. As a result, councils have been established in all parts of Scotland, except for the city of Edinburgh, where both major parties have resisted them as unnecessary. It is difficult to establish just what is the reality of community council activity on the ground but Masterson (1979) has estimated that, allowing for the collapse of some councils after their formation, some 80% of the population and land area of Scotland are still covered.

Generally speaking, it appears that community councils are more active and widely supported in the rural areas and small towns than in the cities. For instance, where elections were contested, differences in turnout have ranged from 94% in a community in Orkney to 0.3% (comprising a single voter) in a part of Aberdeen. This can be explained by the greater sense of community outside the cities, particularly in the former small burghs where citizens were used to electing their own councils on the basis of personal acquaintance. In most cases, elections for community councils are not contested; indeed the usual problem is to find enough candidates to fill the available places. This raises the problem of how representative they really are, particularly when it comes to arguing with local and central governments elected on a much higher poll. If community councillors are, in effect, a self-appointed minority, then they may not be the best spokesmen for the area. Even where community councils do speak for the majority of people in their areas, there may be dangers in seeing them as the 'voice of the community', given that communities themselves are divided by class, age and ideology, with important minority interests needing a voice. Many people have expressed fears that community councils could lead to the demise of voluntary groups which are better at expressing these disparate interests.

This problem revolves around the question of the role of community councils and how one views the dilemma identified by Barker and Keating (1977) between community groups fighting for the self-interest of their members and those fighting for more broadly defined 'public interest' goals. There has been a certain tendency for community councils to see their role as defending the interests of their more vocal residents and to treat public resources and public planning decisions as though they were an extension of the private resources and interests of residents. This is particularly liable to happen in areas of owner-occupation, where public decisions can affect property values. At higher levels of government, from district councils upwards, private interests are to some degree separated from public decisions by the greater size and heterogeneity of areas and the intervening effects of party ideology.

A related problem is one of the most familiar dilemmas of 'participation'. Given that participation in any system of government can never be more than a minority activity, the more scope one gives for participation the more power one gives to that minority, against the 'silent majority'. As, in practice, participants tend to be the middle-class, prosperous and articulate people who already do well out of the system of government, encouraging participation may serve to reinforce rather than reduce political and social inequality. The evidence available does indicate that community councillors are disproportionately middle class though in terms of age and sex they are rather more representative than regional and district councils.

Community councils have no statutory powers or rights and their power depends on how active they are, how far local government is prepared to listen to them and on their resources. These vary greatly. As we have seen, urban councils tend to be less active, though this can vary from time to time according to the personalities involved. In the more deprived areas, there have been some deliberate efforts by local authorities to foster community councils to give local communities more political weight. In some areas, local councillors have taken an interest in them seeing them as partners in securing the welfare of the area. In others, they have seen them as rivals in the representation of the community. Most local authorities have consulted community councils on the preparation of statutory local plans and, in many cases, on development control applications. Where local public enquiries are held, it is usual for the community council to be granted a hearing even though there may not be time to hear other groups. On the other hand, the community council's view is only one of the factors which an authority will take into account in deciding on planning matters, particularly where a development has wider geographical implications or is seen as vital for the authority as a whole. Outside the field of planning mechanisms for participation are less well developed and community councils, like other outsiders, may find some difficulty in locating the best point of access to the system, especially where they do not have the help of a sympathetic councillor. Nevertheless, where a community council does make a representation, about the closure of a school or provision for the elderly, it is likely to carry greater weight than a mere group of individuals, especially where it can demonstrate wide support through public meetings or petitions.

Community councils derive most of their funds from grants from district councils, varying from the generous to the nominal. These funds are used for secretarial services, to publish newsletters, and to meet the expenses of meetings and, in some cases, maintaining premises and community centres. Additional funds are raised by raffles, jumble sales and the usual repertoire of devices used by voluntary groups.

Beyond their role in representing local views to districts and regions, some community councils have developed a social role, organising local festivals and encouraging other community groups. Unlike the representative role, this raises no major problems of principle but does require a great deal of work and organisation. Given that most community council members are often the same people who are most active in other voluntary bodies, this can present difficulties but it does seem that this type of social activity can be a means of recruiting into participation, however slight, into public affairs individuals who might not be attracted by the usual means of recruitment, the political parties.

CHAPTER SIX

CORPORATE MANAGEMENT IN LOCAL GOVERNMENT

The origins of corporate management

The 1960s and 1970s witnessed increasing discontent with the suitability of traditional management in local government for the needs of an increasingly complex, urbanised society, and the beginning of a movement towards corporate management. Traditional forms of management and organisation reflected the piecemeal development of local services. Local government was organised around specialised functions which in most cases had their own department, and, at elected member level, a committee. The management process was viewed as being dominated by technical and professional issues, at the expense of wider policy issues. 'Departmentalism', whereby people think in terms of self-contained policy problems, justify their actions by reference to professional values and attitudes, was described as the 'besetting sin' of local authorities. Traditional management was viewed as being fragmented and unco-ordinated, with little long-term planning.

In the 1960s, however, there was a growing awareness that the major problems faced by local government could not be seen in strictly departmental terms, and this was recorded in a series of government reports, the Buchanan Report (1963), the Report of the Planning Advisory Group (1965), the Dennington Report (1966), the Plowden Report (1967) and the Seebohm Report (1968). All of these reports began by looking at a 'service problem' and concluded that it could not be isolated in this way but needed to be looked at from a wider perspective. The 1970s saw the publication of two reports by the CPRS (1975, 1977), both of which were concerned to improve the corporate links between central and local government, and to facilitate the achievement of a joint, or corporate approach to problems at the point of service delivery, i.e. the locality.

During the same period, people *within* local government were recognising that the fragmented management structures were also contributing to piecemeal approaches to the major, complex issues facing local authorities. At this stage, this reflected a concern for 'administrative efficiency' rather than a focus on the process of management, and various reports echoed similar themes. There was a need for a rationalisation of the organisational structure, central mechanisms to improve co-ordination, and a new type of chief officer. The Wheatley Report in particular argued that the new system of local government "should lay right kind of responsibility in the right places". Thus it expanded its ideas on the "principles of good organisation", but it also developed the need for integrative machinery into a wider concept of the process of management. Once more the absence of 'unified management' was lamented and, to overcome this, there was a need for:

> "a body with definite management functions, including responsibility for such matters as
> (a)   developing and co-ordinating the policy of the authority, assessing priorities and planning the broad assessment of finance;
> (b)   putting up majority policy proposals for the approval of the council;
> (c)   co-ordinating the action needed to implement the policy".

By the time the Bains Committee in England reported, there was a significant consensus on the need for corporate planning and management.

There have been several attempts to define 'corporate management', but perhaps the most fitting definition which captures its strategic nature is that of John Skitt.

> "*Corporate management* means that the major decisions affecting the allocation of scarce resources, determination of long-term objectives, establishing priorities and choosing between alternatives, are taken by the managerial machinery of the authority with a responsibility for strategic decision-making, which is relieved of the burden of day-to-day responsibilities and which can therefore develop its responsibilities from the standpoint of the authority as a whole. It recognises that members and officers with their respective managerial roles must manage together." (Skitt 1974).

This typically implies structural changes, such as:

> —the appointment of a chief executive officer as head of the authority's paid service;

—the creation of a chief officer's management team;

—the establishment of a Policy and Resources Committee to guide the council in the formulation of its policy objectives and priorities.

The Paterson Report

In 1972, a working group was appointed by the then Scottish local authority associations with the Scottish Development Department, to recommend reforms in management structures and processes for adoption by the new Scottish local authorities due to be established in 1975. Chaired by I. V. Paterson, the County Clerk of Lanark, it comprised a *Steering Committee* of elected members, an *Advisory Group* of officers representing the various associations and the Scottish Development Department and a small *Central Advisory Unit* of a management consultant and three local authority officers on full-time secondment.

The Steering Committee's role was limited to approving the terms of reference of the Advisory Group and endorsing a final report. The burden of work was thus taken by the Advisory Group, heavily dominated by officers from urban, 'politicised' authorities; only two members came from 'independent' councils and none from the rural areas.

The Paterson Report, as it became popularly known, regarded the need for a 'corporate approach' to the business of local government as established beyond doubt, and recommended the adoption of what is broadly termed 'corporate management' to the new local authorities. Its immediate impact was such that, when it was published in 1973 the Secretary of State recommended that it would be the first paper to be put before those who are elected to the Regional, Islands and District Councils.

Paterson began with a diagnosis of the failings of existing management structures — excessive specialisation and fragmentation, inadequate arrangements for co-ordination. On the other hand, while professionalism could be a further source of fragmentation, it was also a strength, providing detailed knowledge and expertise for local authorities. A new structure should be able to:

"provide the means of achieving a unified approach to the formulation and implementation of policies and plans to meet the real needs of the community;

preserve the strengths of the professional approach which will still be required for the effective discharge of the local authority's function;

ensure a challenging and worthwhile role for elected members
and officers;

be sufficiently flexible to adapt and respond quickly to
change".

THE CHIEF EXECUTIVE

The report followed its English counterpart (Bains 1972) in suggesting
there was a need for a chief executive as head of the authority's paid
service, and with direct authority over and responsibility for, all other
officers except where they are exercising their professional judgment. He
would be the council's principal adviser on matters of general policy,
responsible for co-ordinating advice on the forward planning of objectives
and services and to lead the management team in securing a corporate
approach to the affairs of the authority. Paterson deviated from the Bains
concept of a chief executive in two ways. First, the report suggested that
whilst in the larger authorities he should not have responsibility for a
conventional service department, in the smaller authorities he could carry
out the duties of a departmental head in addition to his role as chief officer.
Secondly, it stressed that in such large authorities the chief executive
should not be isolated, but have support mechanisms, the *executive* office,
and in the large regions, a *department* of policy planning.

The executive office would comprise two or three chief officers to assist
the chief executive to carry out his responsibilities, the directors of
administration, finance and policy planning (where applicable). The tasks
of the executive office were seen as helping the chief executive to co-
ordinate policy planning, to monitor the effectiveness of programmes, and
to manage central services.

The policy planning department was to be responsible for policy
planning, research and intelligence, and programme area team co-
ordination, and the director a member of the executive office. There are
similarities between the department of policy planning and corporate
planning units in England, but in terms of organisational power, the
department would have the weight of official recognition, in the sense that
it was considered important enough to be a department in its own right,
and not a small unit *within* a department. Its role was to service the chief
executive, management team and policy and resources committee. In
smaller councils, the report suggested that the chief executive should be
directly responsible for some central support functions such as policy
planning.

THE MANAGEMENT TEAM

The next major recommendation was for a team of chief officers to act together as the focal point for the preparation and presentation to the council, via the policy and resources committee and the service committee, of co-ordinated advice on policies and major programmes of work. With regard to the 'best' size of management team, the evidence was regarded as varied, but the report suggested it should be kept small to facilitate discussion and decision-taking, whilst ensuring adequate representation and utilisation of different skills, and to secure the necessary degree of commitment and involvement.

THE POLICY AND RESOURCES COMMITTEE

At elected member level, there was a need for a policy and resources committee with a remit to "guide the council in the formulation of its policy objectives and priorities". The report made few specific recommendations regarding membership of the committee, but there was a feeling that the existence of a majority party as a ruling group should be openly acknowledged and recognised in the authority's procedures. It was assumed that in many councils a *one-party* policy committee would be adopted, but the report stressed the need to make effective arrangements for officers to brief members in advance of decisions being taken. This was quite a radical suggestion, for many local authority officers had traditionally been reluctant to engage in such advice, apart from that given professionally and neutrally to the council as a whole.

COMMITTEE AND DEPARTMENT STRUCTURE

Paterson echoes Bains in its proposals that the departments and committees should be organised, where possible, on a programme area basis, i.e. the grouping of related or linked activities.

At the Regional level, the report recommended a minimum of seven service committees, *Education, Social Work, Transportation and Basic Services, plus the Chief Constable, Firemaster* and *Assessor*. In Strathclyde, *General Purposes*; and similarly seven directorates at officer level, *Education, Social Work, Engineering and Technical Services, Leisure and Recreation, Consumer Protection, Physical Planning* and *Architectural Services, plus the Chief Constable, Firemaster* and *Assessor*. In Strathclyde, however, there was seen to be a need for separate committees for *Roads, Sewerage* and *Water*, and at officer level, for transportation and basic services to be broken up into *Roads, Sewerage* and *Water* (with separate departments) and *Public Transport*.

At District level, the report argued for four service committees, *Housing, Environmental Health, Leisure and Recreation*, and *General Purposes*. However, with regard to officer structure, the report distinguished between large and small districts, although it did not explicitly define these. For large districts, the basic officer structure was *Housing, Physical Planning, Cleansing, Sanitary Services, Libraries and Museums, Leisure and Recreation, Architectural Services*; and for small districts, *Housing, Environmental Health* and *Technical Services*, plus heads (not directors) of leisure and recreation functions.

There is a legal requirement to have an Education committee, and a Director of Education, a Social Work committee and a Director of Social Work. It was not therefore possible to have a programme area approach at departmental level for personal social services. Indeed the only areas in which departments were recommended for programme areas were Engineering and Technical Services; Leisure and Recreation; and Environmental Health. Only in the latter case was there to be a 'programme area' committee. So the traditional departmental structure of local government was left largely untouched by the proposals.

Corporate management has often been attacked as ignoring the issue of power within the system or as attempting to 'take the politics out of local government', substituting 'managerialist' and 'technocratic' means of governing. How far does Paterson meet these criticisms? Certainly, as in many official reports, the question of power is played down, but it does not disappear entirely. The emphasis on the support needed for the Chief Executive suggests an awareness of the need to give him a power base; the proposal for an executive office, in particular, stemmed from a worry that without adequate support he could become isolated and powerless, in face of the departments. On the other hand, we have noted that Paterson recommended the retention of departments and recognised the benefits of professionalism. This and the advocacy of programme area or project team suggests they were not seeking a highly specialised, neatly ordered system, but one which facilitated co-ordination of policy whilst recognising the legitimacy of the professional view beside the corporate view.

The report itself takes a neutral line on whether local government ought to be partisan, recognising the diverse political environments of Scottish local authorities and the need to accommodate management reform within existing political frameworks. The main point is that the members of the Paterson Committee were experienced officers who were acutely aware of the political dimension and some were convinced of the benefits of coherence which a unified political majority can bring to the operations of local government. Indeed, Lawrence Boyle was a well-known advocate of the need to develop the political dimension in local government.

Great emphasis was laid on the process and procedures of management with the adoption of a modified version of 'rational' decision-making, focussing on the analysis of needs, objective setting, options analysis, programme design, implementation, monitoring and review. The procedures for achieving such a cyclical, corporate process were the production of position statements, a policy plan which would be the 'whole core of an authority's activities', and improved budgetary procedures which integrated planning and analysis with the resource allocation process. The approach, however, would need to be more selective and gradualist than more comprehensive reforms such as Planning Programming and Budgeting Systems (PPBS).

All this could help to secure political control over an authority's activities. The report recognised that while convention suggested elected members made policy whilst officers implemented it, reality was more complex. Many councillors were more interested in the details of administration than in strategic policy making. Councils might formally *take* decisions, in committee or the council, but *policy making*, the establishment of a set of guiding principles which provide a general context within which specific decisions could be taken, happened in only a few authorities. Greater emphasis on this aspect of their work was necessary if more coherent decisions were to be reached by councillors, who must be prepared to delegate more detailed matters to officers.

The implementation of the Paterson Report
In this section we seek to describe the management systems of the new local authorities. By management systems is meant the structures, procedures and operations of management in local government, including the roles played by officers *and* members in the management process. We begin by examining the management structures of the new authorities.

It is often argued that the study of structures in themselves is a somewhat sterile exercise. Our argument is simply that the forms of structure adopted reflect the desired approach to management in the various councils. We are interested in the various patterns of organisation and how they facilitate policy formulation, or co-ordination, or affect the allocation of resources. Organisational change has implications for the distribution of power.

We have already commented that organisational reform, though often couched in the soothing language of management, is usually about the distribution of power. It is no surprise, then, to find it meeting opposition. Paterson, however, came at a time when, because of local government reorganisation, the system was in flux, the old power structures shaken though by no means destroyed. The climate for change was fairly favourable and most of the new authorities adopted the main corporate, integrative mechanisms of chief executive and management team. Other aspects of the report have made less impact.

THE STATUS OF THE CHIEF EXECUTIVE

Three types of chief executive have emerged. First, there is the chief executive with a new style department based on specialist functions such as personnel management, public relations, research and intelligence, management services, policy planning and project co-ordination. This differs from Paterson's recommendations in concentrating integrative mechanisms in a powerful central department. Second, there is the chief executive who is also director of administration, responsible for traditional committee administration and legal services, but usually with few new functions, except personnel and management services. Third, there is the Bains style chief executive without departmental responsibility, who has only minimal support staff. An Executive Office, recommended for all regions and large district, was introduced by only five regions and five districts.

Only two of the four large regions recommended to have policy planning departments, Strathclyde and Lothian, introduced them, and Strathclyde have since revised their arrangements. In Grampian, responsibility for policy planning rests with the chief executive, the management team, a deputy chief executive, and a personal assistant. In Tayside, responsibility also rests with the chief executive and the management team, whilst a great deal of the groundwork for corporate documents is done by the planning department. Both councils felt that extensive support was unnecessary for the achievement of corporate management.

INTEGRATIVE MACHINERY

Only three local authorities, all districts, have not adopted the management team. The overwhelming majority, however, included *all* chief officers (directors). Paterson argued that while there was no optimum size for a management team, it should be kept small to facilitate decision-making. However, such a new and potentially important arrangement was bound to attract chief officers wanting to be near the centre of power and it has proved difficult to keep teams down to the small size needed for effective action and decision-making.

The final organisational means to integration was the use of 'functional specialists' in central services. Table 6.1 records the extent to which these functional specialists have been specifically recognised in the organisational structure of local authorities.

Table 6.1

ORGANISATIONAL RECOGNITION OF FUNCTIONAL SPECIALISTS

Functions	Regions			Districts		
	No	%	N	No	%	N
Personnel	8	89	9	21	40	50
Public Relations	3	33	8	7	13	50
Research and Intelligence	—	—	8	1	2	50
Policy Planning	4	44	9	4	9	50
Project Co-ordination	1	11	8	10	19	50

N: Number of respondents

This table suggests that on the whole authorities were much more willing to accept the proposals to improve management through the more conventional mechanisms of personnel management, and to introduce project co-ordination, where the emphasis is still highly professional and technical, than arrangements to foster corporate policy making. Almost half of the Regions had policy planning specialists, but only five (less than 10%) of the fifty-three districts. The table, however, only refers to functions which are specifically recognised in the authorities organisation charts. The research and intelligence function has traditionally been the preserve of the planning departments, although some service departments had also made use of such skills. Paterson wanted the function centralised for the benefit of the organisation as a whole. Authorities have overwhelmingly ignored this advice. In Lothian, R&I remained the responsibility of the Planning Department, while in Strathclyde, both policy and physical planning had a research and intelligence capability, though this was later changed in line with the Paterson recommendations.

THE POLICY AND RESOURCES COMMITTEE

The Paterson Report recommended that all but the smallest authorities should appoint a Policy and Resources committee and three resources committees for Finance, Manpower, and Planning and Development. These latter committees could be either full committees in their own right or subcommittees of the policy and resources committee. The majority of authorities have adopted all four central resource committees, although Manpower is the least common. The very small authorities tended *not* to have a policy and resources committee. The diverse response of the districts reflects their different social, economic and especially political environments. A considerable proportion of districts (30%) are small authorities with limited functions and resources and populations of below 50,000. Politics in those authorities in the main are non-partisan. The necessity for a Policy and Resources committee is less, and the political organisation for ensuring corporate priorities are reflected in departmental programmes is missing. This is reflected in the fact that only 11% of districts limited membership of the Policy and Resources committee to committee chairman, only 21% confined membership to the majority party as we would expect in highly partisan councils. The picture is very much one of authorities adapting the membership of the new committee to their traditional political cultures. Even here, there is no consistent pattern. For instance, Borders Region (Independent) had a mixture of chairmen and backbenchers, whilst Dumfries and Galloway (Independent) had chairmen only. With regard to membership of committee chairmen and backbenchers, the breakdown was as follows:

Table 6.2

MEMBERSHIP OF DISTRICT POLICY AND RESOURCES COMMITTEE

	Number of Councils	Percentage of Councils
Chairmen only	6	11%
Chairmen and backbenchers	21	40%
All members	10	19%
No P&R	8	15%
No response	8	15%
Totals	53	100%

The degree of politicisation of such committees also differs, and three main groups emerge. Single party committees are found mainly in Labour-controlled councils. Conservative councils are more likely to allow opposition representation. Thirdly, there are councils where membership is proportional to the party's share of the council seats.

COMMITTEE AND DEPARTMENTAL STRUCTURES

One of the main aims of organisational change was to improve integration by reducing the total number of committees and departments and reorganising them on a 'programme area' basis. While most authorities had fewer departments than their pre-reorganisation counterparts, the major traditional departments have retained their status. There has been some grouping of functions in the districts which were not specifically recommended by the Paterson Report, e.g. environmental services or technical services (often including housing and planning). In fact, of the traditional departments, housing has had the most varied locations, being linked even with finance. The most extensive use of a Paterson-type programme area is in Leisure and Recreation. Overall, whilst there has been some propensity to break with the separate, profession-based department in favour of regroupings, the professional department has remained the dominant form of organisation in the new authorities. What occurred in Scottish local government was in most cases the grafting on of new corporate mechanisms to a largely traditional structure. In many cases, it was local political factors which decided the issue.

In rural areas, where the tradition of 'Independent' politics exists, there is a view that issues should be decided on their merit rather than within a general policy framework. As the need for co-ordination is less, the more elaborate Paterson recommendations are regarded as unnecessary. In other areas, local jockeying for power was all-important. One authority finalised its committee structure on the basis that all members of the Labour Group wanted to be a committee chairman!

What conclusions can we draw regarding the development of corporate management? All authorities have appointed a Chief Executive, but more than half of the districts and one region have made him responsible for a department, although ten of these are the new form of department noted above. It is over the question of *support for* the chief executive that the Paterson proposals were *least* implemented. Very few districts created the executive office, whilst only three regions did not. A similar pattern emerged for the appointment of functional specialists, and only one region and ten districts introduced a project co-ordination facility. The vast *majority* of authorities therefore had only *minimal* organisational changes which would assist the development of corporate management. Most were relying on the Chief Executive and the Management Team, which suggests that many did not see the corporate approach as something radically new or requiring extensive attention in its development. One survey in 1978 (Rhodes and Midwinter 1978) revealed scepticism about the value of policy planning units, and that the tradition of a professionally dominated structure survived, with new corporate machinery superimposed.

In response to a questionnaire, fifty-six councils stated that they had adopted the principles of the corporate approach to management. However, as was pointed out earlier, there have been various interpretations of the meaning of corporate management. Greenwood *et al* have pointed out that no local authority would admit to operating in a non-rational fashion, and those without a formal system of corporate planning still saw themselves as being able to assess needs, produce objectives, plan programmes on the basis of the best available information and implement such plans in the most efficient manner (Greenwood *et all*, 1976).

PROCEDURES

The Paterson Report identified several procedural reforms to assist the development of corporate management. Some of these, concerned with budgeting, are covered in the next section. Here we examine three related items: *position statements, policy plans* and *issue analysis.*

A position statement was described by Paterson as "the production of a document or series of documents summarising the authority's existing policies and activities". Sheila McDonald (1977) has noted that in Scotland position statements for each authority's service departments were a common feature of the background preparation to Regional Reports.

In Lothian Region, policy planning developed through a format of position statements, policy options and annual budget. Central Region has also introduced position statements, and Strathclyde formalised its approach into the first phase of its annual corporate programme, known as the Data Review. Grampian Region has also utilised this type of management information in its attempt to introduce a Zero-Based Budget System. Of the district councils, Renfrew and Glasgow are examples of authorities using position statements. The majority of districts, however, have not.

Regional authorities were required by Section 173 of the Local Government (Scotland) Act 1973 to submit a Regional Report to the Secretary of State for Scotland. The Regional Report system has been seen as a commendable advance in the operation of a corporate approach to local government. Professor Stewart (1976), when asking "if the Scots had a lesson to teach", suggested that Regional Reports had an important effect on the dialogue between local authorities and central government, and had created a means to stimulate corporate management. Howat (1976) has argued that many councils in fact saw the potential of the Regional Report to fulfil the role of the Paterson policy plan. The authorities themselves were more cautious in the claims made for their reports, some seeing them as assisting in the developing of corporate working (e.g. Central, Lothian) others suggesting that the first report was limited in its contribution to the corporate approach.

Let us analyse the content of Regional Reports using Skelcher's (1980) distinction between *corporate* and *service* priorities and issues. Corporate priorities can be either *issue-based*, e.g. employment levels, *client-based*, e.g. the needs of the elderly, or *area-based*, e.g. identification of geographic areas of acute social need. Three types of priority were identified in the reports, and thus three groups of reports emerge.

(a)   Those which identify corporate policy issues separately from planning or service issues. (Central, Lothian, Strathclyde)

(b)   Those where the emphasis is on planning issues. (Dumfries and Galloway, Grampian, Highland)

(c)   Those where service, planning or corporate issues are not distinguished. (Borders, Fife, Tayside)

This reveals an equal division of authorities and a diverse response to the identification of priorities. Where responsibility for producing the report lay mainly with the physical planning department, strategic planning issues emerged and the report resembled a development plan. Where the management team had been heavily involved, key service issues were included alongside planning issues. Tayside, for instance, had no less than fifteen policy priorities. These service priorities can be used as a framework for the taking of departmental decisions, e.g. social work activities for the elderly or educational provision in areas of social deprivation, will be a priority over their other activities. Thus departmental decisions can be made consistent with overall priorities.

In authorities with more developed policy planning arrangements, an additional dimension, that of *corporate* priorities, which could serve as an overall policy plan, emerged. Thus in Strathclyde, there were two key issues:

—the need to reduce the level of unemployment;

—the need to tackle urban deprivation.

It seems significant that the councils with more extensive policy planning arrangements developed corporate criteria to assist policy making and resource allocation. Often these offered issues of redistribution which are more politically acceptable to Labour councils than to Conservative ones. Past research suggests that Conservative councils prefer to lay emphasis on the 'efficient administration of existing services' rather than take up issues of redistribution, priorities, or new policy development. Tayside Region, for example, doubted the wisdom of identifying and labelling areas as 'socially deprived' in their response to the Secretary of State's comments on their Regional Report. Similarly, non-partisan councils may accept broad goals as laid out by officers, but will not necessarily implement these in decision-making, where issues will often be treated on 'their merits' and vague general policy statements ignored.

To date, Regional Reports have enjoyed extensive favourable comment, and some balancing points require to be made. They were introduced one year after reorganisation into a local government system which was new to the concepts and practice of corporate management. There was a shortage of personnel accustomed to working in a corporate system, and the motivation of most staff remains professional and departmental. So Regional Reports provided an opportunity to *develop* corporate working not to *establish* it.

The reports differ from the Programme Budgets produced in the late 'sixties. They set out broad issues for each service area, but do not develop measures which could be used to evaluate success or review policy. Authorities did recognise the importance of developing such measures but in general relied on professional standards and central department guidelines as the means of relating the implications of strategic analysis to the concept of need. Thus the focus remains on *input* rather than on policy *impact*.

There was an emphasis in several reports on financial constraint and indeed some of them really have to be seen as bargaining documents — pleas to the Scottish Office for capital allocations. Few reports had explicit analyses of the financial implications of the policies adopted. Paterson had stressed the need for objective-setting but, in most reports, the separation of objectives from policies for achieving them is not always clear. In some cases the word 'policy' is interpreted as meaning little more than "we shall carry out our statutory duties", rather than a set of principles which provide a framework within which specific decisions can be taken. However, one should not be too harsh in criticising councils. They are constrained by their statutory duties and the weight of existing commitments. Major capital assets like schools, highways, and water systems cannot be moved around at will. So the scope for politicy initiative is necessarily limited.

For the District Councils, no statutory document comparable to the Regional Reports existed, and only a handful of District Councils had attempted to produce a policy plan, under varying titles (policy plan, corporate plan, district report).

The final procedural reform, *issue analysis*, Paterson described as "the selection of key areas for investigation by multi-disciplinary teams; this stage is usually called policy analysis and review". More extensive use is made of issue analysis than of position statements or policy plans. Some councils have formalised interdepartmental teams, others use them on an *ad hoc* basis, as required. Some authorities use both. Examples of interdepartmental issue analysis which are formalised include Transport Policies and Programmes, Housing Policy, Urban Deprivation, and Industrial Development. *Ad hoc* analysis was carried out for expenditure cuts, supplementary capital allocations, employment strategy, estates of low-letting demand, Housing Action Areas, social and community development.

Overall, as with organisational change, the picture is one of only limited introduction of Paterson-type procedural reforms. We can now merge these two concerns to obtain a broad picture of patterns of management systems in the new authorities.

How then, have the organisational and procedural reforms operated in practice? Three broad types of authority can be found in Scottish local government; those in which little corporate development has taken place, and where the emphasis remains on separatist administration of services; authorities where there is increasing emphasis on co-ordination of programmes which remain separate in origin; and finally a minority of authorities which are actively seeking to promote corporate planning and management.

The majority of councils still display most of the characteristics of the traditional approach. In such departmentally-based systems, service issues dominate the management process, with little discussion of strategic issues. The Chief Executive will almost certainly run a conventional department, probably Administration, with little support for policy planning purposes. The management team will be characterised by factionalism and bureaucratic politics, what has been called 'departmentalism'. Such systems are mainly to be found in non-partisan councils, where the outcomes of council meetings are unpredictable, and issues are decided 'on their merits' rather than in accordance with a general policy.

Such councils' aversion to general policy statements or the development of a corporate strategy, result in the Policy and Resources committee playing the role of the old Finance committee, dealing with technical financial administration rather than questions of policy. This position caused frustration in the eyes of officers who were committed to the development of corporate management. One chief executive described the commitment to corporate management in his authority as a 'veneer', and another said the balance of political groupings made his role difficult. Such chief executives will inevitably have difficult in giving corporate policy advice, and with their joint responsibility for administration, may revert to a role akin to that of the old Town Clerk, simply servicing committees and council meetings. In the absence of an elaborate corporate structure, however, small authorities may still manage some co-ordination by informal contacts and meetings.

The second group of authorities have increased their organisational and administrative emphasis on *co-ordination*. These authorities also do not have a Paterson-type corporate process, but several of the stages may be present. The emphasis has been on aspects of *administrative* co-ordination, to ensure that complementary capital projects are developing simultaneously, rather than a concern to integrate *policy planning* and *budgeting*.

These councils have not identified corporate priorities and have no general policy framework within which specific departmental issues can be resolved. Whilst these councils have recognised the interdependence of services, and occasional interdepartmental reports have been produced, the main emphasis of the management process is reactive, responding to issues as they arise, rather than systematic corporate policy analysis. Initiatives tend to come from service departments working with committees.

The political environment most conducive to this style is one of *party organisation, but often with no overall control*, a situation which was prevalent in Scottish local authorities prior to the Regional Elections of 1978 and the District Elections of 1980. However, in some authorities where there was a political majority, corporate management did not develop because of members' suspicion of the power potential of management teams and the appointment of officers with responsibility for 'policy'. Such politicians like to focus on services as the important areas of council operation. These authorities in the main are urban district councils, but also some urban/rural regions. The existence of party control, however, does not necessarily ensure a co-ordinated approach for even here concern with representative issues is often held more important than policy issues. Emphasis falls on project co-ordination.

There is general acceptance that authorities with large capital programmes (housing accounts for around 50% of *total* local authority capital expenditure in Scotland) need such a sophisticated approach to project management and co-ordination. Techniques such as network analysis are very useful for the management of large expenditure projects. The emphasis remains, nevertheless, on the technical aspects of co-ordination rather than on corporate planning.

The third group of authorities is the very small number of authorities laying emphasis (in addition to co-ordination) on *corporate policy formulation and management*. Such authorities are generally found in urban environments, where the complexity of problems is greater and where Labour is the majority party. These councils lay considerable emphasis on policy planning and have constructed an annual corporate programme around the major decision-documents of the council, the capital and revenue budget, Transport Policies and Programmes in the case of Regions, Housing Plans in the case of Districts. This development is similar to Earwicker's (1979) diagnosis of the development of corporate planning in English local authorities.

The common features of such systems were:

(1) *Planning and Analysis*
    The compilation of strategic planning data, social economic and demographic, which provided a picture of the trends in the local authority as a whole. Secondly, the preparation of position state- ments which provide a basis for discussion about service development.

(2)   *Identification of Corporate Priorities/Problems*
There are several examples of corporate criteria, such as the need to promote services for the 15-19 age group, or the need to protect services for the elderly, or the identification of geographic areas for priority treatment. Whereas PPBS suggested the evaluation and selection of programmes for achieving those objectives, under corporate management, these provide a general framework and additional dimension in policy (which) for the major departmental resource allocations. Thus the system is 'incremental', rather than 'comprehensive', but 'jointed' rather than 'disjointed'.

(3)   *Budget Options Analysis*
Such authorities will have evolved a more rigorous system of budgeting in which initiative has shifted from bids from the departments which are revised by the finance committee on financial rather than policy grounds, to a system of centrally imposed guidelines and cash limits, and the issue of corporate policy guidelines. The budgetary options will be subject to a corporate policy analysis at the centre.

(4)   *Policy Analysis and Review*
Again, the emphasis is on selectivity rather than comprehensiveness. Major issues/policies with corporate implications are reviewed by an interdisciplinary work group, which may include members. An example is one review of community development services which recommended organisational change to facilitate integration between the three very different service departments involved, education, social work and police. Such analysis would involve both quantitative and qualitative aspects.

Midwinter (1978b) identified Strathclyde, Lothian and Central Regions as such authorities. All three councils laid emphasis on the methodology of policy planning, in the development of an annual corporate programme, and in an interdepartmental approach to tackling key issues. There is a close working relationship between the central bureaucracy and political leadership, particularly in the appraisal of departmental expenditure proposals. These councils have established a systematic policy framework within which specific decisions about the allocation of resources could be taken. This is not to suggest that budget-making has become a technical rather than a political exercise, or that the changes from year to year are other than incremental, for much of the budget is already committed. What the framework provides is better information and corporate criteria to assist political decisions and political assessment of the specific proposals made by service directors. In a word, a planned, co-ordinated approach to change.

All authorities, however, have faced recurrent problems which affected the development of corporate management. Such constraints can be classified as structural, analytical and behavioural.

Structural constraints exist in the form of relations with central government, and the two-tier system of local government. Two of the policy instruments introduced after reorganisation, Regional Reports and Financial Plans, were seen as being particularly important for the development of corporate planning in the localities. During this period, however, planning for growth was the major consideration. The introduction of such systems coincided with the change from growth to retrenchment. Thus whereas heavy emphasis on capital investment decisions was seen as being a crucial aspect of promoting corporate management when Financial Plans were introduced, and there were early signs that the Scottish Office would be flexible over transference of expenditure *between* programmes where that suited local priorities, the large reductions in capital spending since reorganisation and the introduction of cash limits resulted in a re-emphasis of functionalism and departmentalism in the Scottish Office. Whilst this system can be viewed as an improvement because of the use of block allocations permitting greater local determination of priorities *within* programmes, it frustrates the full development of corporate management because it makes it difficult to assert local priorities between programmes (Midwinter 1980).

The two-tier structure of local government also frustrates the development of corporate management. There are close relationships between housing and strategic planning and infrastructure provision, but the priorities of district and region may differ because of the different scale of vision which each adopts. Similarly, housing is closely related to social work and educational provision, but again the responsibility is divided by the two-tier structure. Moreover, differences in political partisanship are another factor which complicates relations and makes coherence and consistency in planning and management more difficult to achieve. Some of the problems of two-tier working may be eased by the implementation of the Stodart (1981) Report, but major problems will remain (Keating and Midwinter 1983).

Analytical constraints also make the full implementation of the Paterson model difficult to achieve. Let us take the example of 'needs' and objectives. Needs may be interpreted in terms of the need for the existing services; or it may be interpreted in a wider sense, as referring to the overall needs of the community. Clearly the rational decision-maker ought to start with the latter and work back to the former; yet 'community needs' can be defined only in vague terms which are difficult to operationalise in terms of services on the ground. In turn, it is notoriously difficult to evaluate the impact of services by reference to community needs as opposed to traditional service-based criteria.

Objectives may be set in relation to needs or be the result of political choice. In either case they are difficult to specify except as vague aspirations (e.g. 'to improve the quality of life') useless as a guide to action, or as precise measures (e.g. 'increase the number of teachers') which are really not *objectives* at all but *means* to achieve them.

So it is difficult to set corporate objectives in the way recommended by Paterson and there is little evidence of authorities examining costed options as *alternative ways of meeting objectives*. Instead there have been more limited exercises in the identification of major issues and priorities as a framework for specific decisions about service activities. Generally, most use of options has occurred in the budgetary process when the aim has been to meet a desired level of expenditure rather than to achieve specific desired ends. Of course, there are many occasions when options for meeting a problem are presented, but this is *ad hoc* rather than as part of a systematic corporate process, and there is little analysis of the *impact* of such options; just more emphasis on the relative costs. However, where such issues are tackled in a multi-departmental working group, there will be some recognition and examination of the inter-relationships and inter-actions of different services, as Paterson suggested.

Further analytical problems arise over *implementation* and *evaluation* of strategies. Certainly corporate priorities can provide a framework within which departmental programmes can be judged; but the key stage in evaluation, the measurement of achievement in relation to stated objectives tends in practice to focus on *inputs* such as the number of houses built or teachers employed, rather than *impact*, the effect of such expenditure. Even where improvements can be measured, it is difficult to isolate the effect of new service provision from other effects which might be operating at the same time.

Behavioural constraints come in two forms, the persistence of departmentalism and the pervasiveness of bureaucratic politics, and the extent of political commitment. Functional professionals remain sceptical of corporate mechanisms, and of the ability of the central bureaucracy to give advice on matters affecting their service. Departmentalism has not been greatly touched by the focus on corporate ideology in the post-reorganisation period, and professionalism is a strong countervailing force. This was recognised by one chief executive who went to great pains to avoid using the word 'corporate' in policy discussions, preferring to talk about 'council' policy. Directors of service are not passive actors in corporate decision-making. Most professionals believe strongly in the service they provide, and wish to see it developed, which normally entails more resources. They can be seen as participants in a struggle for scarce resources, and this political conflict, Stewart (1980) argues, has increased with the removal of the increment of growth and the sustained pressure for retrenchment and cutback. Where reliance is placed on the management team in the corporate process, the dual loyalties placed on service directors faced with service reductions may be irreconcilable.

The second behavioural constraint is the degree of political commitment. Political support for the concept of corporate management is a necessary condition of change. Whereas Paterson claimed that the principles of corporate planning were applicable to all local authorities whatever their political environment, the evidence suggests that corporate developments are more likely to occur when there is a strong political majority. This does entail a new way of working for local authority officers, who must recognise the majority party as the administration. The Paterson Report distinguished between the two roles councillors play, managerial and representative, and advocated greater emphasis on the managerial role. Even in partisan authorities, however, the majority of councillors still place greater emphasis on their representative/ constituency role.

There is also the wariness displayed by councillors of the power of the management team and indeed of the Policy and Resources Committee. For some, it has reverted to the traditional finance committee, for others it resembles a general purposes committee, and elsewhere it becomes an additional hurdle for committee decisions to go through before ratification in full council. Committee chairmen face the same conflicting loyalties as service directors. Political groups, whilst rendering a degree of cohesiveness, are often divided ideologically, either on a left-right spectrum, or an urban-rural basis. Corporate management has been developed furthest where a strong, central political leadership can overcome these divisions.

Post-Paterson developments

Local authorities have now had time to consider the suitability of Paterson-type arrangements for the management of their affairs. Since 1980, there are three types of further developments which can be identified: increased use of analysis; changes in central organisation; and trends towards decentralisation.

The continuing environment of economic restraint is providing an impetus to more searching and extensive analysis of the current patterns of service provision, as authorities seek to release resources from within their base expenditure to meet government cutbacks or to permit service development in priority areas. Grampian Region and Stirling District, for instance, have been experimenting with Zero-Based Budgeting, whilst

Tayside Region have been reviewing their own budgetary process. Central Region have been concerned to develop a 'policy studies process', whilst Strathclyde Region and Borders Region have made some use of policy/performance review systems. Glasgow District Council have just completed their first corporate plan. It is, of course, too early to judge the impact of such reforms, but what these developments demonstrate is a continuing concern to improve the analytical element in the decision process.

In many authorities, there is increasing recognition of the need for support for the Chief Executive, of his need for a power base, and conversely, decreasing emphasis on the role of the management team in corporate planning. In one direction, this has led to greater use of policy planning specialists, as in Glasgow where a project co-ordination unit services the Chief Executive, and where use is made of the Policy and Intelligence Section in the Planning Department in the development of corporate planning.

A major reorganisation of management structures in Strathclyde Region resulted in the creation of a Chief Executive's department, after a policy review group study suggested that the 'Executive Office' arrangement of Paterson failed to effect integration, and achieve corporateness. There were problems of policy co-ordination, the separation of responsibility for policy formulation from policy implementation, and dominance of traditional organisation and attitudes. Paterson's Executive Office concept was 'too loose' an arrangement for a huge and complex local authority like Strathclyde. The new department incorporated the Departments of Administration and Policy Planning, the Industrial Development Unit and appropriate elements from the Planning Department. There are now five Depute Chief Executives, whose responsibilities cover central administration (e.g. general services and special projects); corporate planning (strategic issues) and services on a programme-area basis (personal social services and protective and basic services).

The Strathclyde diagnosis also underline the failure of the management team as a vehicle for corporate management, acknowledging that in practice its role is limited. So the management team is not to be a part of the formal decision-making process because of the constraints of time and volume of business. Instead, more use is to be made of multi-disciplinary groups on a programme-area basis. The term 'Chief Officer's Meeting' was considered a more appropriate designation given the limited role envisaged.

Similar changes occurred in Glasgow, where the management team has, in effect, been superseded by a central Policy Core Group, composed of the Town Clerk and Chief Executive, Town Clerk Depute, and the Directors of Finance, Planning and Housing, and four programme-area teams in Housing, Environment, Leisure and Recreation, and Economic Development. Thus, the time-wasting element of comprehensive management teams is eliminated, and service directors only participate on a programme area basis.

In smaller authorities also, there is a recognition of the need for a central power base. Two novel developments are worth commenting upon. In some authorities the chief executive takes over a traditional department, but in this case *finance*, not administration. This reflects the dominance of financial problems in the post-reorganisation period, but also reflects the Paterson concern to link policy with finance. Whether the necessary support to provide policy advice is available in this situation requires closer study, but certainly some appreciation of organisational power relationships is implicit in such a post. Finally, there is the reorganisation in Kilmarnock, which has an executive office structure in which the two supporting officers, the district administrator and the director of finance, each have *operational* service responsibility. There are no departments, just services and managers. It is the particular responsibility of the district administrator to assist in forward planning and its corporate preparation and application in securing a corporate approach.

Two devices have been introduced to counteract the centralising tendencies in corporate management. One is decentralisation, as seen in the Divisional Deprivation Groups or the Area Initiatives in Strathclyde. The most ambitious form of this is Glasgow's system of area management, in which the city is divided into seven areas, with area teams of officers chaired by the District Housing Manager and area committees of elected members and community representatives. The other device is the increased use of procedures for political involvement in policy making such as Strathclyde's Policy Review Groups and Member-Officer Groups. Such new developments demonstrate the growing feeling that 'policy-maker' is a different animal from the 'decision-taker', and that reaction to reports from officers is not the way to ensure political input to the policy process.

Concluding observations

The "Scottish" approach to corporate management was a more limited yet more political reform than its English counterpart. In practice, only a few authorities have sought to introduce Paterson-style corporate management. Where reliance was placed on the management team as the basis of corporate planning, inevitably little corporate development took place. The dual loyalties placed on service directors in the team when faced with the need to defend their service in times of cutback are irreconcilable. Corporate machinery, therefore, provides an alternative power-base, namely the chief executive and his . support staff, and the political leadership, to seek integration in the interests of the organisation. The LAMSAC Report went as far as to advocate that the key to success in the corporate approach lay in the adoption of corporate management and planning as a distinct function within the local authority (LAMSAC 1981). Moreover, it is absolutely crucial that there exists a strong political group which *wants* to make strategic decisions and recognises that corporate planning is a tool which can assist the achievement of their political priorities.

The introduction of corporate planning in English local government has experienced many difficulties and in recent years witnessed a political and managerial retreat from corporate management. There has been no equivalent retreat in Scotland, and in part this reflects the opportunity Scottish authorities had to learn from the English experience, and to rescue corporate planning from PPBS. Expectations were not pitched so high and there was a greater awareness from the outset of the political context within which the corporate approach would have to operate. Accordingly, development has been gradual. The more euphoric claims for corporate planning may not have been realised, but in those authorities pursuing corporate planning, there has been an impact on local decision-making.

CHAPTER SEVEN

LOCAL GOVERNMENT FINANCE

Financing local services

Local government finance is a notoriously complex subject perhaps understood fully only by a few people within the 'local expenditure community', the network of people involved in the key decisions. Yet local authorities do not lack for advice on spending and are faced at budget time with a clamour of demands from interests groups, ratepayers and central government, all trying to push them in different directions. Expenditure decisions, indeed, are at the heart of the local political process; both they and the rates decisions consequent upon them have a rapid and direct impact upon the communities affected. Yet, as we shall see, a council's own decisions are merely one element in determining expenditure and rate levels; other elements are to be found elsewhere in the network.

Local government expenditure falls into two types, capital and revenue, with a small grey area in between. In the main, capital expenditure is financed by borrowing, and the interest due on the loans incurred is paid for from the revenue account over a number of years. Revenue expenditure is financed by the income which a local authority derives annually from a number of sources. The distinguishing feature of *capital* expenditure is that it creates an asset which provides a benefit to the community over a number of years, such as a housing development, a leisure centre, a school, or a residential home for the elderly. Usually such projects generate a flow of benefits over a number of years, so financing them by borrowing ensures that those who benefit from them in the future also make some contribution to their purchase. *Revenue* expenditure by contrast pays for the current running costs of providing the facilities, such as the salaries of teachers, policemen, sewerage workers or administrators, the purchase of certain types of equipment (such as school supplies), certain types of maintenance, energy costs, as well as the loan charges stemming from the capital account. The grey area covers some types of repairs and maintenance, or equipment purchases, which can be classified as either capital or revenue, often offering some margin of choice to local authorities facing expenditure cuts. Revenue expenditure must be met from current income, and therefore local authorities must operate the *balanced budget* rule. They may not deliberately budget for a surplus or for a deficit, though they may maintain a working balance; a particular year's revenue expenditure must be paid for from that year's income, although authorities may borrow to tide them over while waiting for the rates to come in.

The main source of capital finance is borrowing, and every local authority operates a Consolidated Loans Fund. This consolidates *all* an authority's borrowing requirements into one account, so that loans raised by the Loans Fund are *not* earmarked for specific projects; and advances are made as required to the various spending departments' accounts. Local authorities borrow from three main sources: the Public Works Loan Board (a government agency which raises funds for lending to public authorities); the money market; and from internal funds such as superannuation funds. The operations of the local authority in the money market in the issue of stock and bonds, or by mortgage, bond or temporary loan, are regulated by the Bank of England, subject to Treasury regulations.

Over 90% of capital expenditure is financed by borrowing. Other sources are central government or European grants for specific projects, capital projects funded from revenue (which must commence and be completed in the same financial year), the revenue accrued from sales of existing capital assets, and accumulated capital funds. All capital expenditure is subject to control by the Secretary of State under Section 94 of the Local Government (Scotland) Act, 1973. Local authorities submit to the Scottish Office an annual Financial Plan which in effect constitutes a 'bid' for permissions to spend. Consent is given in the form of amounts of capital expenditure allowed in each programme area — roads and transport, water and sewerage, social work, education, police and fire, and general services for Regions; housing, and general services for Districts. This system replaced the former system of requiring consent for each individual capital project, as part of the move to allow local authorities greater freedom over local priorities while retaining overall control by the centre, but it has not eliminated the intricate bargaining which still takes place between central government and the localities (see Chapter Ten).

Revenue expenditure is financed from three main sources, fees and charges for services, local rates, and government grants, the last providing almost 50% of total income. Whilst fees and charges provide overall a fairly small proportion of income (less than 20%), the income from council house rents is very important for district councils. As a result, they obtain only 40% of their income from government grant, in contrast to about 60% in the case of regional councils.

Rates are a property tax which is the subject of continuing criticism by interest groups such as the National Association of the Self-Employed and the Scottish Ratepayers Federation. The arguments for and against rates have been well rehearsed elsewhere (Layfield 1976) and need not concern us here. The 1982 Green Paper review has resulted in only minor tinkering with the present system rather than its abolition. The fear, however, in the light of the failure to find a suitable system of taxation for a Scottish Assembly, is that the abolition of rates would seriously limit the freedom of local authorities if they were funded mainly by government grant. Rates, nevertheless, remain a politically contentious issue, as the response to the increases of the 1975/76 period and the 1979/80/81 increases demonstrate.

Government grants are the largest single source of income for local government, so central government will inevitably be interested in the policy and expenditure decisions of the local authorities. Specific grants exist notably for police but account for less than 9% of total grants (Heald 1980). The main grant is Rate Support Grant (RSG), a general grant introduced in 1967. (Housing expenditure is excluded from this and dealt with separately.) Annual consultation with the Convention of Scottish Local Authorities (COSLA) culminates in the RSG settlement in November. The practice is to determine the total of 'relevant' expenditure, and the aggregate grant (now 61.4%) which the Secretary of State will pay in respect of such expenditure. Specific grants are then deducted, and the balance is the Rate Support Grant. Local authorities have a collective interest in determining this figure. What divides them, however, is how the grant will be distributed between them.

The budgetary context

The budget and rate decisions of a local authority are the culmination of a long process of negotiation and consultation covering several months. In this section we seek to set out the uses of the budget, and the constraints on local budgetary choice.

The revenue budget is a key tool of financial management, and the controls exercised through the budget provide the basis for regulating local authority expenditure and income, and for fixing the size of the rate levy (Hepworth 1980). It does not have to be submitted to central government, but a local authority does have the statutory duty to determine such a rate as will provide sufficient moneys to meet that proportion of total expenditure which is to be funded by rates (Section 108 of the Local Government (Scotland) Act, 1973).

Finance has a crucial impact upon the management and policies of the council. The uses of the budget are then fourfold, an accountancy document, a policy document, a management document, and a document for assisting public accountability. As an accountancy document, it allows the council to fix its income and expenditure levels, balancing the budget, and thus allowing the necessary rate to be levied to meet the gap between planned expenditure and income from grants, charges, or balances. As a policy document, it is the 'handmaid' of policy making (Marshall 1974), and should "flow from the longer-term corporate plans of the local authority" (Hepworth 1980). The annual budget provides the resources through which policies can be implemented, and policy priorities reflected, for the conflict between what is desirable in policy terms, and possible in resource terms, is resolved in budget-making. The aspirations of both members and service departments are inevitably greater than available resources, and thus budgeting is a political process. Policies approved on an ongoing basis *in principle* await in most cases the provision of adequate resources to become operational.

As a management document, it both authorises a plan of action, and provides a basis for control. Approval of expenditure provides a managerial framework for the activities of a department, and also assists managerial accountability, as service committees can monitor departmental expenditure and review performance.

Finally, it promotes public accountability. Budget and rate-fixing face more public attention than any other activity of the council. The essence of democratic government is that taxation necessary to fund expenditure should be voted and authorised by elected members of the public. According to Hepworth it is the 'primary medium' of electoral accountability, although this has become less clear cut recently with the post-rating interventions of central government (see Greenwood 1981; Midwinter 1981).

The first major constraint facing budgeters in local government is the requirement to operate the *balanced budget rule*; local authorities may not *as a matter of policy* budget for a surplus or a deficit, though they may maintain a working balance. This year's income must be met from current income, although local authorities may borrow to fund revenue expenditure pending receipt of rates.

The budgetary framework comprises both external and internal pressures. External pressures include the level and distribution of government grant, inflation, government policies and new legislation, new developments in the private sector, and interest groups. Decisions about the level and distribution of grant by government come late in the financial year, and for the most part, local authorities make reasoned assumptions to assist budget-making. Inflation has to be forecast, and the local authority has to provide for wage awards, price inflation, and perhaps also higher interest rates. Then there is the impact of government policies. Local authorities complain regularly that government continues to impose new duties upon them without providing adequate financial support, whilst exhorting them to reduce spending simultaneously. Local government must also respond to new building developments and provide the necessary infrastructure (roads, water, sewerage). Most importantly, local government faces the ever-rising demands of interest groups, all seeking a small piece of the budget pie for their particular activity. Such groups are far more numerous than groups seeking to restrain expenditure.

The internal pressures on budget size are considerable, particularly existing expenditure. Schools, residential homes, roads, etc. already exist, with union agreements about their continuance. Every year, moreover, new capital projects are completed. Some merely refurbish or replace existing provision, and the main resource implications are in loan charges. Other projects, however, reflect service development, and will add to the running costs of service departments. The view often propounded and recently emphasised by ministers that capital spending should be reflated but current spending cut, ignores the fact that capital spending inevitably pushes current spending upwards. Some capital projects are financed from revenue, but generally these are fairly minor.

Local authorities, facing an uncertain environment, may decide to budget for a contingency, which may allow any unforeseen developments to be met during the financial year. Finally, there is the use of balances/deficits in the previous budget. If the account is in surplus, the balances can be used to fund expenditure in the current year, thus keeping rates down. More concern in recent years, however, has been the accumulation of deficits, as government cash limits on rate support grant have not kept pace with inflation, and local government has been unable or unwilling to make the required reductions in the volume of service in the course of the financial year. Such deficits have to be funded almost completely from the rate in subsequent years.

Budgetary procedures

Descriptions of the stages in budgeting in local government by participants in the process have usually distingushed between 'traditional budgeting' and 'rate rationing'. For analytical purposes, these can be more usefully characterised as 'bottom-up' or 'top-down' approaches. Traditional budgeting, or 'bottom-up', was a common approach in the period of expenditure growth. Departmental officers began by drawing up a budget estimate which in effect represented a 'bid' for resources, as it included an element of growth. Such estimates comprised an estimate of costs of ongoing activities and proposals for new developments. At this stage, agreement was reached with the finance department over appropriate costs of such services.

The estimates were then submitted to the relevant service committee, where they might or might not have been the subject of amendment, and then forwarded to the finance committee. At this stage, the finance department aggregated the proposals of spending departments, assessed the likely available income from charges and government grant, and estimated the likely rate levels necessary to fund the proposed expenditure programmes. Inevitably, 'cuts' in the proposals were necessary, for in the pre-reorganisation period 'bids' inevitably were too high, but 'cuts' were usually cuts in growth. Estimates would then be remitted back to service committees for pruning, with recommendations for specific cuts, or percentage cuts leaving the detail to the service committee. Once the revised estimates had been finalised, the council would then approve the expenditure proposals and strike the requisite rate levy.

The 'top down' approach of rate rationing reversed the process, by fixing a pre-determined rate level, and then proceeding to allocate resources to departments accordingly. Whilst such procedures were common in the 1920s and '30s, there has been some signs of their return in the new era of retrenchment (Greenwood *et al*, 1976). Alternative rate and expenditure levels were projected by the finance department, and a predetermined rate fixed. The total resources were then allocated between departments, usually after some informal consultation with committee chairmen and chief officers on the 'acceptability' of such proposals. This process simplifies the management of the budget process, for departments have little incentive to 'pad the estimates', and there is less need for scrutiny of the detail of departmental estimates.

Both approaches, however, have certain common features which led in England to attempts to reform budgetary procedures and introduce systems such as PPBS (Planning Programming Budgeting Systems) or ZBB (Zero-Based Budgeting), or techniques such as cost-benefit analysis. The actual impact of such reforms to date remains marginal.

The criticisms of traditional local authority budgeting can be summarised as follows:

(1)   There was a focus on resource inputs rather than policy outputs in budgeting. There are serious conceptual problems in measuring the output of local services, notwithstanding the efforts of recent years to develop such measures.

(2)   The organisation of the budget was 'functional', leading to policy considerations being minimal. Policy objectives were often not defined, or where they were in existence, they were imprecise.

(3)   Many of the major problems of government cut across departmental boundaries, but the local budgetary process was not organised to reflect such corporate problems.

(4)   There was little critical expenditure review carried out. The bulk of existing expenditure remained unscrutinised, even though the initial conditions which made it necessary might have changed.

Studies of budgetary processes remain few, but most would agree in seeing budgeting as *incrementalist*, inevitably so given the limits to rationality. Rational decision-making requires perfect knowledge, a clear specification of values and a review of *all* possible alternatives and their impact on society. Such omniscience is impossible in the real world, where knowledge is incomplete, values are unclear and often conflicting, and only a few alternatives are considered, those consistent with existing interests. Economic limits are the time and cost of carrying out extensive research and analysis to assist decision-making. Budgeting takes place over a very short period of the financial year, rendering comprehensiveness impossible. Extensive analysis is only justifiable where large sums of money are involved.

Local government traditions stress specialisation, professionalism and departmentalism, producing several partial views of the 'problem' rather than the single view necessary for 'rational' choice. Finally, and perhaps the most relevant in the local government context of statutory responsibility and extensive capital investment, there are the physical and human limits of the existing situation. Once agreements have been reached (e.g. over staffing standards), they are *not* up for negotiation every year. Once housing, roads, schools, etc. are built, expenditure on maintenance and running costs is inevitable. A typical 'incremental' budgetary process would contain the following features.

(1)   *The starting point is the base budget*
       Budgets are almost never reviewed as a whole, in the sense of considering at one time the value of all existing programmes compared to all possible alternatives. Instead, this year's budget is based on last year's budget (the base) with special attention given to a narrow range of increases/decreases. The greatest part of any budget is a product of previous decisions.

(2)   *Limited parameters of review*
       Given the assumption that the base is sacrosanct, the attention in budget decision-making focuses upon that part of the budget over which an element of choice exists — a few new programmes and possible cuts in old ones.

(3)   *The notion of fair shares*
       Departments assume that they will get close to this year's existing

allocation, plus a *pro rata* share of any increases or decreases. Thus the new share-out of resources will closely resemble the old one.

(4) *Analysis is limited*
The amount of analysis of the purposes of expenditure, standards of performance, the impact of policy change, is limited. There is little attempt to relate choices to policy objectives, and the focus is on inputs to a service.

(5) *Roles and strategies are fixed and predictable*
The rules of budgetary participants are clear cut. It is the task of the service director to advocate/defend his departmental allocation, whilst the finance department attempts to control/cut spending. The budget negotiations are bilateral between the service and finance departments, with very little attempt to evaluate choices across departments.

Given the complexity of the problems they face, local authorities tend to adopt *standard operating procedures*, to simplify the choices and reduce uncertainty. Since reorganisation, the degree of uncertainty has increased, with the announcements about the level of government grants coming too late in the process seriously to affect the decisions, with uncertainty about inflation and cash limits, and with, towards the end of our study, the need to judge the concept of 'excessive and unreasonable' expenditure under the new Local Government (Miscellaneous Provisions) (Scotland) Act (see Chapter Ten). The turbulence of the environment has in effect meant that for most of the expenditure process, officers and members are 'budgeting in the dark'. Yet, despite these problems, local authorities have striven to develop more refined and more rational budget procedures.

Most councils now utilise a clear identification of the budget base as the first stage of the budgetary process. Indeed emphasis on improving the existing data about the base was a common feature. It becomes a key element for reducing uncertainty by setting out the continuing cost of programmes to the authority, provides a convenient starting place for the budget review and shapes the process of renegotiation and bargaining which then takes place between service departments and the central bureaucracy.

At this stage, the finance department makes its best assessment of likely changes in income, setting the parameters for the budget. In recent years the emphasis has been on reducing expenditure. Authorities differ in their approaches to this, some using cash figures as financial targets for departments, some seeking options for alternative levels of financial saving (e.g. departments are asked to state how they would save 3, 5 or 7% of the base budget) whilst others given an across-the-board target for a percentage reduction (the "equal misery" approach).

Budgetary politics — players, roles, relationships

Focussing on the procedures of the budgetary process alone, however, provides only a partial understanding of budgeting. Budgeting is a dynamic process, in which the behaviour of participants is important. The budgetary process is a game, in which different players have different roles to play; so to understand it, we have to identify the key players, examine their roles, and analyse the patterns of interaction which take place.

First, there are bureaucratic players, engaged in what Heclo and Wildavsky called "the politics of advice" in relation to central government (Heclo and Wildavsky 1974). Much of the interdepartmental negotiation and bargaining in the system is bilateral, between the *central bureaucracy* (chief executive/director of finance) and *service departments*. The service departments submit estimates and options for growth/saving, and these are appraised by the centre.

In the finance department, there is a heavy emphasis on the purely financial aspects of budget proposals. There is a concern to ensure that the estimates have been costed accurately, and although this involves working closely with service departments, there are limits to the degree of supervision possible. Finance directors also have to give advice to the council on what the total picture (income and expenditure) looks like. Budgeting, after all, is a financial forecast, and the finance department advises on the impact of government grant decisions, inflation, etc. This has become an area of great uncertainty in recent years, with government announcements on grant coming too late in the financial year for local government to take proper account of the implications of last-minute amendments to spending plans. Advice about inflation has become a crucial factor in recent years, as government assumptions in the grant settlement have usually been lower than actual inflation. Moreover, with the introduction of *cash planning* (see Chapter Ten) directors face a real dilemma. Do they advise the council on the level of inflation they think is accurate, and run the risk of selective action under the Local Government (Miscellaneous Provisions) (Scotland) Act, 1981, as this will inevitably result in a budget in excess of government guidelines, or do they advise the council to follow government advice, and almost certainly accumulate a budget deficit?

This brings us to the final source of uncertainty over which advice must be given, the government's revenue expenditure guidelines (see Chapter

Ten). Each authority now receives a guideline which indicates central government's view of the level of expenditure for the council which would be consistent with the rate support grant settlement. Although these are only advisory, performance against guidelines is one of the factors used in determining 'excessive and unreasonable' expenditure under the Local Government (Miscellaneous Provisions) (Scotland) Act, 1981. The uncertainty stems from the absence of any clearly defined framework, and thus judgments have to be exercised by the council on the basis of the best guesstimate of their director of finance.

In the main, while directors of finance continue to advise on financial issues, policy issues are the preserve of the chief executive and his policy planning support staff (where it exists!). In most cases, however, there are close working relationships between the chief executive and the director of finance. These policy planning staff come closest to the civil service model of the senior administrator, as their role is to give corporate policy advice in the selection of acceptable options for savings. In some cases, corporate planning has resulted in the generation of a strategic policy framework within which specific service decisions can be resolved. In most councils, however, such a framework does not exist, and chief executives often have to judge themselves which options are likely to be politically acceptable. In that case the chief executive and his management team if it is working effectively must either accept the lack of a corporate policy framework or else supply one themselves. The latter can occur where there is a forceful chief executive (Midwinter 1982b). The central bureaucracy therefore, is exercising more strategic control over the financial and policy context within which budgets are made; and retrenchment increases conflict as, in times of cutback, departments seek to protect and maintain existing activities.

In the service department itself, a handful of key people are involved in the collection and presentation of the department's estimates — the director, his deputes, and occasionally, chief administrative officers who handle both manpower and budget work. Almost all officers are interested in seeing the service develop, and indeed *intra* departmental negotiation and bargaining occurs before the final submission to committee is made. In periods of restraint, professionals will usually interpret their role as 'protecting the service'. The conflict and bargaining involved in this has been described as 'bureaucratic politics', a whole area of political activity apart from the usual politics of elections and councillors. So departmental officers are not neutral, disinterested participants in budget decision-making, but have their own aims and sources of power which they use in furtherance of departmental interests.

Service directors have four main sources of power, control of resources, control of information, a monopoly of expertise and political support. By resources we mean both money and manpower. Very few departments do *not* have access to some external sources of funds, such as fees or charges for services. In the case of water, for instance, roughly two-thirds of finance is raised through charges. As most of the emphasis in the budget process is on reducing *rateborne* expenditure, this provides a considerable advantage. Similarly, most local authority services are labour intensive, and very few councils to date have been willing to contemplate redundancies. Departments vary in the extent of labour costs, which limit the scope for reductions. Departments provide the information on which budget decisions are made; and data about staffing levels, capital buildings, client groups, etc. are an important source of power. It is the department which has the expertise to present professional advice about priorities in the budget process, and it often itself sets out the criteria by which the consequences of such options will be evaluated. Departments view committee chairmen as local equivalents to spending ministers in central government, as political spokesmen for the department. Thus keeping the chairman fully briefed about developments is seen as being crucial, particularly when final decisions are taken in party groups without officers present. Again, like central government, a strong chairman is one who fights the departmental corner.

Officers differ in their ability to exert these sources of power. For some services, such as education, the mobilisation of support by creating a favourable political climate is not difficult. In the more technical services like roads and water, professional proposals may rarely be challenged, except by councillors pushing constituency rather than policy interests. Whilst the police are the subject of increasing political interest, their operational autonomy and constitutional relationship with the Secretary of State is an important source of administrative discretion.

All of these sources are utilised to present the best possible case for the department, which most service directors regard as their professional duty, and more important than corporate loyalty. This may often involve use of dramatic but vague statements about the horrendous implications of certain options for services, or the possibility of failing to fulfil statutory duties. All too seldom is the *actual* impact of options clear.

Elected members are heavily involved in budgeting, although this usually involves reacting to the advice and options offered by the officers. These elected players fall into four groups, political leaders, committee chairmen, political groups and individual councillors.

Political leadership is of two kinds, the 'Inner Cabinet' of a party group, or the more charismatic style of individual councillors in independent councils. In partisan councils, there is generally a powerful group of councillors at the centre, the group leader and the chairmen of policy and resources and finance, whose role is to exercise strategic control over the budget ensuring that the overall budget package is politically acceptable, reflects the overall strategy, and can produce a broad consensus in the group. This is not easy, because all councillors are torn between their desire to push their favoured expenditure project and their concern about the necessary rates increase. In some councils, the leaders reconcile the two by getting an expenditure strategy agreed by the group *before* examining detailed options.

The key role of committee chairmen is widely recognised as being spokesmen for "their" service, by both chairmen themselves and others. As such, they tend to be pro-spending, often irrespective of political partisanship. Even Conservative chairmen adopt the role and argue aggressively that expenditure targets cannot be met, and try to build support for their cause. Each chairman argues that others can meet cuts, but not him, though, if he is wise, he will be unspecific.

The third set of political actors are political groups, which vary in their degree of centralised leadership. Many officers regard centralised leadership as a positive virtue as it provides consistency and direction. Many backbench councillors see the group system as an effective force against the traditional alliance of chairmen and directors. In smaller councils some groups tend to be more fluid, with a democratic way of ensuring each member has a say. Group meetings may provide indications of general strategy; and provide a political net through which the recommendations of group leaders and the options offered by professionals must pass. In practice, some groups do provide consistency (Dearlove 1980) whilst others totally fail to provide any comprehensive set of priorities (Danziger 1978).

All elected members have a role to play as constituency representatives. In some councils, such advocacy may well be regarded as parochial, in relation to a wider public interest. In others, it will be regarded as a legitimate form of protest which may succeed through support mobilisation on an individual basis. This is particularly true in rural councils where horse-trading "something in my area for something in yours" is a common practice, and where focus on specific items is regarded as preferable to strategic policy issues. This can cause tension in some partisan councils, where individuals may make a stand in the group meeting, then conform to the group rather than publicly challenge the decision. In others, permission to speak against (and even vote against) a group decision may be permitted so the representative can be seen to be defending his area.

The resolution of political choice
What has emerged from the analysis so far is a picture of a complex game

with bargaining and politicking by both officers and members. This is consistent with previous studies of budgeting and decision-making in local government. The operation of the local political system and the outcomes reflect the interplay of bureaucratic and political players in response to pressures from each other, from central government and community interest and political groups. Officer influence is greatest in setting the context and shaping the options considered by the politicians, who in the main react to these initiatives, modifying them to incorporate political priorities or react to the political exigencies of the situation. This may mean a negative emphasis on the rejection of specific options rather than positive policy guidance. So a typical budgetary cycle would look like this:

(1) Formulation of a budget strategy in terms of expenditure and services, with targets for specific departments.
(2) Submission of options for meeting those targets by departments.
(3) Scrutiny of such options by the central bureaucracy of the authority.
(4) Political rejection/acceptance of the options.
(5) Finalisation of expenditure programmes and rate setting by the council.

Not all councils will conform to this broad outline. In less centralised, corporately based authorities, for instance, corporate discussion of the options may be minimal and unsystematic. Similarly, once the administrative process has resulted in a set of options which reflect both service and corporate priorities, these may conflict with political priorities, particularly if the options have a visible public impact. For example, in one authority the roads departments consistently placed the non-cutting of grass verges as a least-damaging option for cuts in roads maintenance, whilst in a second, a social work department did likewise over a holiday home for the elderly. Each was just as consistently rejected by the politicians. Even when corporate analysis of the options has taken place, the political process may well accept or reject options which administrators would regard as being inconsistent with a corporate strategy.

Budget outcomes in a period of retrenchment
Incrementalist theory was developed in a period of expenditure growth. Since 1979 local government has faced the most sustained period of fiscal pressure (Greenwood 1980b) in recent history. So how have local authorities coped? First, we must assert that government pressure to cut public expenditure has laid much greater emphasis on reducing *net* expenditure (that funded through taxation) than gross expenditure. This

gives a degree of discretion to managers if they can find alternative means of financing their programmes. The most common method is through increased charges for services, such as school meals, hall rents, etc. The attraction for the officer is, that whilst this may be regarded as a reduction in service by politicians and the public, it means that the level of activity is maintained. A similar method is to reclassify expenditure from the revenue budget to the capital budget. This is possible because there is a grey area between capital and revenue expenditure, and again, the organisational activity continues while the method of payment changes. Thirdly, cuts can be made by deferring the introduction of newly completed capital projects. This may be regarded as a financial saving, but it is obviously wasteful in terms of the real economic use of resources. Fourth, departments can make savings on the non-staff elements of their budget, such as supplies, equipment, etc. There is greater scope for this in some departments than others, reflecting the different nature of local services.

All of these are 'short-term' solutions. The evidence suggests that the scope for manoeuvre in these areas had become extremely limited by 1982. Each option can be regarded as progressively less acceptable to local officials. Politicians will rather increase prices than lose staff, although some increases may be less agreeable to Labour politicians (e.g. school meals) than Conservatives, and vice versa (e.g. charges for industrial users). There has been a gradual trend away from these 'softer' options towards savings on staffing. Non-filling of vacancies is the most common method, but it is impossible to pursue in any rational manner in the long term. Overtime cuts, reductions in hours of part-time staff, have all been employed in recent years.

In the long run, however, as the pressure of retrenchment increases, the emphasis on staff savings will increase. To date (1982) redundancies have been avoided, and many councils of all political persuasions have a no-redundancy policy. With reducing scope for soft options, local government is constrained by the labour intensive nature of local services. The big services are *personal* social services where local authority staff *are* the service; productivity cannot be improved by increased capital investment.

So local government faces hard choices for hard times if the present retrenchment continues. Every cause has its interest group. For every ratepayers group seeking to restrain expenditure, there are a hundred promoting it, varying from the construction industry pushing capital investment, to the rural village which does not want to lose its school or its bobby. This suggests that budgeting requires equal emphasis to be given to consideration of policy and priorities as is given to expenditure and rate levels. Very few councils operate any systematic form of expenditure review, yet the need to look more deeply at the budget *base* will increase, if resources are to be released to allow policy priorities to be protected at a time of overall cutback. This will require more radical and more comprehensive forms of budgetary review. How to achieve this against the entrenched interests within the local government system is the greatest challenge faced by the elected councillors whose task it is, at the end of the day, to take the decisions.

Part Four:

POLICY MAKING

CHAPTER EIGHT

HOUSING POLICY MAKING

Scottish housing problems

Housing is a major policy responsibility of the Secretary of State for Scotland. It is the largest programme of capital expenditure of Scottish local authorities (although declining), and there is considerable expenditure by government agencies such as the Scottish Special Housing Association and the Housing Corporation. Housing is also a highly politicised area of public policy. Government intervention has increased since the first world war, and while housing standards have risen dramatically, areas of poor housing in Scotland remain a major problem.

Moreover, housing is inextricably related to other areas of policy. The major impetus to government intervention came from fears of disease caused by inadequate housing rather than from any concern with good housing as desirable in its own right. Housing has increasingly been recognised as having welfare and income implications, for example, in the Labour rent freeze of 1974, part of a counter-inflation policy.

It has also major implications for economic development and the strategic planning which characterised much of government policy between 1960 and 1975 (see Chapter Nine). As the economic problems of the late 'seventies saw a change in attitude towards public spending, this has also had major implications for housing, particularly with the change in priorities following the Conservatives election victory of 1979.

Finally, the importance of housing as a facet of 'multiple deprivation' was increasingly recognised, and the links between bad housing, poor job opportunity, low income and poor social environment became a major theme in government policy in the 'seventies.

Yet as Cullingworth (1979) has pointed out, much of housing policy is the responsibility of local government, which has caused difficulties for central government, because of the inevitable changes in local political control which result from the mid-term unpopularity of government. So a focus on housing policy can help us to understand how policies are made and why their implementation and 'success' will inevitably be partial.

Are there distinctive Scottish housing problems? The answer is an emphatic yes, although some merely differ in *degree* and *intensity* from the rest of the UK (e.g. overcrowding, bad housing) whilst some are unique to Scotland (e.g. limited tenure choice). In part, this is because of Scotland's different process of industrialisation but also because of differences of culture, income, and political environment. The nineteenth century saw a period of rapid social and economic change, leaving an urbanised and industrialised Scotland, with its population concentrated in the central belt. In the age of laissez-faire, housing provision did not keep match with population development, resulting in inadequate and overcrowded housing, with few basic amenities. Between 1780 and 1830, Glasgow's population *quintupled*, from 40,000 to 200,000. This process of uncontrolled, capitalist development left a legacy of housing problems for government in the twentieth century. The latter half of the nineteenth century saw the first acquisition of powers in the housing field by local authorities (demolition), in Edinburgh and Glasgow, although the emphasis was very much on public health. In the main, provision was by private rentiers, and it was not until 1890 that local authorities got powers to provide houses for working-class people, albeit without public subsidy. Already, however, significant differences were emerging between Scotland and the rest of the UK. The Royal Commission on housing of 1912 advocated state responsibility for working-class housing (Niven 1979). But it was not until 1924 that central government made central funds available, allowed contributions from the rates, and controlled rents. This was short lived, however, and housing subsidies ended with the economic depression. By 1935, overcrowding in Scotland was six times greater than in England.

The post-war period saw a rapid expansion of public housing, totalling 970,000 new houses in thirty years. Thus 50% of Scotland's housing and 75% of the public sector stock was built after 1945. This period also saw improvements in the provision of amenities, until by 1971, 86% of Scottish households had all amenities compared to 82% in England and Wales. The census also revealed, however, that overcrowding remained significantly higher than in England and Wales (almost twice as much, although much reduced overall), and also there was a larger proportion of the worst housing. There was no comparable growth in owner-occupation as in England and other European countries, and in 1975, only 33% of households were in owner-occupation, compared to 53% in England and Wales. One explanation offered for this is a cultural one, reinforced by the availability of cheap, rented local authority housing. Council house rents have historically been lower. However, low income is also a contributory factor, as the Housing Green Paper notes, some peope were unable to buy even if they wanted to. Finally, there has been the domination by the Labour Party of the industrial belt where 80% of the Scottish population lives. It was only in the late 'seventies for instance, that serious attempts were made to generate private house building in Glasgow in response to the unmet demands for private housing which contributed to the city's population loss (Hamilton 1978). (This of course had been actively encouraged by regional policy and the availability of housing in new towns or through overspill housing.)

In Scotland, therefore, there are housing problems which differ from the rest of the UK only in their intensity (overcrowding, bad housing) and one problem, the lack of tenure choice, which results from the dominance of the public sector in housing provision. Tackling those problems results in a complex interplay of government departments (Scottish and UK), departmental agencies, local government, pressure groups and the private sector.

The housing policy network

Central government responsibility for housing policy lies with the *Secretary of State for Scotland*, although the detailed work is carried out by the Scottish Development Department and the Minister for Home Affairs and the Environment. Government supervision is not so comprehensive as in other policy areas, such as education, although more detailed controls of local authorities have been introduced since 1979.

Local authorities, namely the fifty-three District and three Islands Councils, carry the main responsibilities for local housing provision. Their functions include the provision, maintenance and management of council housing, improvement, slum clearance, purchase of older housing for improvement, improvement grants to owner-occupiers, mortgage provision for older properties. As noted earlier, the division of responsibility for housing at district level from social work, infrastructure provision, and strategic planning at regional level, has caused administrative and policy problems.

The *Scottish Special Housing Association* is a government-sponsored body established originally in 1937 to build houses for 'distressed' areas, but now with a general power to build and manage houses both on its own account, and on an agency basis, for local authorities. In 1945, its role was extended to allow it to operate in areas of great housing need, and in 1957, to facilitate overspill housing for Glasgow. It is always regarded as being supplementary to local authorities to lessen the financial burden they face, but it is often difficult to see why local government in theory could not have carried out these programmes given sufficient central financial support. It has indeed been seen as a successful instrument of central government. By using a 'quango', government could ensure that *their* priorities were met in areas where local government was unable or unwilling to comply with central directives. Cullingworth (1979) agrees, seeing the SSHA as an amenable and flexible instrument of central control.

Another form of government agency is the *new town development corporation*, of which there are five in Scotland. They may provide housing for either rent or sale, and applicants for housing from outwith the area generally must have obtained local employment. While seen as effective means of implementing government policy, they nevertheless have a degree of managerial independence. In the post '75 era of expenditure cuts, however, local authorities have felt frustrated in planning for their priorities because of their tendency to place heavy demands on the limited capital investment for infrastructure services. Like SSHA, they also raise the issue of democratic control. Ostensibly, the roles are different, new towns fostering economic development, district councils meeting local housing needs, but the problem is further complicated by the strategic planning role of regional councils. Central government simply finds it easier to influence the activities of new towns than local authorities.

Finally, there is the *Housing Corporation*, an agency created in 1964, which operates on a UK basis but is accountable to the Scottish Secretary for its activities in Scotland. Its chief significance lies in its powers to promote and assist the development of housing associations.

The Corporation was an alternative to 'municipalisation' as a way of renovating private-rented accommodation, by providing financial backing for 'non-profit-making' housing associations. Housing associations therefore, provide an alternative to owner-occupation or council housing, by taking over private property, or indeed building new houses for rent.

These are the main national institutions in the housing policy network. Also involved at central government level are the Department of the Environment, in the formulation of UK wide policies, and the Treasury, over expenditure issues. There is a plethora of private sector bodies important in housing development (buildings, building societies) and also pressure groups, who seek to influence policy and legislation (e.g. Shelter, Scottish Campaign for the Single-Homeless) and numerous tenants' associations at the local level, who tend to be reactive rather than promotional.

Policy development since 1970

How then are policies made in this complex environment? In this section, we shall analyse the evolution of four major policy developments, each of which had a different motivating force behind it. These are, the introduction of housing plans, the housing policy review, housing for the homeless, and council house sales.

The origins of the housing plan system can be traced back to the work of the Scottish Housing Advisory Committee (SHAC), which serves as a kind of intellectual sounding board for the Scottish Development Department. Its concern *prima facie* was professional and technical, as it examined the problems of assessing housing need and the inadequacy of reliance on council house waiting lists. Its conclusions, however, had profound political implications, both for the traditional emphasis that the major parties had placed on new housing in their election manifestos, and also for the relationship between central and local government. In 1972, SHAC published a report on housing planning which suggested that the nature of housing problems was changing, and that the traditional emphasis on new housing was now less necessary. Its recommendations had a marked effect on government thinking about housing, for the main features of the report became the basis of the new Housing Plan System. The quantitative shortage which had been the major policy problem was no longer so acute, and greater emphasis should be placed on modernisation and improvement. Account needed to be taken of emerging special needs, such as the elderly or the single homeless, and there was a growing demand for home ownership. In total this meant that local government must adopt a more comprehensive strategic role in planning for housing needs as well as providing council housing. The report called for a comprehensive approach, based on local assessments of needs, leading to policies suited to the diversity of needs which local authorities faced. Central government should provide a manual of guidance on the assessment of housing need.

SHAC of course were 'insiders'. Their ideas were not being sprung new upon the Scottish Development Department, but in fact were complementary to the emerging philosophy of 'disengagement' which was being gradually adopted by the Scottish Office in its relationships with local government. The SDD soon thereafter established a Working Group which carried out a project in the Dundee area and reported in 1975. These recommendations formed the basis of the Scottish Housing Handbook, "Assessing Housing Needs—A Manual of Guidance".

The local authorities were closely consulted with and involved in the emergence of the new philosophy. A joint SDD/COSLA Working Party was established, to work out a new system of policy and programme planning for housing. The ideas were also complementary to those of the Scottish Office Finance Division on capital expenditure control. The existing system of cost controls involved a close degree of scrutiny by the Scottish Office. As such, it was unsuitable both for controlling total expenditure, for consent to borrow was given for a specific project, but there was no control on *when* the expenditure took place, and also for strategic policy planning, for local authorities could find one element of their housing programme being approved but another not, often leading to imbalance in housing development. The practice of using cost controls for macro-economic purposes was crude and disruptive to capital programme management. There was a prevalent belief amongst Scottish Office civil servants that there should be a 'bottom up' approach with the local asssessment of needs the first step in the public expenditure process. The logic of the arrangements was appealing to administrators, and there was an appreciation of the benefits of decentralisation. So what was the political input? Labour's manifesto had concentrated on the repeal of the Housing Finance provisions of the Tory Government, and promised a rent freeze. The policy initiative was very much the result of a professional/administrative/academic consensus, but the ideas were acceptable to the then Secretary of State Bruce Millan, a pragmatic administrator rather than an ideological politician. Millan appreciated the concept of planning for local needs, and was closely consulted at all stages. The introduction of the system was also facilitated by the reduction in number of housing authorities to fifty-six following local government reorganisation. The new system was seen as bringing about a radical change in central-local relations giving greater responsibility to local authorities, and each Housing Plan would contain a comprehensive assessment of need, a policy statement, and a capital plan to meet those needs. According to the Green Paper, this would enable the government to direct resources more effectively to areas with the greatest needs. Assessment of the impact of this policy change requires a long-term perspective. The policy itself, however, emerged from a co-operative consultative process involving ministers, professionals, administrators, academics.

In the earlier chapter on the Scottish Office, we discussed the conditions for policy autonomy. In housing, there certainly is a tradition of Scottish control over the administrative process. The proposals, whilst intended for Scotland only, were broadly similar to the development of Housing Investment Programmes in England, although the details were somewhat different (e.g. number of expenditure blocks). The cross-border spillover effect was therefore unimportant, the implications of the proposals were conducive to firmer control of housing expenditure, and the ideas were generally acceptable to the political disposition of the Secretary of State. Whilst there was a clear overlap with UK policy, Scottish discretion was substantial over the details and administration of the system, within a broad framework which was acceptable to HM Treasury.

The Housing Plan system was in operation by the time the Green Paper on Scottish Housing was published in 1977, although its ideas had a major conditioning effect on the contents of the Green Paper. To provide a broader understanding of the Housing Policy Review, however, it is necessary to go back to the Housing Finance Act of 1972. This Act sought to introduce 'economic' (i.e. market) rents for council housing, and was a response to the search for reductions in public expenditure. The Heath

Government, like the Thatcher Government, concentrated its policy on council house subsidies, which come under the Scottish Office, rather than on tax subsidies to owner-occupiers, which are administered by the Inland Revenue; though it is true that Labour governments have been equally unwilling to tackle the latter. The 1972 provisions were different in Scotland. In England, local authorities could make a 'profit' on the Housing Revenue Account, whereas in Scotland, the only requirement was to balance the Housing Revenue Account with rents based on meeting 'historic costs'. However, it did result in central government fixing rent levels, and the Labour Opposition pledged its repeal. Within four days of their election victory, Labour had frozen council house rents (at a cost of £500 million in the UK), and proceeded to return the right of local authorities to fix their rents, whilst setting maximum permissable increases. The ensuing economic crisis, however, resulted in the Labour Party itself seeking public expenditure reductions, with Tony Crosland, then Minister for the Environment, acknowledging that he had not realised that housing finance was in such a mess. In part, this was a result of counter-inflation policies, and the use of subsidies to reach agreement on incomes with the trade unions. Inflation following the oil crisis was higher than ever before. The result was that, despite the *fall* in capital expenditure, total public expenditure on housing in 1975-6 was 10% higher than in 1970-1, due to the increase in housing subsidies (subsidy to local authorities, rate fund contributions to the housing revenue account, and option mortgage subsidy — this excludes the 'tax expenditure' of mortgage interest tax relief).

Crosland thus set up a Housing Finance Review in the Department of the Environment (although this was later broadened into a Policy Review by Peter Shore when it was realised that any financial changes would be mere tinkering). The Scottish Office Review was carried out simultaneously, and in some aspects was tied to the coat-tails of DoE, where the scale of operations was much greater. There a whole division of the department, set to work under the supervision of a Steering Group, carried out deep academic studies which eventually became technical appendices to the English Policy Review. The central Housing Advisory Committee had hundreds of meetings with research staff. The Scottish Office was consulted about such developments and received all discussion papers, but the amount of data generated was in fact far too great to receive comprehensive comments from the Scottish Office.

In Scotland, by contrast, there was a very small team of civil servants working on the Housing Finance Review. They comprised the Under-Secretary with responsibility for housing, an assistant secretary, a principal, a finance officer, and an administrative trainee. A special Finance Subcommittee under Professor Cullingworth including the chairman of the COSLA Housing Committee and a trade union representative, sat concurrently, and was used as a sounding board to determine the political acceptability of proposals.

Although most of the conclusions of the reviews were common to Scotland and England, a number of distinctive existing practices, such as the block allocations for capital spending had to be accommodated. The subcommittee had got together a number of papers on housing policy which were passed on to the civil servants, covering historical (what needs to be done), technical (assessing housing need), and discussion (sale of council houses) issues. These ideas were sketched out into a basic framework, then a rudimentary draft, which was revised around twenty times, and circulated around the Scottish Office, DoE and the Treasury, with numerous meetings in Whitehall.

A great deal of the work involved pulling together bits of housing policy that ministers had already endorsed. It was a case of filling in the gaps. Contact with ministers was frequent, sometimes in brief meetings, while on other occasions the issue to be dealt with would be laid out in a letter to the minister, either arguing a line and looking for endorsement, or seeking advice on what line the Green Paper ought to take. The Secretary of State was insistent that the final package had to meet the needs of the housing authorities.

Consultation also took place with COSLA, with SHAC, and with Housing Managers over training for housing managers. Shelter had close connections with Department of the Environment, but had little impact on Scottish policy. The Labour Party had a parallel housing group meeting under Robin Cook, MP, and some aspects of the paper did not please the Labour left. Ministers had already endorsed some of the proposals in the Green Paper, but it pointed in directions which the Scottish Conference of the Labour Party subsequently refused to follow, demanding instead public ownership and municipalisation. Cullingworth (1979) regarded the Green Paper as notably non-ideological in its broad discussion. Ministerial input, however, was extensive, and if the recommendations were non-ideological, then that had more to do with the political perspective of Scottish Office ministers than the machinations of the bureaucracy.

Finally, the SHAC Subcommittee was reconvened and their response to the proposals sought. These were relatively uncritical, as the Green Paper reflected their ideas and recommendations, although they were keen to have credit given to local authorities for their housing achievements since the war.

The major recommendations were for:
—a rationalised subsidy system for local government;
—the development of local housing plans as a basis of the
    system;

—the need to promote owner-occupation, and to allow
selective sales of council houses;
—the need to cater for special housing needs;
—the introduction of Tenants' Rights;
—the need for better training for housing management;
—the need to involve/influence building societies through a
Home Ownership Forum.

The Green Paper then, produced three broad types of policy, a UK led
policy on matters such as owner-occupation, distinctive Scottish policies
on housing plans and the subsidy system and Scottish modifications of UK
policy, for example on policy for building societies.

There was extensive consultation with Whitehall, but there was no flood
of evidence as occured in England. In Scotland, the housing policy
community is relatively small and compact, the variety of institutions
notwithstanding; so the management and administration of policy is
somewhat easier than in England and Wales.

In terms of our framework for policy discretion, this is an interesting
case-study, as it does not fall clearly into either the UK or the Scottish
policy field. It is quite clear that the Department of the Environment was
exercising policy leadership. However, traditional Scottish autonomy was
reflected in a selective fashion, for example on block allocations, sale of
council houses; and the Secretary of State personally was able to make a
considerable impact.

The Housing (Homeless Persons) Act, 1977, provides a useful
comparison in policy formulation, as the initiative came from a UK
department, and the lobbying of pressure groups led to its provisions being
applied in Scotland. The problem in a nutshell was the need to locate
responsibility for housing homeless persons to housing authorities and not
to social work departments. The drafting of the bill was the work of the
Department of the Environment, but it was eliminated from the Queen's
Speech in 1976, presumably because of pressure on the legislative
timetable; but according to a participant (Gibson 1979), the Minister of
Housing, Reg Freeson, had let it be known that if one of the Members of
Parliament who had come out near the top of the Private Members' Ballot
were to take over the bill he or she would receive the active support and
co-operation of his department. While the ideas had been the work of the
Morris Committee, no legislative action was proposed, but reliance was
placed on 'voluntary agreement' between the housing and social work
authorities. This was not pleasing to the housing interests groups, who felt
that the English experience showed that voluntarism would not work.

When Liberal MP Stephen Ross took up sponsorship of the bill, he
received all-party support, and Shelter Scotland began private and public

lobbying for the provisions of the bill to be extended to Scotland, then obtained the support of several other pressure groups, forming an alliance as the Scottish Homeless Group. The Scottish Office, however, continued to argue that the 'code of practice' being developed through COSLA was preferable. Gibson argued that the Scottish Office had given a commitment to COSLA (whose housing and social work committees were divided) that there would be no legislation until a voluntary code had been tried (Gibson 1978).

The Scottish Office then attempted some procedural ploys to prevent the bill's passage, but unsuccessfully. The passage of the bill was one of the conditions laid down by the Liberal Party for the parliamentary pact reached with the minority Labour Government, and although Hugh Brown, the junior minister, continued to voice unhappiness with the bill, he indicated that Scottish Office ministers would no longer attempt to frustrate the bill's passage.

Cullingworth (1979) regards the Act as being so vaguely worded that it is quite unenforceable and constituted little more than a moral exhortation wrapped up in legalistic provisions. Nevertheless the spirit of the Act appears to have been followed in the majority of cases.

Page (1982) argues that the evidence suggests a fairly strong impact for the local government system as a whole, and that local authorities are more than fulfilling their statutory duties. 59% of applicants for accommodation under the Act were successfully housed in the period 1979-81. Local authorities have the power to determine priority group status, and have not been over-stringent in their definitions. This left a large area of discretion for local government, varying from a low of 25% of homeless applicants getting accommodation in Aberdeen, to 100% in Shetlands.

Council house sales, by contrast, provide an example where the policy initiative stemmed from the elected government, and previous experience of leaving discretion with local government indicated that successful implementation would require leaving no room for policy discretion.

The Labour Party's reluctance to sell council houses has been well documented. Yet the 1970s saw a weakening of Labour attitudes over this issue, both in the Green Paper and in local policies. Given the dominance of public housing stock in available housing in Scotland, and the marginal impact of new building (2% is the *most* in any year) on housing stock, if the new demand for owner-occupation was to be met, then this would have to be met partly through sales of existing public housing.

Bruce Millan's position on the issue was quite clear. The sale of council houses could only be meaningfully discussed in the context of the total housing supply and the analysis of housing need. He was prepared to sanction schemes where it could be justified on the grounds that such sales were surplus to total needs — the housing policy of selective sales by

Inverclyde District Council in the late 'seventies was a good example of this philosophy.

While Labour were softening their resistance, and offering greater scope for local authority discretion, the Conservatives, having experienced opposition from Labour councils in the past, were moving to a position of giving the 'right' to individuals to buy their council house, irrespective of the council's policies. On winning the election in 1979, they moved quickly and issued a circular which extended to Scotland a general consent to councils to sell to sitting tenants, which had been introduced by the Department of Environment under Labour just before the election. Local authorities were reluctant to implement the government's proposals, and indeed only six councils did so before the new Act made it compulsory, although sixteen councils had a selective scheme of sales. But while local authorities of all persuasions pointed to the administrative problems of implementing a blanket sales policy, they made little impact on government. It was one of COSLA's least impressive performances, and only minor issues were changed as a result of the local government lobby. Conservative ministers (both English and Scottish) were so determined on the right to buy that internal consultation was unnecessary, and external consultation was restricted to matters of detail! Again, however, the government faced problems of implementation following Labour's local electoral successes in 1980, and a series of administrative/political delaying strategies were adopted. In one council, for instance, a NALGO strike delayed progress. In another, application forms were issued without advice, and if filled in wrongly were returned to the tenant, again without advice. Another tactic was the circulation of 'propaganda' devised to deter tenants from purchasing their homes. These, however, were effective only in the short term and could only hinder and obstruct the policy.

The policy remains marginal to housing problems in Scotland, yet it has been a dominant source of political debate since the Conservative election victory. It provides a contrast with the Housing Green Paper and Housing Plans which resulted from an administrative/professional/political consensus involving a long process of review and consultation for it stemmed directly from the Party Manifesto. The council house sales policy has disturbed much of the 1970s consensus, being introduced quickly and with minimal consultation. Indeed, it has implications for the comprehensive approach advocated in the earlier period, by increasing the degree of uncertainty which local authorities must plan and manage.

Policy implementation was ensured by the elimination of local political choice, irrespective of local needs. The few authorities who engaged in delaying tactics appear now to be co-operating, although analysis is not available on the extent to which such anti-sales propaganda deterred would-be purchasers. As Page (1982) notes, the government displayed its willingness to use formal enforcement mechanisms — a public enquiry and the Court of Session, to ensure implementation. By 1981, 6,500 houses were being sold annually, an increase of nearly 900% from the 1973 total under the previous Conservative Government.

These case studies of housing policy formulation demonstrate the diverse origins of policy initiatives in Scotland. How an issue gets onto the political agenda has a dominant influence on how political bargaining and negotiation take place, not just in policy making but also in implementation. Where consensus and accommodation is reached, implementation is facilitated. Where it is absent, delaying and obstructive tactics will be adopted, whether by central government (homelessness), or by local government (council house sales). A structured accommodation, as in housing plans, was possible because of respect for the legitimate rights of the various levels of government in a partnership situation. Where centralist legislation is enforced, part of the price is the destabilisation of central-local relationships.

CHAPTER NINE

ECONOMIC AND INDUSTRIAL POLICY MAKING

IT is a matter of debate whether there is nowadays such a thing as a Scottish economy. In the nineteenth century, the heyday of Scottish private enterprise, there clearly was a distinct economic system and industrial network, albeit one which was closely linked to England. By the First World War, however, there were already signs that Scottish prosperity was dangerously dependent on a limited range of heavy industries — coal, steel, engineering, shipbuilding and locomotive building. The slump in these industries in the early 1920s inaugurated a prolonged period of decline in which control of Scottish industry gradually passed out of Scottish hands. By the 1930s there was a drift to the South of industry and such new industry as was established in Scotland often consisted of branches of non-Scottish companies, especially vulnerable in times of recession. Rearmament and the Second World War gave a temporary boost to the heavy industries and were followed by relatively favourable conditions in the early 1950s, but by the mid '50s the old problems had resurfaced. Between 1954 and 1960, Scottish manufacturing output increased by only 9%, compared with 23% for the UK as a whole (McCrone 1965). As a result, Scottish gross domestic product per head fell from 92% of the UK average to 88%. Indigenous industry was concentrated disproportionately in the slow-growing heavy industrial sector.

This is the background to the efforts since the 1960s to devise a distinctly Scottish arm of the economic and industrial policy making system. The main instruments of economic policy — demand management, fiscal policy, monetary and exchange rate policies — are a UK responsibility and, unless Scotland should become independent, are likely to remain so, albeit subject to EEC and international constraints. So the responsibilities of the Treasury, the Inland Revenue and the Bank of England are identical in England and Scotland. Within the limits set by these policies, however, there has developed scope for distinctive Scottish measures in a number of areas. We consider six areas here: regional policy; planning; state intervention; the promotion of inward investment; the revival of indigenous enterprise; and North Sea oil development.

Regional policy

Regional policy has a history stemming back to the 1930s but it was in the 1960s that the first major efforts were made to bring industry to the areas of high unemployment rather than encouraging workers to migrate. By 1970, a comprehensive system of grants for industrial development was in operation for development areas and special development areas, which included the whole of Scotland except for Edinburgh, Leith and Portobello. The Conservative Government of 1970 replaced these grants with tax allowances but in 1972 reverted to grants some of which are available to all firms in development areas and some of which are awarded selectively. In 1974, the new Labour Government extended development area status to Edinburgh and its neighbours. In 1979, in a review of regional policy, the Conservative Government removed development area status from parts of Scotland. As well as the 'carrot' of investment grants, regional policy included the 'stick' of Industrial Development Certificates which were required until recently for developments of a specified size out-with the development areas. This regional policy is essentially a UK function, involving decisions in Whitehall as to which parts of the country merit priority in industrial development but it has been influenced increasingly over the years, by Scottish considerations. There is now a regional policy division within the Scottish Economic Planning Department which produces statistics on regional policy in Scotland and is involved in discussions on the development of regional policy. Thus while the decision to redefine the development areas in 1979 was the responsibility of the Secretary of State for Industry, the Scottish Offices were closely involved in the discussions leading up to it. In 1975, the position of SEPD was further enhanced when the Secretary of State was given responsibility for the allocation of selective regional assistance to industry under Section 7 of the 1972 Industry Act. The non-selective automatic grants in development areas are still the responsibility of the Department of Industry which also allocates non-regional 'sectoral' aid to specific industries. The Section 7 aid administered by the Scottish Office is not part of the block expenditure allocation (see Chapter Ten) so that the Secretary of State's discretion extends only to its *distribution* not to its overall amount. However, in practice, this has not imposed a severe limitation on the Secretary of State as shortage of suitable cases has meant that available funds have never been fully spent.

In the 1960s and 1970s, Scotland did very well from regional policy, receiving 30% of all British regional development aid between 1960 and

1972 (Scott and Hughes 1980). By the late 1970s, its share had fallen as a result of its relative prosperity, the increasing problems of other regions and the switch from regional to sectoral assistance. In 1978/9, Scotland received 20% of all British regional development grants and 25% of the selective regional assistance. At the same time, the requirements for Industrial Development Certificates came to be interpreted much less stringently as other parts of the UK began to suffer from de-indulstrialisation.

Whether the regional policy has been a success is a matter of political and academic contention but, in the 1960s and early 1970s, a strong regional policy coincided with an improvement in Scotland's relative economic fortunes. According to McCrone (1969), regional policy in the 1960s did have a marked effect. In the early 1970s, too, Scottish industrial output grew at above the average rate for the UK, falling back between 1975 and 1980. This provides strong grounds for belief that, without regional policy, Scotland could have fared worse. However, by the late 1970s, the possibilities of relocating 'footloose' industry were diminishing as total investment fell and formerly prosperous areas began to feel the effects of recession. Attention then shifted to backing potentially profitable industries wherever they were, to attracting overseas investment and to stimulating indigenous enterprise.

Regional planning
Regional planning started in Scotland in the early 1960s and the Scottish Office was a pioneer in the field. In 1961, it joined with the Scottish Council (Development and Industry) to commission the Toothill Report on the Scottish economy and in 1963 the newly established Scottish Development Department produced *Central Scotland: A Programme for Development and Growth* (Cmnd. 2188). In 1964, the new Labour Government, committed to economic planning as the mainstay of its economic programme, gave the Scottish Office a central role. As the Scottish Office later noted in evidence to the Select Committee on Scottish Affairs:

> "The Secretary of State for Scotland's involvement in problems of economic development flowing from the increasing expectation by Scottish opinion generally that he should interest himself in any matter affecting Scotland, whether or not it comes within the scope of his statutory functions, led in 1964 to his being assigned more explicit responsibilities in the compre-

hensive machinery for economic planning which was
introduced on the advent of a new administration (S.O. Memo
to Select Committee on Scottish Affairs, April 1969)."

The Scottish Office was responsible for the Scottish Plan to fit into the 1965
National Plan. This it did in conjunction with the advisory Scottish
Economic Planning Council consisting of representatives of industry,
trade unions, local authorities and others, under the chairmanship of the
Secretary of State and the Scottish Economic Planning Board, consisting
of civil servants from the main economic departments of government,
under the chairmanship of a Scottish Office official. In 1966, the *Plan for
Expansion* for the Scottish Economy was published, only to fail with the
National Plan in the devaluation crisis of 1967. Thereafter, economic
planning went rather out of fashion generally, but the Scottish Office's
economic role nevertheless grew. In 1973, the Regional Development
Division was taken out of the SDD and became part of the new Scottish
Economic Planning Department. The formation of SEPD was a
recognition of the Secretary of State's expanded economic role and a
consolidation of various economic functions but, ironically, may have
weakened the chances of comprehensive economic planning by separating
these functions from the land-use, infrastructure and local government
responsibilities of the SDD. However, one positive result of the creation of
SEPD was that it was no longer necessary to retain the co-ordinating
machinery of the Economic Planning Board, which has fallen into
desuetude. The advisory council has been retained, under the title Scottish
Economic Council.

SEPD does not now produce a Scottish economic plan but the Secretary
of State retains a general responsibility for the Scottish economy. What
this amounts to in practice is often hard to determine but it certainly
includes a monitoring and research role, the use and co-ordination of his
functional responsibilities in electricity, selective assistance, manpower
and the SDA and HIDB and participation in economic and industrial
policy making for the UK as a whole. Thus, his economic and industrial
responsibilities and his official status as an industry minister mean that the
Secretary of State and his officials are party to all major decisions on
industrial policy including aid to industry and the investment programmes
of nationalised industries. Of course, it is the Department of Industry
which is the lead department here but, depending on the political and other
conditions, the Scottish input can be considerable. Similarly, while the
Department of Employment is the lead department on employment policy,
the Secretary of State, as an employment minister, has a say in the
development of policy. In the case of energy, his responsibility for
electricity entitles him to participate in policy making for energy as a whole

and for this purpose SEPD maintains a small section to monitor general policy developments and contribute where appropriate.

State intervention

Direct government intervention in industry is a politically controversial matter but, with the decline in indigenous private industry in Scotland, it has probably aroused less opposition there than elsewhere in Britain. The first major acts of intervention were the nationalisations of basic industries by the 1945-51 Labour Government. These were placed under the control of corporations which, with the exception of the electricity boards, were responsible to UK departments, provoking the Conservative politician Walter Elliot to remark that, 'for Scotland, nationalisation means denationalisation'. In the 1960s the Wilson government tried a more selective approach to intervention and industrial rationalisation with the Industrial Reorganisation Corporation but, again, the strategy was a UK one, except for the Highlands and Islands, where the HIDB was set up, with considerable industrial powers (see Chapter Three). In 1970, the Conservatives abolished the IRC but kept the HIDB. Two years later, a series of industrial collapses, notably that of Upper Clyde Shipbuilders, forced them to reverse the policy of non-intervention in the 1972 Industry Act. In 1974, Labour came to office with plans to establish a National Enterprise Board, with wide powers of industrial intervention, to engage in state-sponsored entrepreneurship where private enterprise was said to have failed. This time there was a specifically Scottish dimension as Labour was also pledged to establish a Scottish Development Agency to revive Scottish industry and co-ordinate industrial strategy with environmental improvement (see Chapter Three). On their return to office in 1979, the Conservatives kept both the NEB — with a much reduced status — and the SDA. Scotland thus has three industrial agencies with power to take stakes in firms, start new industries or give loans and advice — the NEB, the SDA and the HIDB. In addition, there are the selective powers of assistance possessed by the Scottish Office. This gives a complexity to Scottish industrial policy not seen elsewhere.

This complexity is managed by means of agreed guidelines, a sense of common purpose and a close network of consultation. So, while the Department of Industry is responsible for non-selective assistance and selective sectoral assistance and the Scottish Office for selective regional assistance, each consults the other on important cases. Clearly the Department of Industry is the lead department here, not only in making policy but also in monitoring its implementation and ensuring consistency throughout the UK (Hogwood 1982a). Similarly, there are guidelines laid down for the NEB and the SDA, the former by the Department of Industry and the latter by the Scottish Office but in both cases representing agreed government policy. Generally speaking, the NEB deals with large and UK-wide firms and the SDA with purely Scottish operations, though the distinction is not always a clear one and consultation is necessary when the actions of one agency might affect the other, as where the NEB-sponsored firm proposes an investment or closure in Scotland (Hogwood 1982b). Demarcation between the SDA and SEPD is rather more confused. Papers on important cases are copied for both and are often followed by case meetings where the lead is, by and large, taken by the agency with which the inquiry originated but, by 1980, the SDA was still of the opinion that 'we have not yet reached an ideal state of affairs' (HC 769-11, 1979-80, p. 191 quoted in Hogwood 1982b). Between the SDA and the HIDB there is an agreement that small companies should go to the latter while larger ones involve the SDA and that, where a company has Scottish-wide operations, the SDA takes the lead role.

Consultation, however, does not always lead to harmonious relationships amongst the agencies. Policy differences can arise on matters like the SDA's plans to build a Scottish micro-electronics industry, which cut across similar NEB plans or some of the more ambitious plans of the HIDB. Where conflict is set to assume major proportions though, central government will intervene and the problem will be thrashed out within the government machine.

Inward investment
Inward investment from the rest of the UK and from overseas has played a crucial role in the post-war Scottish economy. By 1973, Scottish-owned firms accounted for just over 40% of manufacturing employment, with English firms accounting for slightly less. United States firms had increased their proportion from 8% in the mid 1960s to 15% (Scott and Hughes 1980) and Scotland had the second largest figure for US investment in Europe (after Eire). Further, it was the fastest growing sectors particularly in oil and electronics and the largest firms that saw the greatest concentration of external control (Firn 1975). So Scotland had become crucially dependent on overseas investment, with government encouraging this through a variety of instruments. For the UK as a whole, the Department of Trade maintains the Invest in Britain Bureau (IBB) whose efforts are backed up by the Foreign and Commonwealth Office. The major independent Scottish effort was for many years run by the Scottish Council (Development and Industry) which, as an essentially private organisation, albeit in receipt of funds for this purpose, was less inhibited than a government department in lobbying for one part of the UK as against others. In the 1970s, attitudes towards a separate Scottish

effort became more relaxed as investment in Scotland was no longer seen as being necessarily at the expense of another part of the UK — it could equally well be at the expense of another part of Europe. So on its establishment, the SDA was given the task of attracting inward investment, gradually taking over the Scottish Council's role here and opening offices in New York, San Francisco and Tokyo. At the same time, the SEPD itself became more interested in inward investment, as did regional and district councils and new town development corporations. In 1980, for instance, Glasgow District Council appointed an investment promotion officer in California and during the last decade both regional and district councils have joined in promotional trips organised by the Scottish Council and, later, the SDA and SEPD.

The result was a picture of considerable complexity, with a number of Scottish organisations competing against each other as well as against other parts of the UK and Europe. Strong resentment built up in the Foreign and Commonwealth Offices against the SDA offices abroad, there were jealousies between the SEPD and SDA and often a lack of communication between the IBB and the SDA. As a result of the proliferation of agencies, a potential investor might have to deal with any or all of the Consular Services, the IBB, the SDA, the SEPD (for advice and selective assistance), the Department of Industry (for sectoral and automatic assistance), the HIDB (in the Highlands and Islands), regional and district councils (for sites and planning permissions) and new town development corporations. The confusion and conflict which this could engender was vividly illustrated in the late 1970s Mostek incident, when the SDA only heard by chance of a potential micro-electronics investment which was about to go to the Republic of Ireland. Suspicions were raised that the Department of Industry, which knew of Mostek, had deliberately failed to inform the Scots as they saw it as a competitor to an NEB-sponsored scheme of their own. The divisions within Scotland were illustrated in the 1981 Nissan car plant affair. This time, SEPD were determined to impose some coherence on the Scottish effort to attract this major investment. They therefore engaged in wide consultation and came up with a list of four Scottish sites for presentation to IBB which would, in turn, present Nissan's consultants with a list of three or four sites in the UK. However, immediately the preferred sites became known, those local councils whose areas had been rejected prepared their own representations to IBB and Nissan. All this led to repeated calls for a 'one-door' approach to investment promotion on the lines of the Republic of Ireland's Irish Development Authority, which is able to present potential investors with an integrated package of sites, permissions, incentives and taxes, assembled with the minimum of delay. The problems of adopting such an approach for Scotland are immense. The Republic of Ireland is a single country whereas in Scotland there is a need to work with the UK departments and agencies. In Scotland, moreover, there is a strong system of local government with powers over land-use and infrastructure and keen to join the promotion effort. So it is quite unrealistic to foresee the concentration of all powers in a single agency. Attention has therefore focussed on the need to co-ordinate efforts, to avoid duplication and conflict and to present potential investors with, as far as possible, a single channel of communication. Under the Labour Government in the late 1970s, the SDA took the lead role here, organising and co-ordinating overseas missions and setting up a Development Consultative Committee and a Regional Development Officers' Liaison Committee to link with local authorities. Under the Conservatives after 1979, the SEPD and its newly designated 'minister for industry' began to assert more of a leading role and complaints about duplication and conflict — not to mention skulduggery by UK departments — resurfaced. This issue came to a head with the 1980 report of the Select Committee on Scottish Affairs, on inward investment. Amid vigorous lobbying and interdepartmental argument of an unusually open kind (Hogwood 1982b), the committee divided on party lines, the Conservative majority recommending closure of the SDA overseas offices and concentration of investment promotion in IBB and the consular service, with Scottish secondments where appropriate. Labour members, supporting their own creation, defended the overseas offices. The government's response was a compromise. A new unit, *Locate in Scotland*, was established to bring together the investment functions of the SDA and SEPD and take over the offices abroad. So a Scottish presence was saved but placed more closely under government control and thus less likely to embark on separate Scottish ventures which could embarrass other departments.

Further, in response to the recommendations of the Stodart Committee on local government, the Secretary of State proposed to require local authorities to obtain permission before making promotional trips abroad. So the Scottish Office has sought to reduce complexity and to establish a clear role for itself but, in such a competitive field, conflict is likely to remain, with local authorities seeking to use all means at their disposal to attract investment and competition between Scotland and the rest of the UK continuing and intensifying.

Indigenous enterprise
Despite government efforts to promote inward investment, the resulting overseas control of much of Scottish industry may carry its own disadvantages. Branch factories are unlikely to encourage entrepreneurship or a spirit of innovation or to provide a large research and

development effort or many senior management posts. Profits may be remitted overseas rather than invested in Scotland and the integration of Scotland into the wider western industrial system may make it particularly vulnerable to economic downturns originating in the United States or elsewhere. For Conservative governments, hostile to state ownership, the rebuilding of a strong indigenous private industrial sector is politically vital. So concern has often been expressed about the need to encourage indigenous Scottish industry and small firms. Government powers here are, by the very nature of the field, limited, but some initiatives have been taken. Biases formerly existing in the award of industrial assistance to incoming firms as opposed to those already present have been eliminated and the Scottish Office's powers of selective industrial assistance can be used here. The SDA has the task of encouraging indigenous industry through the backing of new ventures and the grant of aid and loans to firms which, though potentially viable, have difficulty in the medium term in raising investment funds. It also helps through the provision of management advice and has a Small Business Division specifically to help that sector. The Scottish Council (Development and Industry) also helps small firms, with its research effort, its advice and conferences and its links with government, although most of the funds for the Council come from large firms, who also provide most of the members of the research and working parties.

One sector in which Scotland still has a strong indigenous presence is in banking and finance. Of the three Scottish clearing banks, the Clydesdale is wholly owned by the English-based Midland but has considerable operational independence, the Bank of Scotland is partly owned by Barclays but is independent and the Royal Bank of Scotland remains completely independent.

North Sea oil provided new opportunities for the Scottish banks which by mid-1976 had placed 11% of their committed assets in oil operations (Perman n.d.). The 1970s also saw the establishment of three new Scottish merchant banks to join the British Linen Bank and R.B. Development, merchant subsidiaries of the Bank of Scotland and the Royal Bank respectively. Scotland is also a major centre for insurance companies including nine of the leading 'life' companies and General Accident which has its headquarters in Perth. Consequently, about a third of all UK investment funds are managed from Scotland (Perman n.d.).

The present degree of independence, maintained in the face of considerable pressure as overseas financiers seek a way into the UK market, is widely considered a key element in maintaining a viable Scottish private financial and hence industrial sector. It is because of this that so much passion was raised over two takeover bids for the Royal made in 1981. As a result of the outcry, the government referred both bids to the

Monopolies Commission to which the Scottish Office then made a strong submission, pointing out the importance of the Scottish independent banking sector to industrialists and voicing fears that a major takeover could have a 'domino' effect on other Scottish financial institutions. The merger was blocked largely on the grounds of the need to preserve an independent Scottish banking sector. We are not concerned here to assess whether the existence of a Scottish financial sector is indeed of vital importance — other commentators (Scott and Hughes 1980) have stressed the past role of Scottish finance houses in channelling funds *out* of the country. What is clear, however, is that Scottish ministers and officials have seen this as a key element in the maintenance and encouragement of indigenous enterprise and have exerted their influence accordingly.

The argument about the Royal and its outcome created a legend of a political 'ring fence' around Scottish companies, reinforced when bids for Highland Distilleries and House of Fraser were blocked after Monopolies Commission investigations. However, it seems that the 'regional' arguments were of little account in these cases and the idea of a 'ring fence' to protect industrial, as opposed to financial, companies is a myth (*Scotsman*, 28.10.82). Such a barrier could hardly function in an open integrated economy like that of the UK. On the other hand, the Scottish Council (Development and Industry) and the STUC have made efforts to get government and the Monopolies Commission to recognise the legitimacy of 'regional' arguments against mergers and the SDA has acted to protect promising Scottish companies from 'foreign predators'. The position is thus thoroughly confused, with no clear policy emerging from government as a whole on the position of locally based private firms because no department is in a position to take such an overall view. The confusion was yet further compounded in 1983 when the government overturned a Monopolies Commission recommendation against a takeover bid for Anderson Strathclyde.

North Sea oil

The final area of economic and industrial policy to be considered is the development of North Sea oil.

North Sea oil and gas has had a profound impact on the Scottish economy, creating, directly or indirectly, between 85,000 and 100,000 new jobs on and offshore. Although all the oil fields lie off the Scottish coast and are for legal and administrative purposes considered to be in Scotland, statutory responsibility for oil and gas development policy and the issues of licences lies with the Department of Energy. However, the Scottish Office does enter the picture at several points. In Cabinet, the Secretary of State is able to contribute to the major policy decisions and, to brief him, there is a unit in SEPD concerned with North Sea oil and gas. This unit monitors developments and maintains close links with the Department of Energy and other Whitehall departments as well as oil companies operating in Scotland. Within the Scottish Office, it acts as co-ordinator for all matters concerned with the North Sea developments. It is also represented on the Oil Industry Liaison Committee, chaired by the Minister of State for Energy (by convention, a Scottish MP), a UK body bringing together government departments, companies and trade unions.

At the same time, other aspects of the Scottish Office's work impinge on North Sea developments, notably the planning and infrastructural responsibilities of SDD. Roads, housing, schools, hospitals, airports, ports and harbours have been needed to accommodate the industry, requiring investment by central and local government as well as the private sector. While, in the early years, SEPD had a major role in co-ordinating this activity, in bringing together the actors involved, nowadays relationships are well established, with firms able to find their own way around the network. There are now close links between the Scottish branches of oil companies and SDD and local authorities on matters to do with planning and infrastructure while their London headquarters deal with the Department of Energy on major policy issues.

Help for UK firms in securing orders for North Sea development is provided by the Offshore Supplies Office in Glasgow sponsored by the Department of Energy. The Scottish Office has no direct role here but, given the location of the North Sea operation, Scottish business is well placed to take advantage of opportunities, with the encouragement of the Scottish Office and the SDA. Many of the enterprises engaged in the oil-related industries such as platform construction have been joint ventures between Scottish and English or overseas firms.

Economic and industrial policy making in Scotland is thus a complex matter, involving the interaction of a number of UK and Scottish agencies. Clearly, the UK level of decision-making is paramount here, with the Treasury determining macro-economic policy and the Departments of Industry, Energy and Trade taking strong leads in their respective spheres, though they in turn are constrained by the wider international environment, including the EEC. However, the Scottish Office does occupy a place in the network, with its broadly defined economic responsibilities which, together with the more specific responsibilities in fields such as manpower and industrial assistance, gives the Secretary of State the status of an economic and industrial minister. His power and influence will depend on the range of factors which we have analysed in Chapter Two. In some cases, it is spectacularly evident. Such a case was the Chrysler rescue of 1976 when William Ross played a major part in the Cabinet decision to save the firm and thus the Linwood factory originally established at the insistence of one of his predecessors some fifteen years before. This decision is generally believed to have been influenced by the SNP threat to the Labour Party in Scotland and by Ross's determination to assert his developing role as an industrial minister. Five years later, in very different political conditions, Linwood was closed down by its new French owners. Another tussle took place in the early 1980s over the fate of the Ravenscraig steel complex, another development brought to Scotland by Scottish Office pressure in the 1960s. The Secretary of State in this case made no secret of his opposition to closure, in order to mobilise opinion in Scotland. In other cases, the influence of the Scottish Office is more difficult to pin down, exercised, as it is, through the network of Cabinet and civil service committees dealing with matters such as changes in regional incentives, investment programmes of nationalised industries or oil development policy. But unlike education policy or even housing policy, economic and industrial policy leaves little scope for independent policy initiatives as opposed to reacting to or modifying UK initiatives.

The Scottish Office is also important as a channel for interest group demands. It has, as we have noted (Chapter Four), close links with a number of Scottish interest groups who are able to use this not only to influence policy made within the Scottish Office but also to gain a hearing for their case in Whitehall. So many groups concentrate their efforts on convincing Scottish Office ministers and officials of their case, knowing that these in turn can carry the battle into Whitehall. At the same time, interest groups will usually apply pressure at every other point available to them, as appropriate. Where they are a branch of a UK organisation, as with the CBI, contacts can be conducted at Scottish and UK levels simultaneously. In other cases, there may be a UK or English sister organisation with which the Scottish group co-operates. So, in this, as in other fields, politics is played at two levels — the UK and the Scottish — simultaneously and the Scottish Office has to look both ways. It makes the Scottish case in Whitehall and explains government policy in Whitehall. This sometimes allows Scotland to get the best of both worlds, the benefits of being part of the wider UK economy *and* the advantage of special Scottish measures. On the other hand, it can give rise to confusion as to responsibility for Scottish economic and industrial matters. There is no clear responsibility for *planning* the Scottish economy, for relating economic and industrial planning to land use and environmental planning — SEPD and SDD remain separate departments — or for developing an overall Scottish policy for industrial development. We take up some of the implications of this in our conclusion.

In recent years, Scottish economic performance has shown a relative improvement and, though the 1980s recession has hit the whole UK hard, Scotland's position has deteriorated less than that of some other parts. By

1980, Gross Domestic Product per capita was up to 96% of the UK average, higher than any region except the South East and East Midlands of England. Unemployment in Scotland as elsewhere increased dramatically during the recession so it is perhaps no consolation that it went up less rapidly than in some of the former boom regions. However, the industrial structure of the country had been diversified considerably with the aid of the interventions we have discussed. By the mid 1970s, Scotland was less dependent than the UK as a whole on metal manufacturing and engineering but well represented in the food, drink and tobacco and electrical sectors. In 1973 43% of total good and services were exported to the rest of the UK and a further 23% abroad. So Scotland is quite well placed to take advantage of an upturn in world economic conditions with good prospects for growth, if not for employment.

CHAPTER TEN

PUBLIC EXPENDITURE POLICY

Public expenditure in Scotland

Public expenditure is one of the most vital issues in modern government affecting, as it does, practically every other area of policy. For Scotland, this is particularly true given the key role of the public sector in fields such as housing provision and economic development. In principle, public expenditure is easily defined as the current and capital spending of central government and local authorities and the borrowing and losses of nationalised industries and certain other public corporations. In practice, it is sometimes difficult to draw the line as governments can alter the figures by relabelling unchanged activities, for example by converting a nationalised industry from a public corporation into a limited company; or by financing services from charges instead of taxes. As only the net cost of an activity to the *taxpayer* or ratepayer counts as public expenditure, alternative means of paying for services count as reductions in the total. Then there is the problem of 'tax expenditure' such as the tax relief given on mortgage interest payments by owner-occupiers. Although this imposes a cost to the Treasurer in terms of lost revenue when mortgage interest rates or house prices rise, it does not count as public expenditure.

These qualifications must be borne in mind when assessing how well Scotland fares from the distribution of public expenditure. For instance, its low owner-occupancy rate will reduce the amount of tax expenditures in Scotland, though this will not be reflected in the published figures. Subsidies for council houses, on the other hand, do count as public expenditure and are included in the figures. Even allowing for this, however, we can confidently say that Scotland does relatively well out of public spending. Short's (1982) figures show that, in the period 1968-74, Scottish expenditure was some 20% above the British average, with dramatic differences in Agriculture, Fisheries and Forestry, Trade, Industry and Employment and Housing. Table 10.1 shows that, at this time, Scotland fared better than Wales or any English region. Heald (Table 10.2) shows that the Scottish advantage remained stable at around 20% in the following years.* There are several reasons for this. Some of the differential is accounted for by need. Scotland's poor housing conditions are well known. Industrial decline had resulted in the whole country being declared an assisted area by 1974; and half the UK fishing industry and some of the most difficult farming is located in Scotland. However, the Treasury's Needs Assessment Study (Treasury 1980), produced originally to provide a basis for financing a Scottish Assembly, calculated that, on the basis of need alone, Scotland should get less and Wales more — a finding that was not surprisingly better received in the Welsh Office than in St Andrew's House! We can agree with the Scottish Office judgment that the methodology of the Needs Assessment Study was seriously flawed; but the broad finding that Scottish spending differentials are not simply the product of greater needs must be accepted.

Another reason for Scotland's advantage may be the inertia of past spending patterns. At one time, spending was allocated to Scottish Office programmes on population basis. The Goschen formula, giving Scotland 11/80ths of British spending for individual programmes gradually died out after the war, lingering on in education until 1958. By that time, such had been the decline in Scotland's share of population, 11/80ths was over-generous but public spending patterns tend to change only gradually, allowing Scotland to keep this advantage. However, this Goschen effect would not apply to programmes like Industry which are relatively new and do not come under the Scottish Office.

A third factor explaining the Scottish differential is the role of the Secretary of State as a lobbyist for Scotland in the Cabinet. There are two types of public expenditure in Scotland, that within the responsibility of the Secretary of State, for example health or education, and that incurred in Scotland on which are the responsibility of UK departments such as defence or social security. In the former group, the Secretary of State is the *spending minister*, whose role in Whitehall culture is regarded as defending and promoting his department's interests, and in the Public Expenditure Survey, advocating spending. Success is measured in terms of obtaining resources, and the minister who does so is seen as a "strong" minister (Heclo and Wildavsky 1974). This role differs little between Labour and Conservative Governments. Former Labour Secretary of State Willie Ross is often regarded as a combative spending minister. Mrs Thatcher herself succeeded remarkably well in this role (Richardson and Jordan 1979) at the Department of Education and Science, and although it has since been asserted that spending ministers must now prove their virility by the size of their spending cuts, there is little sign that this revolution has actually

* Percipient readers may note that Short uses Great Britain figures and Heald UK figures but the inclusion of Northern Ireland in the latter hardly affects the percentage figure.

occurred. Russell Fairgrieve (former Scottish Office junior minister), for instance, announced that he was the "good news" minister; spending was growing on the health service! Since the introduction of the 'Barnett formula' (see below) it has become much more difficult for the Secretary of State to argue for more resources for Scottish Office programmes as happened in the past with notable success. Instead, he must support other spending ministers with functional English programmes and then await Scotland's share.

Where UK programmes administered by UK departments are concerned, the Secretary of State has a different role. As 'Scotland's Minister' he can legitimately claim a direct interest in any matter affecting Scotland and can argue in Cabinet or Cabinet Committee on items like saving industrial plants in Scotland, investment and closure programmes for nationalised industries or the drawing of assisted area boundaries to benefit Scotland. Table 10.3 shows the Secretary of State's spending (Programme 15) as a percentage of all Scottish identifiable expenditure between 1976-7 and 1980-1.

Expenditure planning and decision-making

The Public Expenditure Survey system was introduced following the report of the Plowden Committee in 1961, whose main conclusion was that decisions involving substantial future expenditure should always be taken in the light of surveys of public expenditure as a whole, over a period of years, and in relation to prospective resources. The aim was a comprehensive planning system, covering *all* types of public expenditure, irrespective of the source of finance (e.g. including local authority rateborne expenditure). This was seen as being necessary to bring the *growth* of public expenditure under better control. Arrangements were developed to collect and collate information about the whole range of public expenditure, to classify and analyse it, and forecast its development over a five-year period on a constant price basis (abandoned, 1982-3) so that changing demands could be measured.

The surveys therefore cover all expenditure by the public sector and the forecasts of expenditure represent costings of existing policies. The figures are analysed by function (health, education, etc.) and also by economic category (current expenditure, grants, etc.). Originally, forecasts were made for five years ahead, but this has now been reduced to three years.

The process falls into three main stages. From December to July, an administrative exercise is co-ordinated by the Treasury. Departments submit preliminary expenditure returns by the end of February, and then a process of bilateral negotiation between the Treasury and spending departments takes place, to reach agreement on the figures and on the underlying policy and statistical assumptions, with a view to reaching agreement about the current cost of expenditure programmes. Departments can also make submissions for additional expenditure, and outline options for making expenditure reductions if these become necessary.

A draft report on public expenditure is drawn up by the Treasury and considered by the Public Expenditure Survey Committee (PESC), which is an interdepartmental committee chaired by a Deputy Secretary in the Treasury, and on which sit the Principal Finance Officers of all major spending departments. But this report does not seek to recommend a *level* of expenditure to ministers, nor the pattern of resource allocation. The main purpose is to provide a context for expenditure decisions, showing the cost of current policies, and the implications of possible changes in policy.

From July to October, the Cabinet takes its decisions on the total and the functional allocation of public expenditure. At one time, the Secretary of State was able to bargain for a Scottish Office share of each of the appropriate functional totals. However, the English backlash to devolution, the move towards expenditure costs and the weakened status of the Secretary of State led to a change in the system in 1978 with the introduction of the 'Barnett formula' (Heald 1980). Under this, spending totals are set for Britain for functional programmes. Any increase or decrease in spending is then allocated, 85% to England, 10% to Scotland and 5% to Wales. This, it must be emphasised, only applies to those programmes within the Secretary of State's responsibility and not to the spending of UK departments like Industry or Social Security in Scotland.

The effect of the Barnett formula is to protect Scotland's position in a period of retrenchment. It has, in fact, resulted in a small fall in the Scottish Office share of total public spending but this is because many of the programmes administered by the Scottish Office have been cut throughout the UK — for example housing — while programmes such as defence which have been increased fall outwith the Secretary of State's ambit (Table 10.3).

Another change introduced at the same time allows the Secretary of State, once his expenditure totals are set, to treat these as a block within which he can reallocate. Within the Scottish Office there is what Parry (1982) has called a 'mini PESC' with the Management Group and Central Services assisting the Secretary of State in reaching decisions. In practice, however, the scope for reallocation of spending is limited. Past patterns of spending determine future to a considerable extent and any shift implying a policy change will need to be cleared with the Treasury and the Whitehall network. In any case, Central Services does not have the analytical capacity or the bargaining leverage over the Scottish Office departments to conduct a Scottish PESC. There is thus no overall Scottish view of public spending but rather a series of reactions to decisions taken at UK level, though of course the Secretary of State is party to these. Some reallocations have, nevertheless, been made for Scotland. In 1982, George Younger allocated rather less to transport and housing and rather more to education and law than the comparable English and Welsh programmes.

When the Secretary of State has finalised the Scottish Office expenditure programmes, however, that is not the end of the story. Just over half the expenditure in the Secretary of State's block is passed on to Scotland's sixty-five local authorities who are able again to reallocate spending among services. The main transfers take place through the Rate Support Grant and Housing Support Grant (discussed later). Rate Support Grant is negotiated between the Scottish Office and the Convention of Scottish Local Authorities (COSLA). First, a figure is set for Relevant Expenditure, the total of local government spending on which grant will be payable. An Aggregate Grant is then set as a percentage of this and divided into three elements: Domestic Element is a subsidy to domestic ratepayers set at a standard rate for Scotland; Resource Element compensates poor authorities by equalising the income raised for a penny rate on a per capita basis; Needs Element gives more to authorities with greater assessed needs. The Needs Element is distributed in three stages: first, among regions and islands authorities; secondly between regional and district councils within each region; thirdly among the districts within each region. Local authorities are able to supplement their RSG allocation by levying higher rates, so that any target the government might set for overall levels of public spending is dependent crucially on the response of local authorities. In transmitting central directives to cut spending to local authorities, the Secretary of State finds himself the 'man in the middle'. He is required by the Treasury to contribute Scotland's share of expenditure cuts and to force austerity on local authorities. On the other hand, as a 'spending minister' and as 'Scotland's Minister' he will argue with the Treasury for Scotland to be allowed more, via the Barnett formula or local authority spending.

While the Secretary of State is responsible for the final figures, then, he is open to influence. For example, when the initial target of 7½% reduction in local expenditures was being discussed in 1979, the Convention argued this was impossible. The Secretary of State's role as spending minister required him to argue this case with the Treasury, who gave him a favourable hearing, and the final target cut was much less than anticipated. Similarly, COSLA's advice that cuts ought to fall predominantly on capital expenditure was accepted.

The Rate Support Grant and Housing Support Grant settlements are announced around November. In 1982-3, the announcement was delayed until January 1982, reflecting the delay in setting the overall level of public expenditure because of disagreements between Treasury and spending ministers. Local authorities have complained that the settlement comes too late to influence their budget decisions, and for 1983-4 the Scottish Office made an interim announcement in the late summer of 1982 to give broad guidance to councils on the likely level of government support.

Expenditure managment and control

Over the years, the Public Expenditure Survey has seen a change in emphasis. From the mid 1950s to the mid 1970s, the main focus of macro-economic policies was demand management, with public expenditure as an important component of the strategy. The aim was to plan for public expenditure levels which would be consistent with likely available resources. In practice, there was much greater emphasis on "planning" rather than "controlling" public expenditure. The annual review of government plans was, until 1982, planned and controlled in "volume" terms, by using constant prices. The review was based on prices prevailing at the time the survey began, a constant price base rolled forward each year.

The use of constant prices brought some benefits for planning and decision-making, in assisting operational decisions, the accurate measurement of resource inputs, and assisting in the discussion of a change in priorities. However, the weakness of this approach as a system for controlling public expenditure was that once decisions had been taken on a constant price basis, the cash needed to finance the agreed volume was provided automatically, irrespective of inflation, and this flaw was revealed dramatically in the period of hyper-inflation from 1973-6. In 1975-6, outturn expenditure was £5 billion greater than planned in 1971, leading to allegations that public expenditure was out of control. The rapid expansion of public spending between 1973-75, financed by borrowing in a period of high inflation and aimed at maintaining the level of economic activity in the recession, resulted in a 'crisis of confidence' in sterling and the negotiation of a loan from the International Monetary Fund, with the condition that the Public Sector Borrowing Requirement would be reduced by cuts in public spending.

This period marked the change of emphasis in economic policy away from full employment through demand management to controlling inflation by a tight monetary and fiscal policy. The new mechanisms for controlling public expenditure were cash limits and the financial information system. First introduced in 1976-7, Cash Limits are administrative ceilings representing the maximum amount which the government propose should be spent on the service during the coming financial year.

There are now around 160 blocks of capital and current expenditure covered by Cash Limits, and each spending authority has to manage within its cash block. Cash Limits now cover around 60% of public expenditure, the main excpetions being demand-determined expenditures such as welfare benefits, and some aspects of industrial policy. Cash Limits apply to three groups in the public sector, central departments and their agencies, local authorities, and nationalised industries. In the case of central departments, they are administered in two blocks, one for non-pay costs, and one for pay and administrative costs. For local government, they apply to Rate Support Grant and most capital expenditure. For nationalised industries, Cash Limits only apply to the External Financing Limit, and not on current spending. The EFL relates to the difference between each industry's capital expenditure plans and its ability to generate financial resources internally from revenue and depreciation provisions.

The logic of Cash Limits is devastatingly simple. When inflation exceeds that allowed for, the volume of service should be reduced so that expenditure remains with the Cash Limit. The early result of Cash Limits was underspending of programmes by a substantial 7% in 1977-78, much greater than the planned cuts of 3%. By 1978-79, however, the degree of under-spending was being reduced. Unfortunately, the expenditure plans of the incoming Conservative Government were based on a return to actual expenditure in 1977-78, the year of the biggest underspend! Since 1979-80, despite a more overt political commitment to the restraint/ reduction of public expenditure, the divergence between planned and actual expenditure has now widened. This is perhaps not surprising, given the incremental nature of public spending, the culture of Whitehall and the role of spending ministers, for only in years of extreme crisis (1967, 1977) have severe cuts in planned expenditure been achieved. Whilst there has been a shift of priorities *within* the public sector, total public spending has grown because of increased welfare benefits, and the ability of local government to resist cuts in grant by increasing rates. This has led the current government to utilise Cash Limits for means other than financial control.

Cash Limits originally were introduced as a control system grafted on to the volume system of planning. They prevented public expenditure from rising automatically as a result of unforeseen price increases without questioning the priority attributed to programmes in the light of changed circumstances. The system, however, is heavily dependent on accuracy in forecasting, so that government decided its volume plans in the light of the best available estimates. In recent years, given the reluctance of spending ministers to accept the necessity of spending cuts, one way round this has been to set unrealistic Cash Limits which inevitably require a reduction of the planned volume of expenditure in mid-financial year. A succinct quote from one participant in the process was found in the *Guardian* of 15 January 1980.

> "We have a great argument about the volume of spending next year. When the Treasury is defeated by the forces of the anti-Christ, they regroup and try again through the back door of Cash Limits."

In the absence of a coherent prices and incomes policy, then, the prevailing tendency is for government to fix Cash Limits in terms of what they would like inflation to be rather than what it is likely to be. The result is a somewhat arbitrary and inequitable 'pay policy'. Whilst the government has argued that this cash limit is not a "norm", but a block within which there can be variation, the reality is that it becomes a 'minimum' level of settlement, with higher increases in the public sector organisations less dependent on government finance. Central departments and their agencies, for instance, have little scope for manoeuvre now that "staging" is frowned upon. Local authorities, however, have some discretion via local rates. Minimum settlements are generally 1-2% *above* RSG Cash Limit, with "special cases" like the police, fire and water services in excess of this settlement. Finally, in the nationalised industries, flexibility is determined by the degree of dependence on government to finance a deficit, by the ability to increase prices, and by the proportion of costs attributable to pay. The result is that more "powerful" groups of workers like miners, electricity supply workers, or water engineers can negotiate increases substantially above the public sector target.

Cash limits did not, however, have a cumulative effect. The focus on volume planning required the updating of the price base as the first stage in the next expenditure planning process. The Treasury view is that this system gave programme managers little incentive to adapt their expenditures in response to the annual cash limits. Expenditure savings made to accommodate the pressure of cash limits were not carried forward into future plans. Whilst cash limits succeed in restraining expenditure in the short term, they are not effective as a way of ensuring long-term reductions in public expenditure.

The government's answer to this problem is to convert the planning system into a *cash basis*, bringing it into line with the control system. As a result, changes in the revaluation in PES will no longer result in the *actual* movements in pay and prices being reflected in the base budget, which made good retrospectively any inflationary squeeze due to previous cash limits, thus putting an end to automatic compensation in the subsequent year for unrealistic cash limits. In the government's view, this will result in efficiency savings being carried forward. This is problematic, for unrealistic cash limits are not normally met by efficiency savings, but short-term expediencies such as temporary freezing of vacancies or delay of implementing new projects. Government argue that the volume system did not supply any pressure to reduce costs, but costs *have been* reduced, nevertheless. Cash planning is, therefore, a device which emphasises cutting expenditure rather than controlling expenditure.

Mr Younger, in his evidence to the Select Committee on Scottish Affairs, argued that the volume system was inflationary. Managers of programmes saw the volume figures as an inflation-proof entitlement and they gave no adequate measure or incentive towards efficiency or value for money. However, the gap between actual cost increases and government forecasts in recent years has been so large that it is extremely doubtful if such a gap could be met by efficiency savings on an annual basis, particularly as most public services are labour intensive. Cash limits have already led to stop-go tactics. Spending agencies are told at the beginning of the financial year that money is short, then later on when underspending becomes likely, are urged to commit new expenditures before the end of the financial year. These may *not* be priorities, but have the simple virtue that the expenditure can be incurred before 31st March. David Heald (1982) has argued that the absence of volume figures make the development of expenditure priorities within Scottish Office expenditure programmes more difficult to identify, and the figures give little "feel" of what is happening to service levels.

Unless government forecasts of inflation become more realistic, then the Public Expenditure Survey process will degenerate into a crude system of financial control with wasteful use of resources. Indeed, the very phrase, cash planning, is something of a misnomer, as the figures give little useful indication of service developments. Choices about priorities are in fact avoided, and concealed under the mystique of 'efficiency'. The political choices about cuts are being clouded by tinkering with the expenditure system. The government's difficulty has been reinforced by its own priorities for cutting public spending being heavily dependent on local government to implement them, revealing the tension between a centralised expenditure system and a decentralised political system.

The local government expenditure issue
The expenditure programmes of local government in total account for 52% of public expenditure in Scotland under the direction of the Secretary of State. This makes it important for two reasons, one political, and the other, administrative. First, the Conservative Government identified local authority services as the policy areas where its planned expenditure reductions will take place. The other major area of spending, health, had

expenditure growth built in, meaning that bigger reductions in local government spending would be necessary if the overall reduction in public expenditure was to be achieved. Second, the mechanics of the Public Expenditure Survey system require government departments to spend within their cash limits. Rateborne expenditure is *included* within the Treasury definition of public expenditure, and therefore the Secretary of State does require to maintain a great influence over local spending of he is to keep his expenditure programmes within the Treasury's cash limits. This arrangement creates an inevitable tension between central control and local discretion, for it would be remarkable if the spending decisions of sixty-five diverse local authorities in aggregate met the target of central government.

Academic studies of central-local relations have traditionally drawn a distinction between the *agent* and *partnership* models of the relationship. Under the *agent* model, local authorities have little or no discretion over matters of policy, and the relationship is a hierarchical one. Local authorities merely administer national policies under the supervision of central departments. Under the *partnership* model, local authorities and central departments are co-equals under Parliament. Local government has a degree of choice over policy and the extent of pattern of expenditure and service provision. The rhetoric of the Scottish Office for most of the period since reorganisation has been that the 'proper' relationship was one of constructive partnership in a common cause. Moreover, the distinctive features of those relations have attracted much attention by both practitioners and academics in the post-reorganisation period (Layfield 1976, CPRS 1978, Stewart 1977, Page 1978). The pattern of central-local relations in Scotland was viewed favourably as having lessons to offer the rest of the UK. The existence of only one government department responsible to one minister; the existence of only one local authority association, and relatively small number of authorities, led to the assumption of closer, more corporate, relations. The development of the family of plans, Regional Reports, Structure Plans, Financial Plans, Transport Policies and Programmes, and Housing Plans, reflected the philosophy of disengagement which was regarded as providing a basis for a constructive partnership between centre and locality. These assist the centre in strategic decision-making, and allow local determination of priorities (Midwinter 1980).

The election of a Conservative Government in 1979 with a manifesto commitment to reduce central controls was further welcomed in some quarters, yet after only two years, David Scott of *The Scotsman* newspaper wrote of the deterioration of the relationships being the dominant theme of the annual conference of the Scottish Branch of the Rating and Valuation Association, and the Association of Metropolitan Authorities took the unique step of intervening in Scottish affairs, claiming that changes proposed in the Local Government (Miscellaneous Provisions) (Scotland) Bill would shift the balance of power even further towards the government and could spell the end of local democracy.

Page has argued (1978) that in fact there are factors in the financial framework which suggest 'central control' should be easier in Scotland. Local government receives a larger proportion of its total funds from government grants than do English authorities. Capital expenditure is also higher, and is seen as being subject to stringent control. The local expenditure issue has been the dominant feature of central-local relationships since reorganisation, and is a crucial element of public expenditure decision-making. The Conservative Government may be prosecuting the policy with greater ideological commitment than their Labour predecessors, but the difference in practice has been of degree rather than substance. This has led inevitably to some ambivalence in central-local relations. Whilst both parties have made manifesto commitments to the concept of local democracy, they have become increasingly concerned to control local spending whatever the source of revenue. Thus the rates, which have long been seen as providing a degree of independence to local government, have become the object of increasing central concern, reflecting their status as an 'uncontrollable' aspect in the Public Expenditure Survey System (Wright 1977). Whilst capital expenditure requires the consent of the Secretary of State, no such statutory control exists with regard to the levying of the rate. What then are the mechanisms by which central government influences local spending decisions?

It should be emphasised that what central government is concerned to control is not *gross* local authority expenditure but *net* expenditure, i.e. the proportion of total expenditure financed by central government grant and the local rates. There are both *before* and *after the event* controls on revenue spending. First, the Secretary of State can adjust the total sum of relevant expenditure on which grant is payable. From 1977-1981, this could be affected in two ways; by adjusting the *base* (which was determined in volume terms), or by fixing a cash limit which was considerably below the likely level of inflation. The new cash planning system does not distinguish between these two factors, making it difficult to have any objective analysis of the real changes in grant which are taking place.

Second, the Secretary of State can adjust the *percentage* of relevant expenditure provided by central government. This was increased from 68% to 75% in the first two years after reorganisation but has since been reduced progressively to the current 61% for 1983-4. The implication of such a cut is to transfer the burden of financing expenditure from central to local government. In theory, rates ought to rise to compensate. In practice, it is a means of applying the "squeeze" on local government. For example, in 1977-8, Bruce Millan reduced the level of support from 75% to 71%, on the grounds that when grant was high, expenditure was high, and effected the most dramatic *fall* in local spending in the post-reorganisation period; indeed, local authorities underspent central targets that year.

Third, the Secretary of State can adjust the formula by which grant is distributed, either by altering the relevant factors in the needs element of RSG, of by adjusting the share of needs and resources elements in the grant. David Heald (1980b) has argued that the needs element is devised to produce the desired pattern of grant allocation.

The Secretary of State can also exert pressure on local government through the issuing of current expenditure guidelines. These give authorities an *indication* of the level of expenditure consistent with the provisions of the Rate Support Grant settlement against which they can plan their own spending but they are not *mandatory*. There have been four stages of development in six years. The first set of guidelines (1977-8) were calculated on the basis of historic budgets. In 1980, this was changed to base the guidelines on 1978 outturn figures. In 1981, the guidelines were issued pro rata with grant entitlements under Rate Support Grant, and in 1982, to the current system known as the Client Group Approach. The guidelines have assumed increasing importance as a key factor under the new Local Government (Miscellaneous Provisions) (Scotland) Act, 1981.

There are now important after the event controls on expenditure, namely abatement (commonly known as 'clawback'), and the Local Government (Miscellaneous Provisions) (Scotland) Act, 1981 (hereinafter described as the Miscellaneous Provisions Act). Clawback is the term being used to describe the withdrawal of grant across the board because councils have incurred 'overspending' in previous years. The new powers under the Miscellaneous Provisions Act increase the government's ability to effect *individual* authorities, and introduce a major change in constitutional principle, whereby the government can now order a reduction in planned expenditure *and*, under the Local Government and Planning Act 1982, order an adjustment in rate levels, in cases where he has convinced Parliament that the councils' planned expenditure is excessive and unreasonable (Midwinter, Keating and Taylor 1982).

Housing expenditure is subject to a separate system, being divided into three categories: Housing Support Grant, payable by central government to local authorities in much the same way as Rate Support Grant; Rate Fund Contribution, the amount local authorities themselves pay out of the rates to subsidise council house rents; and Capital Allocations, the amount the Scottish Office allows local authorities to spend on the capital programme for housing each year. Council house rents themselves do not count as part of this system though in recent years central government has been reducing Housing Support Grant, so forcing councils to put up rents or the Rate Fund Contribution or both. Recently, the government has been trying to ensure that the necessary increases fall on rents rather than the Rate Fund Contribution and thus the rates by reducing Capital Allocations where Rate Fund Contributions have been above targets which it has set. So it has attempted to link up the various elements of the system to strengthen central control.

How, then, have these mechanisms been used, and how successful have they been, in the post-reorganisation period? To understand recent events it is necessary to review the development of local finance over a longer period.

In the 1950s local expenditure grew relatively slowly. Over the whole period 1948-59 the increase in expenditure was only 15% in real terms. From the mid 1960s onwards local services and expenditure developed at a faster rate. Even when inflation is taken into account, local expenditure on Rate Fund services *doubled* in the period from 1964 to 1975, and as the Layfield Report pointed out, the major part of this growth was funded by increased central grant, thus sheltering the ratepayer from the true cost of increasing local services.

Local government reorganisation in 1975 coincided with a changed approach to local spending, after more than twenty years of expenditure growth. The RSG order for 1975/76 called for a *reduction in the rate of growth* by local government. Although it raised the percentage of expenditure to be financed by government grant from 68% to 75%, it allowed for only 3.8% growth in relevant local expenditure. However, the momentum of expenditure cannot be reversed overnight, and spending was *5% above* that figure. By 1976-77 the emphasis was on *standstill budgets*, the cash limit system, and 'indicative guidelines' were issued to individual authorities which suggested to them the level of spending consistent with the provision of the RSG order. The intriguing feature of the squeeze on local government is that with regard to net expenditure, government were prepared to sanction 'growth', and the 'cuts' were enforced by reducing the percentage support (thus inviting rate increases) and by cash limits being generally around 3% less than the actual cost increases. Government could thus claim they were 'maintaining' expenditure levels while reducing their own contribution to local spending.

1979/80 saw a change in tactics, as the Labour Government's incomes policy had ended and it was through the cash limit system that the squeeze was enforced, the allowance being almost 7% *below* the eventual level of cost increases. The Labour Government, of course, were in the run-up to an election. At the same time, they announced a growth of 3% in volume expenditure, which was eliminated by the shortfall in cash limit. One other important feature was the change of the distribution formula which gave a greater share of the resources to urban districts and Strathclyde in particular, the Labour heartland. This year had a crucial implication for later years. Given the imminence of the general election and district elections in 1980, authorities were keen to have low rate increases and budgeted in accordance with the cash limit guidelines and eliminated balances, with resultant deficits which would have to be funded in subsequent years.

The Conservative election victory of 1979 led to a more enthusiastic approach to cutting local spending, much of which it had been assumed would be achieved by the elimination of 'waste', and the reduction of bureaucracy. The first finance circular issued to local authorities offered a sharp contrast to Labour's assessment of the "welcome recovery of some aspects of the economy" by drawing attention to the "serious decline in the British economy in recent years", which pointed out that local budgets were 3.3% in excess of RSG settlement, and that budgets should be reduced to that level, and that the government intended to seek a 7½% *reduction* in 1980-1, with "the prospect of *continuing* and *increasing* reductions in future years". They increased the allowance for inflation inherited by the Labour Government, but not by the full amount, which was some £35m short of actual cost increases. Over the next two full RSG settlements, the government modified their targets in volume terms, to 2.3% in 1980/1 (from 7½%, but with cuts of 10% in Housing Support Grant and 9% in capital expenditure) and 2.7% in 1981-2. Two trends became apparent, however. The tendency of enforcing the squeeze through the cash limit was continued (Midwinter and Page 1981) and in 1981-2, changes in the distribution formula withdrew grants from urban districts and increased the share of rural authorities, and ironically, in 'wealthy' councils such as Central Region and Edinburgh District. This is because the Secretary of State changed the ratio of the needs and resources element of RSG from 4:1 to 7:1 in 1980 and 9:1 in 1981, which Heald (1980) has seen as an attempt to punish profligate Labour authorities. In the case of Lothian Region, this cost them £20m, which was a major cause of their rate increase.

One difference does emerge, however. Whilst Labour succeeded in achieving spending restrictions in 1977-78, and then maintained that level overall for the next two years, *actual* revenue spending in total has not fallen under the Conservative Government. Outturn for 1980-1 was around 3% above, and for 1981-2 was about 5% above the government's target, which means the overall spending has been maintained, although some councils have reduced whilst others have increased their spending and funded it from the rates. In the main, the reductions in expenditure fall on capital budgets. So whereas local spending in aggregate was broadly in line with the plans of the Labour councils, overall councils have not made the further cuts sought by the Conservative Government. The result, in a period of high inflation, inadequate cash limits, has been high rates increases. Rates is an issue which affects the client groups which support the Conservative Party. There is no doubt that the high rates increases brought increasing pressure from domestic ratepayers and business interests. The evidence is that government policy was an important contributory factor to those increases (Midwinter 1981) but the government have managed somewhat successfully to present these as the result of "profligate" local government. The Conservative Party Conference of 1980 had numerous motions calling for controls on local government spending. More militant Labour councillors had emerged in control of Lothian, Dundee and Stirling, who were unwilling to accept the traditional consensus on central government's terms, and indeed were eager for a showdown over public expenditure, particularly, as they saw it, after the performance of the previous Labour Government on this issue. The government therefore sought selective powers, which it could use to bring the few left-wing councils into line.

The Local Government (Miscellaneous Provisions) (Scotland) Act of 1981 amended an existing power of a 1966 Act, which allowed the withdrawal of Rate Support Grant *retrospectively* from an authority which has engaged in 'excessive and unreasonable' expenditure, to allow him to exercise this power *prospectively* in relation to budgets. In deciding whether planned expenditure was excessive and unreasonable, the Secretary of State was to have regard to:

(a)   the expenditure or estimated expenses in that or any preceding year, of other local authorities which are, in the opinion of the Secretary of State closely comparable (or as closely comparable as is practicable) with the local authority concerned;

(b)   to general economic conditions;

(c)   to such other criteria as he considers appropriate.

In June 1981, the Secretary of State announced he would be taking action against seven councils: Lothian Region, and Cumnock and Doon Valley, Dundee, Dumbarton, East Lothian, Renfrew and Stirling District Councils, seeking reductions in expenditure of £76m. Under the Act, the Secretary of State must inform the local authority why he is proposing to reduce RSG, and allow them to make representations. So there then followed a lengthy and complex process of negotiation and bargaining. The government's methodology has been under severe criticism (Heald *et al* 1982; Sewel and Young 1981; Midwinter 1981), and later research showed that two factors of crucial importance to the government were considerably flawed, the use of guidelines, and the use of rate poundages (Midwinter, Keating and Taylor 1982). The guidelines have no legal status, they are not approved by Parliament, and have always been regarded as indicative. With four changes of methodology in six years, there is an element of volatility. For example, in 1981-2, only five of the sixty-five authorities were at or below their guidelines, and twenty-eight councils more than 20% above.

Table 10.4

DEGREE OF EXCESS OF LOCAL AUTHORITY BUDGETS OVER
SCOTTISH OFFICE GUIDELINES

% Above Guidelines	*1981-82*	*1982-83*
	Number of Councils	
	%	%
On Target	5	9
1 to 10% above	17	27
11 to 20% above	14	22
21 to 30% above	15	5
31 to 40% above	10	Nil
Over 40% above	4	2
Scottish average	8.9%	8.3%

In 1982-3, the disparity *between* authorities had been reduced, till only seven councils were 20% or more above guidelines. Yet little change occurred in the total gap between central targets and local budgets. Dramatic changes in guidelines brought some members of the 1981 "hit list" (e.g. Dundee) back into the mainstream of local spending without any great changes in their budgets. The guidelines have been the subject of much criticism by local authorities, and their credibility challenged so that COSLA have now formally requested the government to end the practice of issuing guidelines.

It is the use of rate poundages which is perhaps the most serious flaw in the methodology. Expenditure growth is only one factor which contributes to rate increases. The use of balances, changes in the level and structure of grant, cash limits, and changes in the value of the penny rate product, all affect authorities in different ways. Even more critically for district councils, a major factor in determining rates is the decision on the Rate Fund Contribution to the Housing Revenue Account, which is *not* considered as part of relevant expenditure to which the Act refers. As Midwinter, Keating and Taylor (1982) have shown, the use of rate poundage "saved" several councils, which had incurred greater increases in expenditure than some of the councils on Mr Younger's list, from selective action.

The process of negotiation culminated in spending reductions of about £34m, less than half the target. The Act requires a time-consuming process, whose virtue as a means of expenditure control lies more in bringing into play the "law of anticipated reactions" in council budgeting.

Control and accountability in public expenditure

Britain has a highly centralist public expenditure system. Concern to control public spending, and a centralist interpretation of the framework needed to exercise that control, has resulted in the failure to devise an economically acceptable form of taxation for a Scottish Assembly under Labour, or any serious alternative to domestic rates under the Conservatives. Scottish public expenditure is determined by the government of the day, which means that patterns of expenditure will change in a uniform way, although the expenditure needs of the various areas of Great Britain may be moving in different directions.

The Treasury insistence on controlling all public expenditure has resulted in a constitutional conflict with local authorities. The ambiguity and confusion of the partnership concept was unproblematic during a period of expenditure growth and political consensus. Cutback and political polarisation have demonstrated the absence of a coherent framework for accountable government.

Central government has consistently tried to shift the 'blame' for high levels of public spending on to local government. Yet, during the period 1975-81, while central government spending grew by 10.7%, local government spending actually *fell* by 16%. It is true that most of the cuts in local expenditure were in capital spending, putting the cost of adjustment onto private sector contractors. But, while this may be a problem in itself, it was not something about which the government should have been concerned if, as the Treasury maintains, it is *total* expenditure that matters.

Why should cutting revenue expenditure be so difficult? It is partly because few politicians are willing to contemplate the redundancies and closures this would entail. Reliance on non-filling of vacancies means a much slower process of cutting than the government would have liked, but manpower levels have been falling in 1982. Moreover, there is tremendous pressure from the public and interest groups to maintain current services. The CBI view that revenue can be cut whilst capital spending is increased is really unrealistic within the public services. Most public services are labour intensive, and even capital intensive expenditure (such as roads or sewerage) generates revenue spending in the form of new running costs.

Few politicians themselves are enthusiastic "cutters". We quoted earlier examples of Conservative ministers seeing success as diminishing cuts or increasing spending. This is equally true at the local level. In 1979, Brian Meek, the leader of the Tory Group in Lothian Region, argued that the initial cutbacks in council spending should not be too savage, for even

Conservative-controlled authorities would baulk at slashing long-planned schemes they had promised their electorate. Leonard Turpie, Tory leader in Strathclyde, argued that large cuts (7½%) were not possible in one year and should be phased over three years. The minority Conservative administration in Glasgow argued that Glasgow was a special case and should not suffer to the same extent as elsewhere in Scotland. Borders Region, whose convener was a senior member of the Conservative Party in Scotland, announced that no further cuts could be made in 1981-2. Tayside Region, a Conservative authority, have lobbied both governments for extra capital allocations. The block allocation system permits *both sides* to blame the other for the non-provision of specific amenities. Scottish Office ministers will reply to parliamentary questions on specific projects by MPs that priorities are a matter for the local council to decide, while local government will argue that their allocations are too small.

Confusion has been commonplace over the Miscellaneous Provisions Act, for there has been little discussion of the change in principle in central-local relations from a concern by the centre with local spending in general, to controlling the specific actions of individual authorities. Mr Younger astutely presented the bill as being necessary to control 'profligate' Labour councils, thus avoiding conflict over inroads to local autonomy with local Conservative groups. Edinburgh Conservative MPs in the Commons saw the bill as a way of controlling Lothian Region, and their contributions to debates focussed on their budgeting record rather than central-local relations. Labour MPs responded equally polemically, promising to ensure Tayside Region did not cut so far that statutory obligations were not met. Perhaps Labour's strength in local government in Scotland actually assisted the Secretary of State in ignoring the constitutional implications of his proposals. He has presented it successfully as being necessary to control excessive spending and protect ratepayers. The public debate, therefore, has confused rather than clarified issues. Mr Younger has blamed high rates increases on high spending, when high rates increases were being incurred in authorities regarded as moderate (Tayside, Central, Strathclyde). Local authorities rhetoric predicting the end of local democracy is equally exaggerated. There has been an erosion of the margins of choice, but considerable diversity over rates and spending is occurring.

But the arguments that local spending can frustrate central public expenditure control, and thus economic management, have little substance. The centralist case is not supported by the facts. Pursuit of excessively tight expenditure control, however, has resulted in a deterioration in central-local relationships, and demonstrated the limitations of the partnership concept when local democracy rests on no constitutional guarantees and a fragile political base. If local democracy had been more strongly rooted, it might have prevented the centre from unilaterally altering the rules as events evolved. As it was, the centre could not rely on the electorate to exercise its sanction on the few high-spending councils.

Table 10.1

Index GB = 100

REGIONALLY RELEVANT PUBLIC EXPENDITURE 1969/70-1973-74 AVERAGE PER CAPITA

Programme	N	YH	EM	EA	SE	SW	WM	NW	W	S
Agriculture, fisheries and forestry	120.0	98.9	103.3	277.8	55.6	163.3	71.1	36.7	174.7	201.3
Trade, industry and employment	210.1	60.7	117.6	61.4	64.0	119.1	59.6	111.2	150.6	171.9
Roads and Transport	129.2	81.9	66.3	87.2	95.9	123.9	86.8	104.9	214.7	113.6
Housing	111.3	68.8	66.8	77.9	126.0	56.0	74.3	87.7	79.3	149.3
Other Environmental Services	93.0	85.3	95.4	117.2	100.0	108.1	88.1	97.2	121.0	112.6
Law, Order and Protective Services	96.6	76.9	89.8	81.6	121.1	93.9	83.0	95.9	88.4	98.6
Education and Libraries, Science and Arts	93.4	91.9	93.6	101.5	107.0	89.4	89.9	94.5	101.7	116.5
Health and Personal Social Services	89.4	92.7	91.3	90.5	109.7	98.4	84.8	94.0	103.0	113.3
Social Security	112.8	104.4	93.1	92.9	93.2	103.7	91.1	107.2	117.2	105.3
Total	110.9	89.3	90.3	95.6	100.8	98.6	84.7	98.0	111.2	120.9
Central Government	116.0	93.1	91.7	98.2	94.5	106.6	83.0	99.4	118.5	123.4
Local Authorities	104.1	85.1	86.6	86.9	111.4	85.0	85.9	95.8	98.8	117.3
Public Corporations	98.0	69.7	117.2	170.7	83.8	122.2	105.1	98.0	137.4	120.2
Current Expenditure	104.3	95.3	93.6	93.9	99.9	101.0	86.3	97.5	111.1	118.7
Capital Expenditure	131.2	71.2	80.6	100.8	103.9	91.2	79.7	99.7	111.9	128.1

The index is calculated as per capita expenditure as a percentage of per capita GB expenditure on relevant functions.
Source: John Short, "Public Expenditure in the English Regions," in B. W. Hogwood and M. Keating (eds.), *Regional Government in England* (Oxford, 1982).

Key:
N	North (of England)	YH	Yorkshire and Humberside	EM	East Midlands	EA	East Anglia
SE	South East	SW	South West	WM	West Midlands	NW	North West
W	Wales	S	Scotland				

Table 10.2

Index UK = 100

IDENTIFIABLE PUBLIC EXPENDITURE IN SCOTLAND

OUTTURNS (£ million cash)

	1976-77		1977-78		1978-79		1979-80		1980-81	
	£m	index	£m	index	£m	index	£m	index	£m	index
Agriculture, Fisheries, Food and Forestry	148	200	125	200	106	167	161	194	194	211
Industry, Energy, Trade and Employment	426	216	356	197	386	174	385	163	522	155
Transport	236	110	273	132	327	140	376	138	455	142
Housing	559	123	572	131	610	136	780	138	801	140
Other Environmental Services	311	130	312	125	375	131	470	140	535	139
Law, Order and Protective Services	177	97	187	95	214	95	278	100	344	100
Education, Science, Arts and Libraries	908	117	956	117	1073	119	1213	117	1512	122
Health and Personal Social Services	794	117	883	117	1026	120	1232	121	1550	119
Social Security	1105	102	1340	103	1547	101	1869	103	2087	96
Other Public Services	137	126	140	180	154	187	176	179	216	183
Common Services	32	75	36	87	39	78	40	80	57	100
Government lending to Nationalised Industries	−1	—	40	—	14	—	217	—	466	—
Scottish Identifiable Expenditure	4832	120	5220	120	5871	119	7197	121	8739	121

Table compiled by David Heald from *Hansard*, 8 December 1981, Cmnd. 8494-1 and Cmnd. 8494-11.

Table 10.3

SECRETARY OF STATE'S EXPENDITURE (PROGRAMME 15) AS PERCENTAGE
OF SCOTTISH AND UK EXPENDITURE

	1976-77 £m	*1977-78* £m	*1978-79* £m	*1979-80* £m	*1980-81* £m
Expenditure on Programme 15	3060	3234	3679	4423	5292
Programme 15 as % of Scottish Indentifiable Expenditure	63.3	61.95	62.66	61.46	60.56
Programme 15 as % of Planning Total	5.60	5.66	5.58	5.73	5.66

Notes: The index is calculated as per capita identifiable expenditure in Scotland as a percentage of UK identifiable expenditure per capita on relevant functions.

Table compiled by David Heald from *Hansard*, 8 December 1981, Cmnd. 8494-1 and Cmnd. 8494-11.

CONCLUSIONS

CHAPTER ELEVEN

THE FUTURE OF SCOTTISH DEMOCRACY

We have in these pages described the main institutions of *Scottish* government, that is, those which are peculiar to Scotland; and we have analysed the process of policy making. We have seen how policy outcomes depend on a complex interplay of Scottish and UK elements. What has become clear is that the UK element is usually dominant, that areas of Scottish autonomy are tolerated as long as they do not infringe on UK priorities or concern relatively non-controversial matters. Two questions remain to be asked about the system — is it effective? and is it democratic and accountable?

Effectiveness is a difficult concept which could be measured in any of a variety of ways. Scotland has a system of government which is generally honest and bureaucratically efficient. Policies are made, adapted and applied in Scotland; public services are administered. Indeed, some Scottish innovations have won admiration elsewhere in the UK. The regions provide local government units large enough to plan and, potentially at least, powerful enough to engage many of the problems faced by deprived communities. Their existence and that of a Scottish level of central administration in Edinburgh cuts out the need for many of the regional offices joint committees and *ad hoc* agencies found in the English regions (Hogwood and Keating 1982). Policy initiatives like the Social Work (Scotland) Act of 1968 and institutional innovations like the SDA and the HIDB have aroused interest elsewhere in the UK and beyond. Special Scottish interests can be taken up at UK level; and Scotland has got more than its share of public expenditure. Public acceptance of the system of government is high in comparison, for instance, with Northern Ireland; and social stability is greater than in many parts of England.

However, all is not well with the system of government in Scotland. While St Andrew's House and the regional councils are evidence of some recognition of the need for co-ordination and integration of government activities at these levels, Scottish government, like that of the rest of the UK, remains riddled with functional divisions both within and between public agencies. At the local authority level, regions and districts have found co-operation notoriously difficult (Keating and Midwinter 1983) though the complementary nature of their functions — housing with social work, strategic with local planning for example — makes it imperative for effective government. At the small area, community level, both tiers of local government, central government and agencies like the SDA and the Health Boards agree on the need for a common information base and a common policy approach yet in practice have found this difficult to achieve.

At the Scottish level, too, despite the administrative achievements of the Scottish Office, there is cause for concern. Functional and departmental divisions within the Scottish Office together with the strength of 'policy leadership' from Whitehall departments undermine much of the potential for innovation and for a comprehensive examination of Scotland's problems. We have seen, for instance, that the Scottish Office's economic and industrial powers, acquired piecemeal over the years, give it some scope for independent action but for the most part force it to work in a lobbying role within Whitehall. The establishment of the SDD in the 1960s was a Scottish innovation but later developments followed the English pattern in separating the departments responsible for economic and physical planning. This would be even more of a problem if there was any serious economic planning being done within SEPD; but there is no Scottish economic plan — nor a social or physical one, for that matter. So much of the potential of a Scottish level of government is being lost. The Scottish Office can fight last-ditch battles to defend Scotland's steel industry or independent banking sector, but there is little by way of a forward strategy. The SDA has tried to look ahead, to seek out opportunities, to innovate, but is handicapped by its limited power and resources — and neither could be substantially increased to a non-elected body.

UK policy leadership, perhaps inevitable while the Scottish Office is part of central government and a unified civil service exists, results in unsuitable policies being forced on Scotland for the sake of administrative and political consistency. Everyone will have his own list of these but one might mention council house sales; the bungled housing repairs grants scheme of 1982; the pay beds legislation of the 1970s. Whatever the political merits of the basic principles behind these initiatives, their form and timing failed to take into account the distinctive circumstances in Scotland.

The effectiveness of the system is further undermined by its sheer complexity. With UK and Scottish levels of central government, two tiers of local government and an array of miscellaneous agencies and 'quangos', the implementation of major physical, economic and social renewal programmes can become a nightmare. Effective implementation of major projects requires a strong lead agency to plan and cajole and the capacity to negotiate strategies and resources to meet the programme's aims. We saw some evidence of the SDA doing this in its area projects but, quite apart from its limited role and capacity, it suffers from the political weakness of being a non-elected agency.

Nor should the system's survival and apparent public acquiescence lead us into complacency. The elaborate device for containing Scottish demands within the framework of the United Kingdom came close to collapse in the 1970s when the political parties sustaining them found themselves outbid. Traditionally, they had argued that any increase in autonomy for Scotland would result in material loss, as access to the UK level was prejudiced. The SNP challenged this autonomy — wealth trade-off by promising both. Few people now believe that North Sea oil could, in itself, resurrect Scottish industry and employment; but faith in UK solutions, too, has declined as regional policy has found itself, in the recession, with very little spare resources to redistribute northwards. We have seen how table-thumping by the Secretary of State is no longer effective in boosting Scotland's share of public spending. The 'Barnett formula' can be no more than a holding operation before the big battles about Scottish spending resume. Further challenges to the system can already be discerned, within as well as outwith the main parties and the system seems as little equipped to respond as it was last time round.

What all this points to is the weakness of the political as opposed to the purely 'administrative' element in Scottish government. At local level, democracy is weakened by increasing central controls such as those of the Miscellaneous Provisions Act of 1981 (Midwinter, Keating and Taylor 1982) giving the Secretary of State, in theory subject to parliamentary approval, in practice quite arbitrary powers to reduce the rate of grant to individual authorities. The move back from the planning systems of the 1970s towards detailed intervention and the single-minded emphasis on reducing spending makes local planning well-nigh impossible. Declining turnout and general apathy about local elections are a further sign of the malaise of local democracy but may reflect a realistic judgment as to the value of voting for councils. Those electors who do turn out are perhaps not so misguided in the circumstances in regarding local elections as a referendum on the national government.

In the contemporary world, no local authority can ever be completely independent; the demands of modern economic management and the welfare state dictate interdependence for the whole system of government. Nor can conflict ever be banished from the central-local relationship as long as differences of interest and ideology in public policy persist. A democratic system must allow for the accommodation of these differences through negotiation and bargaining. Scotland's diversity of needs, interests and opinions mean that policy cannot be applied in a uniform way from one end of the country to another. Local authorities are the only elected bodies at their territorial level and it is inevitable and quite proper that they should take an interest in the welfare of their inhabitants across the whole policy field, though recognising that in many areas national needs may be paramount and the central government must have the last word. At the community level, local authorities themselves must come to recognise that needs and wishes differ and accept the legitimacy of *local* political choices.

At Scottish level, again, it is the elected political element which is lacking. The Scottish Office's status as a central department is, as we have seen, its most important feature and its responsibility to Westminster means that it is bound to follow the programme of the majority party there whatever the conditions or expressed political choices in Scotland. This is indeed the fundamental weakness of this form of administrative decentralisation. It exists to administer to distinctive Scottish needs and traditions — otherwise everything could be run from Whitehall departments — but it has no right to depart from the common UK line on major policy items.

An elected Scottish Assembly could provide an alternative mandate for the Scottish administration and provide the democratic political input which is necessary effectively to plan and pull the various activities together behind a common set of purposes. Accountability for Scottish administration, blurred at the moment in the complex of pressures and parliamentary devices, could be clearly established. This is not to say that Scottish affairs could be run independently of the rest of the United Kingdom, any more than local government could be run in isolation from central government. Common concerns and interdependence would remain but a Scottish administration with the weight of an elected assembly behind it and committed to social and economic planning would be a more effective interlocutor with Whitehall than is the present structure.

This is a question still needing a great deal of thought. Labour's proposals of 1978 would have set up an Assembly with many of the weaknesses of the present local government system — tied down functionally to a prescribed bundle of tasks and financially dependent. What we see as needed is a strengthened *area* perspective in government, from the local community to the European level, one which recognises both the *horizontal* interconnections of policies and the *vertical* interconnections of units of territorial government. Of course, there must be a distribution of functions to units of government but these can never be absolute. Rather, each level should be able to take the lead in those functions allocated to it but in partnership with others (we would emphasise that this 'lead' is by an elected body). Such partnerships cannot be created by a wave of the legislative wand or merely wished into existence. They must be *negotiated* and this can only be done effectively and accountably by elected government, whether party-political or not.

The same is true of local government. Calls for further reforms are made in the interests of efficiency and democracy. This debate continually focuses on the wrong question, i.e. "what is the appropriate level of government for specific functions?", and with an assumption that "more local" means "more democratic". Single-tier local government would *not* eliminate the divisions and disagreements which stem from the functional organisation of local government. It would merely change the arena within which these conflicts take place. Nor are we enamoured with the argument that this would reduce political conflict. Partisan political debate is a healthy feature of pluralist democracy, not something to be eliminated. It is necessary to expose and clarify choices.

There is little evidence that small-scale local government encouraged democratic discussion. It was heavily dependent on central advice, and major issues of local priority were in effect settled by the centre. Reorganised local government offers the prospect of locally determined strategic decisions, within a more flexible political structure but only if the centre is prepared to allow local authorities the necessary freedom to plan their own futures.

The growth of 'ad hocracy' is as alarming in Scotland as elsewhere; the proliferation of appointed agencies threatens both efficiency and accountability in government. Three agencies, in particular, the SDA, the MSC and the National Health Service need to be integrated into a system of democratic control. The SDA has some important achievements to its credit, but it can only come near to meeting the original expectations of it as part of a co-ordinated approach to Scottish economic, industrial and physical planning. Democratic control through a Scottish Assembly — while still leaving a considerable degree of operational freedom to the Agency — could give it the political legitimacy to intervene on a bolder scale. It could also justify increasing the Agency's powers and resources. Manpower planning would be an important element in a Scottish plan and would need to be co-ordinated with industrial planning and educational provision. So we see a strong case on efficiency as well as democratic grounds for bringing the MSC's Scottish operations under the Assembly which would then have to co-ordinate its plans, where appropriate, with those made at UK level.

The National Health Service has remained outside the scope of elective government on the grounds that its concerns are not susceptible to political judgment; rather they are purely professional, medical matters. We do not find this convincing. Naturally, in medicine as in other fields, there is an area where professional judgment must be respected. On the other hand, the broad direction of health policy, the relative weight to be given to preventive or curative medicine and the allocation of resources among social groups, geographical areas and medical specialities are essentially political matters, to be settled properly by elected authorities.

We do not have space here to present a complete blueprint for the future system of government for Scotland, though we have both written extensively about the options for change. We can, however, point to some specific changes which we would like to see. First, we see an elected Scottish Assembly as a vital element in the revival of Scottish democracy. Labour's 1978 plans do not, in our view, go far enough and we would like to see the Assembly have its own taxation powers, control over the SDA and MSC, powers of selective industrial intervention and the right to take the lead in preparing, in conjunction with other levels of government, a Scottish economic and land-use plan. We would also like to see a revival of planning at the UK level for only through medium and long-term planning based upon negotiation and not central dictat, can inter-governmental relations be turned from destructive conflict into constructive co-operation. This, in turn, means rescuing planning from the delusions of the 1960s when it was often assumed that the mere formulation of a plan could produce consensus on its objectives and the means of implementation. In our vision, planning would provide mechanisms whereby conflicts can be exposed and negotiated, uncertainty reduced and areas of collaboration identified. It is *essentially* a political process and can only be undertaken by political, elected bodies.

We also see a need for a more rational, planned approach to allocating public expenditure in the UK. The old system whereby the Secretary of State bargained for what he could get for Scotland was, rightly, resented by English MPs once they became fully aware of what it entailed. Nor was it a healthy feature of Scottish political life to concentrate so much time and energy on passing the begging bowl around the Treasury. A dangerous feeling of dependence had undoubtedly developed to debilitate Scottish political life by the 1970s. We would support Heald's (1980) proposals for an independent board to provide information on the relative spending needs of parts of the UK, with the final decision on the allocation of funds taken openly in Parliament. If the Scottish Assembly wished to spend more than the rest of the UK, it would be free to raise its own taxes to do so.

We also believe that there are strong arguments for the health service to become part of local government, a question 'ducked' by the Wheatley Commission. The interdependence we identified at all levels of government is particularly relevant in the case of health, which has close links with housing, social work and environmental health. Integration of the health service with local government would enhance the prospects of both corporate planning and democratic control. The power of professionalism in the health service seems an invalid reason for not including it in local government. At the end of the day, decisions about priorities within and between services have elements of political judgment which are not being exposed at the moment.

Finally, we would argue for a further strengthening of local government's democratic base. A viable local democracy will not be achieved by tinkering with the present structure and distribution of powers in the way that the numerous options for reform have been discussed, if no change in the constitutional and financial framework take place. John Stewart's argument on the need for a "Bill of Rights" for local government (Stewart 1981) may well be one avenue to pursue. Related to this is the need to produce a financial framework whereby local government raises more of its finance locally. The 1981 Green Paper on Alternatives to Domestic Rates was produced within a framework which ruled out radical change, on the grounds of central economic management. Yet countries throughout the Western world operate local income and sales taxes. These are only "off" the agenda within a highly centralised, unitary, political system and a centralist perspective about the need for tight central control over public expenditure. We would support the introduction of local income tax as recommended by the Layfield Committee (1976) and a reduction in the amount of local expenditure met by the centre. Of course, there would still be a need for an equalisation of revenue between rich and poor authorities, as there would be within the UK generally, but this does not require the massive central intervention of the present system.

So 'effectiveness' and 'democracy' are not, as is so often implied, in conflict with each other. Rather, the one requires the other. This book has concentrated on the administrative arrangements for handling Scottish affairs and on the policy process. If what is usually thought of as 'politics' has been played down, this reflects no value judgment on our part. It reflects the reality of the policy process in Scottish affairs where the 'political' in the sense of democratic, elective, elements are the weakest point.

We are moving inexorably to a quasi-federalist view of the political system. These changes are *not* incompatible with central economic management, and would promote the scope for the politically diverse responses which are needed to cope with Scottish social and economic diversity, both between Scotland and other areas of the UK, but also among the different regions of Scotland.

The absence of a Scottish political dimension, the growth of quangos and government agencies, the fragile constitutional base of local government, all call for radical solutions if democracy in Scotland is to survive and grow.

APPENDIX

THE PRESENT STRUCTURE OF LOCAL GOVERNMENT

3 ISLAND COUNCILS
9 REGIONAL COUNCILS
53 DISTRICT COUNCILS

Powers

Regional and Islands
Major planning and related services, including strategic planning, industrial development,† transportation, roads, water, sewerage.

Education, social work, police, fire, registration of births, deaths and marriages, registration of electors. Some joint activities in Island areas.

Districts and Islands
Local planning and associated services,* industrial development† including urban development and countryside,* building controls,* housing, community centres, parks and recreation, museums and art galleries, libraries,* tourism, nature conservation, war memorials, environmental health, including cleansing, refuse, Shops Act, burials, regulation and licensing, including cinemas and theatres, betting and taxis, caravan sites.

† Concurrent.
* Except in Highland, Dumfries and Galloway, and Borders Regions, where function is regional.

INDEX